Baedeker's

MADRID

Hints for using this Guide

Following the tradition established by Karl Baedeker in 1844, buildings, places of natural beauty and sights of particular interest, as well as hotels and restaurants of particular quality, are distinguished by either one or two stars.

To make it easier to locate the various places listed in the "A to Z" section of the Guide, their co-ordinates on the large city map are shown in red at the head of each entry.

Coloured lines down the right-hand side of the page are an aid to finding the main headings in the Guide: blue stands for the Introduction (Nature, Culture, History, etc.), red for the "Sights from A to Z" section, while yellow indicates Practical Information.

Only a selection of hotels and restaurants can be given. No reflection is implied, therefore, on establishments not included.

In a time of rapid change it is difficult to ensure that all the information given is entirely accurate and up-to-date, and the possibility of error can never be entirely eliminated. Although the publishers can accept no responsibility for inaccuracies and omissions, they are always grateful for corrections and suggestions for improvement.

Preface

This guide to Madrid is one of the new generation of Baedeker guides.

These guides, illustrated throughout in colour, are designed to meet the needs of the modern traveller. They are quick and easy to consult, with the principal features of interest described in alphabetical order, and the information is presented in a format that is both attractive and easy to follow.

The subject of this guide is Madrid, the Spanish capital; in addition it includes a number of places of tourist interest in the vicinity of the city including the towns of Aranjuez, Segovia, Toledo, Alcalá de Henares, La Granja and Guadalajara, the monastery of El Escorial and the Sierra de Guadarrama.

The guide is divided into three parts. The first part gives a general account of the city, its population and administration, climate, economy, transport, culture and history, and famous people. A brief selection of quotations leads into the second part, in which the principal sights in Madrid and the surrounding area are described. The third part contains a variety of practical information designed to help visitors to find their way about and to make the most of their stay. A number of "Baedeker Specials" feature the Madrid tapestry manufactory and the glass factory at La Granja, the zarzuela, bullfighting, shopping, night life and eating and drinking in Madrid. Both the sights and the Practical Information section are in alphabetical order.

A peaceful Sunday afternoon in the Retiro Park

Baedeker guides are noted for their concentration on essentials and their convenience of use. They contain many coloured illustrations and specially drawn plans, and at the back of the book will be found a large plan of the city. Each main entry in the A to Z section gives the co-ordinates of the square on the plan in which the particular feature can be located. Users of this guide, therefore, should have no difficulty in finding what they want to see.

Baedeker
Verlag Karl Baedeker

Contents

Baedeker Specials

5

A City

The capital of Spain is proud of its style as "La Nobla Villa de Madrid" – though the word *villa* now means a small town or in modern idiom, rather less flatteringly, a "dump". Of course this city in the centre of Spain, with a population of three million, is very different from the sleepy little market village of 1561 which Philip II, with political considerations in mind, made his capital. But even then Madrid was too small for its new role, and things are still very much the same today. The city is growing steadily beyond its capacity, in terms both of its infrastructure and the attitudes of its inhabitants. Madrid is the very essence of Spain, of its history and the varying characters of its regions. Here visitors with an interest in culinary matters will be in their element, for – borrowing the idea from Zola's novel "Le Ventre de Paris" – Madrid is the "belly of Spain", where fish and seafood come as fresh to the table as in a harbourside bar in Andalusia. Here too Basque delicacies compete with Mediterranean dishes and the sophisticated cuisine of Catalonia.

Madrid has been the melting-pot of the Spanish way of life since it began in the 16th and 17th centuries to attract immigrants from all over the Iberian

Palacio Real

There is a fine view of the Royal Palace from the Campo del Moro park, from which the Moors besieged Madrid

Don Quixote

You will often come across Don Quixote and Sancho Panza in Madrid

Bird's-eye view

There are only a few points from which there is such a wide view of the city

Eternally New

peninsula. In the time of the Habsburgs it was the scene of Spain's first cultural flowering since the decline of Moorish culture. After the "Siglo de Oro", the Golden Age of Calderón, Cervantes and Velázquez, it remained under the Bourbons one of Europe's cultural centres, even though it declined in political importance in the latter part of the 19th century. And so visitors to Madrid make first for the Prado, the Centro de Arte Reina Sofía and the Thyssen-Bornemisza Museum. But Madrid is much more than a place of pilgrimage for the art-lovers who come to see its Picassos, Velázquezes and Goyas, its profusion of churches and monasteries and the Royal Palace. In addition, in contrast to Rome – to whose history the Hispanic provinces contributed four emperors – it is an eternally new city.

Segovia

The Alcázar of Segovia – within easy reach of Madrid

Here people are not so much concerned with history, but eagerly absorb anything new. It is perhaps because of this that in the 1990s Madrid, in a Europe tired of Europe, became one of the continent's great metropolises.

After Franco's death, in the new conditions of freedom, Madrid blossomed. The twisting lanes of the old town, the shady avenues and the city's streets, forever gridlocked with traffic, are a great stage for the enjoyment of life's pleasures. Anyone who has spent a hot summer night on Madrid's airy terraces, who has eaten his way through its *tapa* culture, who has visited its *tabernas* and *tascas,* its bars and discos on the *marcha madrileña,* is well on the way to becoming a Madrileño.

Paella

Along with beer, one of Spain's culinary delights

**Nature, Culture
History**

Facts and Figures

Madrid's coat of arms

General

Madrid is the capital of the kingdom of Spain and of the autonomous Madrid Region (Comunidad de Madrid). In 1561 the Habsburg king Philip II declared it the country's *única corte* and moved his court to Madrid. With his decision to make the youngest of Spain's cities its capital he rejected the claims of Zaragoza in Aragon, the Castilian towns of Burgos and León, the Visigothic town of Toledo and the Moorish towns of Córdoba and Seville. Madrid is now the largest city in the Iberian peninsula, the seat of government and the Cortes (the Spanish parliament), the residence of the Spanish king and thus the political, cultural, financial, commercial and transport centre of Spain.

Location

Madrid lies in the centre of the Iberian peninsula on a karstic plateau, rising towards the north-east, 80 m (260 ft) above the water-starved and now partly canalised Río de Manzanares. At 650 m (2100 ft) above sea level, it is Europe's highest capital city. On the north the city is bounded by the Sierra de Guadarrama, whose highest peaks rise to 2400 m (7900 ft); to the south and east extend the wide plains of La Mancha.

Area

The administrative district of Madrid occupies an area of 531 sq. km (205 sq. mi.). The autonomous Madrid Region has an area of 8000 sq. km (3000 sq. mi.).

Society

Population

Madrid has long been a magnet for the population of the Spanish provinces. In the 16th and still more in the 17th century Madrid, as the administrative centre of a flourishing colonial empire, the seat of the court and a lively commercial and intellectual centre, housed a shifting and partly rootless population drawn to the Villa y Corte (city and court). The town's attractive power was still further increased by the Industrial Revolution, and by 1880 it had a population of 400,000. During the wave of industrialisation in the 1950s and 1960s Madrid developed into an industrial conurbation.

Between 1950 and 1970 the population of the Madrid region rose from 1.9 to 4.8 million, and it is still attracting incomers from Andalusia, the Asturias, the Basque country, Extremadura and Galicia in quest of a better life in the capital, in accordance with the proverbial phrase "de Madrid al cielo", "from Madrid direct to heaven". The region now has a population of just under 5.2 million, the city around 3.2 million – though in 1997 it showed a decline for the first time for decades. (This compares

◀ *Calle de Alcalá, one of Madrid's principal traffic arteries, seen from an unusual point of view*

Madrid

Capital of Spain and of the autonomous region Comunidad de Madrid	Position 40°25'N, 3°42'W
	Population 3.1 million

with Barcelona's population of 2 million). The population includes some 130,000 foreigners. According to the charitable organisation Caritas more than 700,000 can be classed as poor, with an income of under £250 a month, while 30,500 suffer hunger.

The religious diversity of mediaeval Spain, with Christians, Jews and Muslims living side by side, came to an end after the conquest of the last Moorish kingdom, Granada, by the Catholic Monarchs in 1492. The expulsion of the Moors in 1492 and of Jews in 1502 put the seal on the religious uniformity which was enforced by the tribunals of the Inquisition.

Religion

The Reformation met with resolute resistance in the Spain of Charles V and Philip II, and the Counter-Reformation maintained the country's allegiance to orthodox Catholicism, which remained the state religion under the Bourbons (from 1713). The First Republic (1873–74) made a short-lived attempt to liberalise religious attitudes, but this was negatived following the restoration of the monarchy under Alfonso XII. The anti-church legislation and expropriation of church property in 1931–33 by the left-wing coalition government in the early days of the Second Republic was followed by a reaction under the right-wing CEDA coalition which came to power in 1933 but was then displaced by the republican Popular Front in the last democratic election before the Civil War. Under the Franco dictatorship the Church regained its powerful influence on politics and education. Finally the democratic constitution introduced after Franco's death established liberty of religious belief and practice and the separation of church and state. The Catholic faith continues to be predominant in Spain; but the Centro Cultural Islámico in Madrid, opened in 1990, is the largest mosque of the largest Islamic community

Colourful street name-plates in Madrid

in Europe, while Jewish communities have rediscovered the land of their Sephardic ancestors.

Administration

The administration of Madrid is headed by the Alcalde (Mayor), who is elected by a simple majority of the Asamblea, the city council or parliament. He is assisted by deputy mayors *(tenencias de alcaldía),* and the administration is run by various municipal departments *(concejalías).*

Districts

The city is divided into 21 wards or districts: Centro, Arganzuela, Retiro, Salamanca, Chamartín, Tetuán, Chamberí, Fuencarral, Moncloa, La Latina, Carabanchel, Villaverde, Usera, Mediodía, Vallecas Puente, Vallecas Villa, Vicálvaro, Moratalaz, Ciudad Lineal, San Blas, Barajas and Hortaleza. From the visitor's point of view a more helpful division is into the following areas of tourist interest:

Habsburg Madrid

The area round the Plaza Mayor and the Plaza de la Villa in the Centro district bears the mark of the period of the Habsburg kings. It extends from the Royal Palace in the west – though this was given its present form only in the 18th century under the Bourbons – by way of Calle Segovia to the Puerta del Sol in the east, turning back from the Plaza de Callao to the gardens of the palace. The quarter extending along Calle del Sacramento from the Plaza Mayor has buildings of the late mediaeval period and Renaissance, while the area round the palace, with the

Opera House, is characterised by its Baroque and neo-classical architecture. Between the Puerta del Sol, the Opera House and the Gran Vía late mediaeval buildings rub shoulders with the commercial world of the 20th century.

The western part of the Centro district, from the Puerta del Sol to the Paseo del Prado, was given its stamp by the Bourbon kings from the 18th century onwards, though the neighbourhoods in this area – Sol, Cortes and Las Huertas – were already being created in the Baroque period. While Calle de Alcalá and the Gran Vía show the spacious planning of the 18th and 19th centuries, developed most fully beyond the Paseo del Prado, the Huertas quarter round the Plaza de Santa Ana is an area of narrow lanes and old town houses, now the centre of much of Madrid's night life. In the Baroque period the town's principal theatres were in this district, which accordingly became known as the Barrio de las Musas, the Muses' Quarter.

Bourbon Madrid

The Lavapiés and Embajadores quarter, named after squares in the southern part of the Centro district, and the Latina district to the south of Calle Segovia form a distinctive area of the city. La Latina is the popular quarter of Bourbon Madrid. Its most important buildings were erected in the mediaeval period round the Plaza de la Paja on the foundations of the Moorish quarter. The cleaning-up and rehabilitation of the old town has given a new lease of life to this quarter, in which Madrid's patron saint, San Isidro, is revered. To the east is the Rastro quarter, a part of the city with its own distinctive character, merging at Calle de Embajadores into the Lavapiés quarter, which extends to the Centro de Arte Reina Sofía.

La Latina and Lavapiés

The Reales Sitios del Buen Retiro, laid out in the time of Philip I, extended to the Paseo del Prado. This area was built up during the reign of Charles II, contrasting in the spaciousness of its layout with the older part of the town in the Centro district. Along the magnificent Paseo del Prado lie the city's three great museums – the Prado, the Centro de Arte Reina Sofía and the Thyssen-Bornemisza Museum. The Retiro Park is enclosed on the north and east by middle-class residential districts, with art galleries, fashion shops and elegant tapa bars to attract the visitor. To the west are monumental buildings such as the Palacio de Comunicaciones, the Stock Exchange and the Army Museum, housed in the old palatial buildings of the Retiro or in modern buildings which have replaced them. To the south-west are the Botanic Gardens and the Atocha Station.

Retiro

To the north of the Retiro quarter are the Recoletos and Salamanca quarters, laid out on a geometric grid of streets and lanes, with exclusive fashion shops, restaurants, middle-class houses and palatial 19th century mansions. These districts are bounded on the west by the Paseo de la Castellana, the northward continuation of the Paseo del Prado.

Recoletos and Salamanca

In the Justicia and Malasaña quarter, which also lies within the Centro district, extending from the Gran Vía in the south and the Paseo de Recoletos up to the *bulevares* running between the Plaza de Colón and the Glorieta de Bilbao, all periods of the city's history are represented. Interesting contrasts are provided by Baroque convents like that of the Iglesia de San Antonio de los Alemanes, Art Nouveau buildings like the Casa Longoria, lawcourts like the Tribunal Supremo and the brash architecture of our own age like the Torres de Colón. Round Calle Almirante is Spain's avantgarde fashion scene; the Plaza Dos de Mayo and Plaza de Chueca are favourite resorts of young Madrid.

Justicia and Malasaña

Around the turn of the 20th century Argüelles developed into a middle-class residential area, offering coolness in summer above the Parque del

Argüelles

The fine view of the Royal Palace and the Almudena Cathedral from the cableway in the Casa de Campo park

Moncloa

Oeste and the Río de Manzanares. In the 1950s high-rise blocks built round the Plaza de España marked the northern termination of the Gran Vía. To the north of the Moncloa district is the Ciudad Universitaria, the University City.

Chamberí and Nuevos Ministerios

The Paseo de la Castellana is lined on both sides by office blocks and high-rise buildings occupied by banks and businesses. Behind the Estadio Santiago Bernabéu, home of the famous Real Madrid football team, and the Museo de Ciencias Naturales lie the city's most select residential areas, while behind the tower blocks of the Azca quarter and the huge office complex of the Nuevos Ministerios extend endless streets of middle-class houses, with such features as the town villa of the Valencian painter Joachín Sorolla and the lively Plaza de Olavide.

Climate

Lying in the same latitude as Naples and Istanbul, Madrid has a markedly continental variant of a Mediterranean climate. The average annual temperature is 13.3°C (55.9°F). Summers are long and hotter than on the coast. As a result of high pressure areas over the Azores, absence of cloud cover and high irradiation the summer heat reaches its maximum mainly in July but also in August, with average day temperatures of 30°C (86°F). During the summer months the central regions of Spain are overlaid by the *calina,* a layer of dry dust carried up from the arid soil by hot rising currents of air. Because of the absence of troughs of low pressure over the Atlantic at this time of year the only cooling influences are summer storms coming from the Montes de Toledo or the Sierra de Guadarrama, which sometimes, after cloudbursts of rainfall, lead to local flooding. Rain falls mainly in spring and autumn, with average annual rainfalls in Madrid of between 400 and 500 mm (16 and 20 in.) and in the Sierra of over 1000 m (40 in). There are, however, wide variations, with years of high rainfall alternating with dry periods.

Madrid's winters are also colder than in coastal areas, though not so harsh as on the northern Meseta, even though temperatures may some-

times fall some degrees below freezing point. In the mountains rising out of the plateau much of the winter precipitations falls in the form of snow, offering scope for winter sports in the nearby Sierra de Guadarrama. The frequency of snowfalls and the duration of snow cover increase with height and from south to north. In the Madrid area snowfalls are likely at heights over 600 m (2000 ft). In the Sierra de Guadarrama, at a height of 1350 m (4430 ft), there are snowfalls on 56 days in the year.

Economy

Since Madrid, situated at the geographical centre of the Iberian peninsula, does not lie on the coast and has no local sources of raw materials it was late in developing into the country's economic and financial centre. Until the 1960s small and middle-sized enterprises still dominated the economic life of the city, whose oldest-established industries were the royal tapestry manufactory and glass factory (see Baedeker Special, p. 76). It was also famed for its leather goods, jewellery and musical instruments.

In recent decades Madrid has grown into one of Spain's leading industrial centres. 40 per cent of the working population are now employed in industry, more than 15 per cent of Spain's industrial output comes from the Madrid region and 70 per cent of multinational enterprises operating in Spain, over half the country's research institutes, staffed by 5000 scientists, and leading high-tech manufacturers are established in and around the capital.

Madrid is the seat of Spain's central bank, the Banco de España – though with the introduction of a common European currency the fixing of interest rates becomes the responsibility of the European Central Bank in Frankfurt. The five major Spanish private banks – the Banco Central Hispano (BCH), the Banco Hispano Americano, the Banco Argentaria (a postal bank privatised in 1998), the Banco Español de Crédito (Banesto, taken over in 1998 by the Banco Santander) and the

(Palacio de la Bolsa) is Spain's leading stock exchange, well ahead of Barcelona, Bilbao and Valencia.

Commerce and industry

Madrid has a varied pattern of industry. The most important employers are the consumption goods industries (cosmetics, clothing), publishing (80 per cent of all Spanish publishers are based in Madrid), aircraft construction, the automobile industry – goods vehicles (Pegaso), motorcycles, tractors (Lanza Ibérica, John Deere, Hanomag) – and electrical appliances (Marconi, Zanussi, AEG, Siemens).

Madrid, with its steadily increasing population, is one of Spain's leading commercial areas (with 14 per cent of the Spanish domestic market), a major housebuilding centre, a great congress city and the hub of Spain's tourist trade. In 1997 it attracted some 4.8 million visitors, 48 per cent of them from abroad.

Housing

Madrid's development into an international metropolis has had unfortunate effects on the housing market. A huge property boom drove house prices to great heights, leading many Madrileños to leave the capital, at the cost of long daily commuting journeys. More than 2 million cars make for Madrid every day, leading to increasing air pollution by exhaust gases. The poor quality of the air is felt particularly by the southern and eastern parts of the city where the poorer members of the population live, often in densely packed high-rise apartment blocks. The northern and western districts, occupied by the more prosperous inhabitants, benefit from the prevalent westerly and north-westerly winds which make smog conditions rare in Madrid.

The poorest inhabitants of Madrid live in *chabolas* (shanty towns), of which there are several dozen round the M 30 and M 40 motorway rings circling the city on the north, east and south. The city's policy of siting the *chabolas* in these areas, sometimes bordering municipal rubbish dumps, has been for many years an affront to the European Convention on Human Rights. The city's income structure follows a similar pattern: household incomes in the north-west of the city are more than five times as high as in the south.

Transport

Airport

Barajas (16 km (10 mi.) east of the city) is Madrid's principal airport and the central point for Spanish air traffic, both passengers and freight. Its geographical situation makes Barajas the hub of much of the international air traffic to North and South America, as well as of Spanish domestic traffic (which accounts for around 50 per cent of its total traffic).

The airport carries a heavy traffic (with a throughput of 24 million passengers in 1997), and has been in course of expansion for some years, with a large new terminal due to open in 2001. A new Metro link between the airport and the city centre is due to come into operation by the end of 1999. Hitherto there have been only motorway and expressway connections, which are heavily overcrowded at rush hours.

Rail services

All the main railway lines radiate from Madrid. The lines to the north by way of San Sebastián and Irún and to the north-east by way of Barcelona and Port Bou link the city with France and Central Europe; the lines to the west provide a link with Portugal.

Madrid's principal railway stations are the Estación de Chamartín (services to the Asturias, Santander, the Basque country and France) and the Estación de Atocha (services to the Levante and Andalusia). Services to north-western Spain (La Coruña) depart from the Estación de Príncipe Pío.

Roads

Madrid's situation in the heart of Spain means that all the country's main roads radiate from here. A slab in the ground at the Puerta del Sol marks the zero point from which distances on all the national highways are measured.

Although the main roads within a wide radius of the capital are of motorway standard and much of the traffic is diverted on to orbital motorways and bypasses (M 30, M 40), the city is almost strangled by its enormous road traffic. One in every three inhabitants of Madrid has a car. The average rate of progress within the city is only 14 km (8 mi.) an hour. The city planners have been striving to find a solution to this steadily growing problem. A modest beginning was made with the introduction in 1997 of "Metrobus" tickets valid on both the Metro and municipal buses; but these

did not cover transfers, so that changing between Metro and bus or between one bus service and another meant additional expense. The separate lanes for buses and taxis, of which there are many in Madrid, are usually blocked by parked vehicles or used with impunity by private cars. There are few cycle tracks, and these are mainly designed for the use of leisure cyclists travelling from the city into the country.

The following trunk roads start from Madrid:
N I to Burgos, San Sebastián and France
N II to Barajas and Barcelona
N III to Valencia
N IV to Cádiz and Andalusia
N V to Badajoz, Extremadura and Portugal
N VI to La Coruña and Galicia

Public transport within the city is provided by the Empresa Municipal de Transportes (EMT), the state-owned Compañía Metropolitana de Transportes (Metro) and various private bus companies.

Public transport

The Madrid Metro, inaugurated by Alfonso XII in 1919, is one of Europe's oldest underground railway systems (preceded by London in 1884 and Paris in 1900). With ten lines, a total length of 124 km (77 mi.) and 167 stations, it operates daily from 6 am to 1.30 am the following morning.

Metro

More than 170 bus lines fight their way through Madrid's traffic, including the red EMT buses, night buses – known as *buhos* ("owls") – and various regional buses, mostly privately run. Most of them start from Chamartín, Moncloa and the new bus station on the M 30 south. Timetables can be obtained at the information counters in the main junction points like Atocha and Moncloa or from tourist information offices (see Practical Information, Information).

Buses

Madrid has around 15,500 taxis. Given their numbers, they are not usually ordered by telephone from taxi offices or taxi ranks, but can be picked up at taxi ranks or hailed in the street. Taxis which are free show the word *libre* in green behind the windscreen; if they are engaged they show *ocupado* in red.

Taxis

See also Practical Information, Public Transport

Culture

Madrid's position as the intellectual and cultural centre of Spain is reflected in the number of its museums, including some of international standing. They are headed by the Museo del Prado, with Spain's principal art treasures; the Thyssen-Bornemisza Museum in the Palacio de

Museums

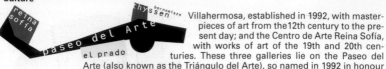

Villahermosa, established in 1992, with masterpieces of art from the 12th century to the present day; and the Centro de Arte Reina Sofía, with works of art of the 19th and 20th centuries. These three galleries lie on the Paseo del Arte (also known as the Triángulo del Arte), so named in 1992 in honour of Madrid's selection as European City of Culture.

Other major museums are the National Archaeological Museum; numerous monasteries and palaces containing art treasures such as Las Descalzas and the Encarnación; the Romantic Museum; the Sorolla Museum; the Real Academia de Bellas Artes de San Fernando; the art and weapons collections in the Palacio Real; and there are many more. There are also innumerable galleries and foundations, as well as the Contemporary Art Fair (ARCO).

For further information, see the entries on Museums and Galleries in the Practical Information section.

Universities

Madrid is the seat of the Scientific Research Council, the Royal Spanish Academy and the Academies of Fine Art, History, Language, Natural Science, Jurisprudence, Philosophy and Politics. It also has four universities, with 25 per cent of Spain's total student population. Among them is the Universidad Complutense, successor to the famous university of that name established in Alcalá de Henares in 1508 and transferred to Madrid in 1836. Originally situated in Calle San Bernardo, it moved to the University City, in north-western Madrid, in 1927. The city's second university is the Universidad Autónoma de Madrid, founded in the suburb of Canto Blanco in 1968 to relieve pressure on the overcrowded Universidad Complutense. The other two are the Universidad Pontífica Cornillas and the Open University (UNED), founded in 1972.

Madrid is also home to the National Library and numerous other libraries.

Theatres

Madrid is the centre of Spanish theatrical and musical life. It is the seat of the National Drama Centre, the National Ballet and the National Orchestra. Over 30 theatres, outstanding among them the Teatro Nacional María Guerrero and the municipal Teatro Español, offer a varied repertoire, from the classics to modern works by Spanish and foreign playwrights. In the field of music the leading establishments are the Auditorio Nacional de Música, opened in 1988, the Teatro de la Zarzuela and the Teatro Real (also known as the Teatro de la Ópera), one of the world's finest opera houses, which reopened in 1998 after many years of renovation and modernisation. In addition Madrid has a great range of jazz, reggae, pop, rock and flamenco performances.

Media

Some of Spain's leading daily newspapers – El País, El Mundo, ABC – are published in Madrid, as well as important regional dailies such as Ya and Diario 16, which as a result of changes of publisher are regularly closed down. Spain's most widely read daily, the sports paper Marco, is also produced in the capital.

Television

Since the introduction of commercial television in 1990 the state television corporation RTVE with its two channels has just retained its leading position with a very narrow majority. The private television companies Antena 3, Telecinco and Canal Plus España are based, like RTVE, in Madrid. There are also two digital channels, Satélite Digital and Vía Digital.

Radio

The leading radio stations (Cadena Ser, Radio COPE, Onda Cero, Antena 3 and Nacional) are also based in Madrid.

Cinema

Madrid once had the only film studios in Spain, Estudios Chamartín, but film production is now shared with Barcelona. With over 130 cinemas in

The Royal Opera House, recently reopened after thorough renovation, is now set to achieve international standing

the different parts of the city, including many on the Gran Vía, Madrid offers a large audience for both Spanish and international films. The Madrid Film Festival (IMAGFIC), originally devoted to science fiction, is now known far beyond the bounds of Spain as a showcase for international cinema.

Since the description of the Museo del Prado in the "Sights from A to Z" section of this guide gives an introduction to the history of Spanish art from the 12th to the early 20th century, no separate account is given in this section.

Spanish art

History

Finds of stone implements and sherds of pottery have shown that the Madrid area, between the rivers Jarama and Manzanares, was occupied by nomadic peoples after 6000 BC. Around 1000 BC Celtic tribes moved into the interior of the Iberian peninsula from the north-west. There they encountered the Iberians, a people made up of independent tribes who had settled between Languedoc in southern France and the southern tip of Spain and with whom they now mingled to form the group known as the Celtiberians.

Neither under Roman rule (from the 2nd century BC) or under the Visigoths (AD 409–711) was there any permanent settlement on the site of Madrid. The only surviving remains of these periods are a few grave slabs found in the old town area.

Middle Ages

In 711 Arab and Berber armies landed in Spain and advanced as far as the Río Duero, to the north of Madrid. The Visigothic kingdom fell apart, and Córdoba became the capital of a Moorish kingdom which existed until the conquest of Granada in 1492.

Mayrit

Around 860 the Moorish Emir of Córdoba, Mohammed I, established the stronghold of Mayrit or Magerit ("town of many waters", or according to another interpretation "healthy hill") on the site now occupied by the Royal Palace. It served as a frontier fortress against the Christian kingdoms in the north of the country. Under the protection of the fortress, which was situation on an important trade route, a settlement grew up. Between 1085 and 1095 Alfonso VI, the Bold, conquered Toledo and the Arab settlement of Mayrit. Legend has it that the Christian conquerors found in the ruins of the stronghold a figure of the Virgin, who became the first patroness of the town as the Virgen de la Almudena.

By the beginning of the 12th century the little market township had so grown in size as to need a new circuit of walls. Surviving from this period are a few remains of walls on the Cuesta de la Vega and the towers of two medieval churches, San Nicolás de los Senitas and San Pedro el Viejo (or el Real). In 1202 Madrid, which already comprised ten parishes, was granted special rights and privileges *(fueros)* by Alfonso VIII. It received a municipal charter from Alfonso X, the Wise (1252–84). The Moors who still remained in the town lived in their own quarter outside the south gate, still known as the Puerta del Moro. In 1309 Ferdinand IV of Castile summoned the Cortes, the assembly of the three estates (churchmen, the secular nobility and the towns) to meet in Madrid for the first time.

Catholic Monarchs

The marriage of the Catholic Monarchs, Ferdinand II of Aragon and Isabella I of Castile, in 1469 led to the union of the two kingdoms, which had hitherto been rivals. The Reconquista, which was completed in 1492 by the surrender of Granada, the last Moorish stronghold and the Inquisition ended the previously peaceful cohabitation of Muslims, Christians and Jews. Although Ferdinand and Isabella lived only occasionally in Madrid they built the church and monastery of San Jerónimo el Real to the east of the town (1478 onwards). From this period also date the Casa de los Lujanes and Casa de Cisneros, as well as parts of the palace of the Emperor Charles V's treasurer Alonso Gutiérrez, later converted into the Monasterio de las Descalzas Reales. Another example of Isabelline Gothic is the renovated Capilla del Obispo in the church of San Andrés. There is a description of Madrid at this time in the account of the German doctor, geographer and astronomer

Hieronymus Münzer, who travelled in Spain in 1494–95. He wrote that it had "many fountains, cheap food and two Moorish quarters inhabited by numerous Saracens".

Spanish Kings

Habsburg Kings

Charles I (as Holy Roman
Emperor Charles V)   1517–1556
    m. Isabel of Portugal Philip IV
    illegit. daughter: Margaret of Parma
    illegit. son: Don John of Austria
Philip II   1556–1598
    m. 1 Maria of Portugal
    m. 2 Mary Tudor
    m. 3 Elizabeth of Valois
    m. 4 Anne of Austria
    son: Don Carlos
    daughter: Isabel Clara Eugenia

Philip III
    m. Margaret of Austria
1621–1665
    m. Maria Anna of Austria
    daughter: Margareta Teresa
    (m. Emperor Leopold I)
Charles II   1665–1700
    m. Marie Louise of Orleans

Bourbon Kings

Philip V   1700–1746
Ferdinand VI   1748–1759
Charles III   1759–1700
    m. Maria Amalia of Saxony
    son: Fernando IV, king of the
    Two Sicilies
Charles IV   1788–1808
    m. Maria Luisa of Parma
    son: Don Carlos (supported by
    the Carlists)

Ferdinand VII   1814–1833
    m. 1 Maria Antonia of Naples
    m. 2 Maria Isabel of Braganza
    m. 3 Maria Josepha of Saxony
    m. 4 Maria Cristina of Naples
Isabella II   1833–1868
Alfonso XII   1874–1885
    m. Maria Christina of Austria
Alfonso XIII   1886–1931
Juan, Count of Barcelona (uncrowned)
Juan Carlos   1975
    proclaimed king

Habsburg Madrid

After the deaths of Isabella I and Philip II the crowns of Castile and Aragon did not pass to the legitimate successor, Juana, who was declared mad and shut up in a convent for the rest of her life.

In 1517 their son Charles, a grandson of the Emperor Maximilian of Austria, became king. This was the beginning of Habsburg rule in Spain. In the same year, after the death of his grandfather, he was elected Holy Roman Emperor in Frankfurt. As the Emperor Charles V he reigned over Spain, the Netherlands, Sardinia, Naples, Sicily, Milan, the Franche-Comté and numerous American colonies. As a result he did not spend even half his time in Spain. In Castile there was a rising by the Comuneros, the petty nobility and the prosperous burghers, who sought to curtail the powers of the crown. Charles suppressed the revolt and had its leaders executed. Even the Cortes, representing the nobility and the upper clergy, lost any importance. When Philip was in Spain he liked to stay in Madrid. In 1537 he extended the old Alcázar and gave it a more imposing façade, and in 1544 he began to build the palace of El Pardo, to the north of the town. In the same year he granted Madrid the style of "imperial y coronada villa", the imperial and crowned town. Twelve years later he abdicated. During his reign the population of the town had grown from 3000 to some 25,000.

Emperor Charles V

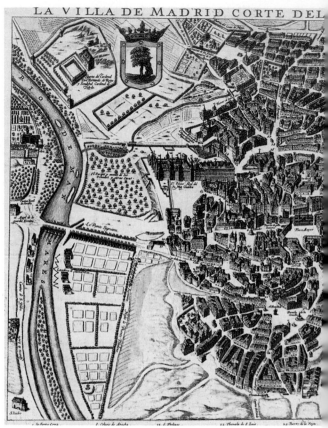

Madrid in the time of the Catholic Monarchs

Philip II

In 1561 Charles's son and successor, Philip II (1556–98), made Madrid the capital of his empire, in which "the sun never set", and the town's old fortress, the Alcázar, became the centre of Spanish political life. As his second residence Philip built the palace of Buen Retiro, near the monastery of San Jerónimo el Real, then well out of the town to the east. The nobility were now drawn to the capital and the seat of the court. Apart from the Palacio de Uceda, however, no new palaces were built, and the new arrivals found accommodation in the Alcázar. Religious buildings were given priority. The direction of the new projects was in the hands of the court architects Juan de Herrera, Juan Bautista de Toledo and Juan Gómez de Mora. They put their stamp on the new capital, building eighteen churches and seven religious houses. Philip's main interest was in the Escorial, which swallowed up vast amounts of government money. Little was left over, therefore, for the redevelopment of the town, now with a population of 60,000, which was urgently necessary. In order to house the army of officials and courtiers the king issued a decree requiring house-owners in Madrid to reserve the upper floors for the court. The result of this was that three-quarters of Madrid's houses had only a single storey. As the

papal nuncio Camillo Borghese (later Pope Paul V) wrote: "The houses are poor and ugly, almost all being built of clay. Among other defects they lack pavements and lavatories; for natural needs chamber pots are used, the contents being thrown out of the window during the night."

In 1601, three years after Philip's death, His successor Philip III moved the court temporarily to Valladolid. After it returned to Madrid in 1606 he commissioned a bronze equestrian statue of himself which was set up in the Casa de Campo (removed to the Plaza Mayor in 1847).

Philip III

Although the 17th century saw the decline of Spain's economic and political power – more than 500,000 Moors and Jews had been driven out of the country at the beginning of the century, after the wars with France and the Netherlands Spain's former predominance on the European continent passed to France, the country's economic situation was desperate, and the population lived in the bitterest poverty – Spain enjoyed a great artistic flowering in what became known as the Siglo de Oro, the Golden Age. The city too benefited from it. It had reached a population of around 100,000, and contained some 60 monasteries and other

Siglo de Oro

23

religious houses. Among the principal monuments of this period are the Town Hall in the Plaza de la Villa, the Plaza Mayor, the Convento de la Encarnación and the Puente de Segovia. Examples of the Baroque architecture of period are the Capilla de San Isidro in the church of San Andrés and the church of San Antonio de los Portugueses (later rededicated to San Antonio de los Alemanes). Madrid's fame was based on the presence in the city of Cervantes, Calderón, Lope de Vega, Quevedo and Philip IV's court painters, Velázquez (from 1623) and Zurbarán (from 1634).

Bourbon Madrid

War of the Spanish Succession

On 1st November 1700 the last Spanish Habsburg ruler, Charles II, died without leaving an heir, and war broke out between the Austrian Habsburgs and the French Bourbons over the succession. It was to last twelve years. Finally, under the treaty of Utrecht in 1713, Philip of Anjou, a grandson of Louis XIV, was victorious over his rival Karl von Habsburg and, as Philip V, founded the Spanish Bourbon dynasty. Spain, on the brink of ruin, now became a centrally organised state on the French model and began to recover, though it had lost its position as a European great power.

Madrid was now embellished in the style of French absolutism. The dominant architects in the first half of the century were José Churriguera, Pedro de Ribera and Francisco Moradillo, whose work displays the superabundance of ornament characteristic of Spanish Baroque. Among the principal monuments of this period are the Puente de Toledo, the Hospicio de San Fernando (now the Museo Municipal), the Cuartel del Conde-Duque, the churches of Montserrat, Santa Bárbara and San Andrés and the Miraflores, Ugena and Perales palaces. Thereafter this style ceased to be favoured by the Bourbons, and later buildings were designed by French and Italian architects, who carried through the transition from Baroque to neoclassicism.

Neo-classical Madrid was mainly the work of the architects Francesco Sabatini, Ventura Rodríguez, Juan de Villanueva, Filippo Juvara and Giovanni Battista Sacchetti. All over the city fountains, bridges and palaces of the nobility were built. The Alcázar was burned down, and this offered the opportunity to built a magnificent new palace in 18th century style, the Palacio Real. At Aranjuez and La Granja royal country palaces were built, set in extensive parks.

Ferdinand IV

Ferdinand IV, Philip V's son and successor, improved the Spanish road system, founded large hospitals such as the Hospicio de San Fernando (now the Museo Municipal) and the Hospital General de San Carlos, and built the Academy of Fine Art, which bears his name. Reflecting the influence of the Enlightenment, the Royal Academies of Language, Pharmacy and History were founded. There was also an upsurge of house-building, and the number of four- and five-floored houses increased considerably.

Charles III

The third Bourbon king, Charles III, who had previously been king of Naples and Sicily, came to the throne in 1759. In his 29-year reign this enlightened ruler left a stronger mark on Madrid than any other king, and was later called "Madrid's first and best mayor". He was responsible for the main streets, boulevards, fountains and avenues which still dominate the city's layout, for a long overdue improvement of Madrid's sewerage system and for the paving and lighting of streets. He ordered the construction of the Puerta de Alcalá (designed by his favourite architect, Sabatini), making Calle de Alcalá the principal approach to the capital from the east. At the end of Calle de Alcalá, at the Puerta del Sol, the Palacio de Correos (Head Post Office) was built. Charles moved into the

Palacio Real in 1764. The present Paseo del Prado, the middle section skirting the Retiro, was laid out in 1782. Numerous other buildings were erected in this area in strictly classical style. Charles established the porcelain manufactory which had been brought from Naples to Madrid in the Hermitage of San Antonio in the Retiro Park. He was anxious to promote the natural sciences, and founded the Botanic Gardens and the Prado (designed by Juan de Villanueva), which was originally planned as a museum of natural history. In 1762 he brought the painter Giovanni Battista Tiepolo to Madrid, which now became the last centre of late Baroque painting. At the same time the young German neo-classical painter Raphael Mengs also came to Madrid. He became one of the most influential figures in the development of Spanish art, enabling Francisco Bayeu, Goya and other artists to gain court employment. Goya made his name by the altarpiece he painted for the church of San Franciso el Grande, built in 1770.

In 1788 Charles's son Charles IV succeeded to the throne. The government was run by a young prime minister, Manuel Godoy, who became the lover of Queen Maria Luisa. A rising in Aragon overthrew Godoy and forced Charles IV to abdicate in favour of his son Ferdinand.

In 1808 French troops marched into Spain, on the pretext that British forces had occupied Portugal and thus threatened Napoleon's interests in the Iberian peninsula.

French occupation

19th century Madrid

Spain's history in the 19th century was marked by military coups d'état *(pronunciamientos)*, two civil wars over the succession to the throne (the Carlist wars) and a number of popular risings. In addition the country lost almost all its overseas colonies.

First, Napoleon compelled the royal family, which was riven by divisions, to abdicate and appointed his brother Joseph Bonaparte – known contemptuously to the people of Madrid as "Pepe Botella" – king of Spain. On May 2nd 1808 the people of Madrid rose against the French intruders, but were compelled to surrender after long and bloody street fighting in which more than 1500 lives were lost. The shootings that followed were pilloried in Goya's fiercely expressive picture, "El 3 de Mayo" (illustration, p. 26; now in the Prado). They also sparked off the six-year war of liberation, which finally led to the expulsion of the French forces. During the brief reign of Joseph Bonaparte no major buildings were erected in Madrid, but he paved the way for later important developments by pulling down churches, monasteries and whole blocks of houses and thus making room for the city's spacious squares, including Santa Ana, Oriente, Ramales and the Puerta del Sol.

Spain's first liberal constitution was adopted at Cádiz in 1812, and for a brief period a liberal atmosphere prevailed. This was abruptly ended, however, when Ferdinand III returned in 1814. With the help of French troops he restored the old absolutist order, repealed the constitution, closed universities, banned the press and re-established the Inquisition. In 1819 the Prado was opened as the Royal Picture Gallery, and in 1820 the Ateneo.

Ferdinand III

Ferdinand's death in 1833 gave rise to a conflict over the succession between his daughter Isabella and his brother Charles. At the end of the Carlist wars, in 1843, Isabella II, then only thirteen years old, emerged victorious. In 1836 the University of Alcalá was transferred to Madrid. The building of the Canal de Isabel II ensured a good water supply for the capital, which now also gained a gas lighting system. The equestrian statue of Philip IV in the Buen Retiro Park was moved to the Plaza de Oriente in 1843, the statue of Philip III in the Casa de

Isabella II

Francisco de Goya: "The Shootings of May 3rd 1808"

Campo to the Plaza Mayor in 1847. The Palacio de las Cortes (now Congreso de los Diputados) was built in 1843, the Teatro Real or Teatro de la Ópera (now altered) and the National Library in 1850. In 1860 the Plan Castro, a development plan for the growing capital, provided for the extension of the city to the north-east and south. (This followed Haussmann's plans of 1851 for Paris and was contemporaneous with the Plan Cerdá for Barcelona). Under the plan particular population groups were to have their own neighbourhoods. The plan was followed by the development, on a strictly rectangular grid, of the Chamberí and Salamanca districts, extensions of the residential areas round the Retiro Park which had been laid out in the reign of Charles III. These are still favoured residential districts for prosperous Madrileños. In 1851 the first railway line between Madrid and Aranjuez was opened.

First Spanish Republic

A revolution in September 1868 deposed Isabella and led to the establishment of the First Spanish Republic. This lasted only a short time, for in 1874 Isabella's son Alfonso XII returned to power with the help of the military. In 1875 he entered Madrid, which now had a population of almost 500,000, amid popular rejoicing. Alfonso was responsible for giving the city its first telephone system, introducing general and equal suffrage and promulgating the code of civil law which is still in force. Other modern innovations were electric light and a tramway system. In architecture Historicism was the fashionable mode, and new buildings were erected following a variety of models – Gothic, Romanesque (Almudena Cathedral, 1881), Venetian (Banco de España, 1882). The first steel-framed buildings were now erected (Atocha Station; Palacio de Velázquez, whose brick façade is purely ornamental; Palacio de Cristal).

20th-century Madrid

In 1898, after the war with the United States, Spain lost its last remaining colonies – Cuba, Puerto Rico and the Philippines. Alfonso XIII came to the throne in 1902. In the architecture of Madrid Historicism still predominated. Art Nouveau failed to establish itself, and the Casa Longoria (1902) is one of the very few examples of the Modernist style. In 1910 large and imposing buildings started to be erected along the Gran Vía. One of the leading architects of the 1920s was Antonio Palacios, builder of the Palacio de Comunicaciones, who contrived, on the model of the American skyscrapers, to add modern elements to the vocabulary of Historicism and forge a very individual style. His buildings dominated the townscape of Madrid (Círculo de Bellas Artes, Banco Central, etc.). House-fronts began to be decorated with brightly coloured tiles *(azulejos)*. In 1919 the first section of Madrid's underground system, the Metro, was opened. In 1929 the Telefónica Building, the city's first high-rise block, was built.

On April 14th 1931 the Second Republic was proclaimed, and Alfonso XIII, who since 1923 had only managed to hold on to power with the help of General Primo de Rivera's military dictatorship, went into exile. The *niña bonita* ("fair maiden"), as the Second Republic was popularly known, was faced with insoluble problems, which led to violent confrontations. On July 18th 1936 the army, under the leadership of General Francisco Franco, seized power in a military coup. Madrid bitterly resisted the military takeover, under the slogan "No pasarán!" The bloody civil war which followed cost some 500,000 lives. Franco's victorious march into the capital on April 1st 1939 marked not only the end of the three-year battle for Madrid but the defeat of the Republic. The dictatorship which now followed was to end only with Franco's death in 1975.

The five years of the Second Republic up to the outbreak of the Civil War were too brief to permit any major building development in Madrid. The Ciudad Universitaria (begun in the early 1930s), the Casa de las Flores (1930–32) and the Barceló cinema (1930) show, however, that the younger generation of Spanish architects were no longer tied to Historicism but favoured Realism, the functional style which was already popular in Germany and Holland. At the end of the Civil War the priority was the rebuilding of the destroyed areas of the capital, and the first buildings erected were again in the Historicist manner (Ministerio del Ejército del Aire, 1942–51); but the buildings erected only a little later (Edificio España, Torre de Madrid) show a return to American models.

Spain's admission to UNESCO (1950) and the United Nations (1955) promoted the opening up of the country in both economic and cultural respects. In the early 1960s Spain enjoyed an economic upswing. Madrid reached a population of a million and became an industrial centre. People flocked to the capital from all over the country in quest of work. In 1960 Madrid's population passed the 2 million mark; by 1970 it was over 3 million. This growth was reflected in a number of major projects, including the development of the Paseo de la Castellana, which now became *the* financial and economic centre of the city, and the building of the Azca district and La Vaguada, the very model of a modern shopping centre, in the early 1980s (architect César Manrique).

Franco's death in 1975 had opened up the way for political reforms. Juan Carlos of Bourbon, Alfonso XIII's grandson, became king. In December 1978 the people of Spain voted in favour of a new constitution which made the country a parliamentary monarchy (the Reino de España) and a democratic state based on the rule of law. Madrid's first democratically elected Mayor was the socialist Enrique Tierno Galván, under whose aegis the city flourished in an atmosphere of liberalism and became the capital of the cultural movement of the early 1980s known as La Movida.

On February 23rd 1981 members of the Guardía Civil attempted, unsuccessfully, to launch a coup d'état in the Congreso de los Diputados. In 1982 a socialist, Felipe Gonzales, was elected prime minister, continuing in office until a change of government in 1996.

On February 22nd 1983 Madrid became an autonomous Region, one of a total of 17 *comunidades autónomos*. In 1986 Spain joined the European Community. In the same year the Centro de Arte Reina Sofía was opened.

In 1992 Spain celebrated the 500th anniversary of Columbus's discovery of America. Also in that year Barcelona hosted the Summer Olympics, Seville put on the World's Fair and Madrid became the European City of Culture.

1997

As a result of a movement of population from the city into the outlying districts Madrid's population fell slightly below the 3 million mark in 1997. In the same year Spain showed for the first time a slight rise in the birth rate.

On July 14th 1997 Madrid was the scene of the largest demonstration in its history, when 1.5 million people gathered between the Plaza de Colón and the Puerta del Sol to protest against the murder of a Basque town councillor by the Basque terrorist organisation ETA.

The birth rate was around 1.16 children per women – the lowest in the world.

1998

The extension of Madrid's Metro system continued. The link with the IFEMA exhibition centre was completed; that with the airport is due for completion by the end of 1999.

Famous People

This section contains brief biographies of notable people who were born, lived or worked in Madrid or died there.

The Duchess of Alba earns her place in history as the patroness of the great Spanish painter Francisco de Goya. As a member of the powerful Alba family she dominated the social life of Madrid at the end of the 18th century. Her receptions, her dramatic performances and her literary salon contrasted sharply with the dull and tedious court of Charles IV and his wife Maria Luisa of Parma. Goya immortalised the restless and vital Duchess in many paintings and drawings which bear witness to the enigmatic attraction and celebrated charm of this aristocrat who also had a very human appeal. (See Sights from A to Z, Palacio de Liria).

Cayetana de Alba (1762–1802)

The beautiful Teresa de Cabarrús, daughter of the Conde de Cabarrús, was born in Madrid. She married a Frenchman, the Marquis de Fontenay, and became involved in the turmoil of the French Revolution. After separating from her husband she moved to Bordeaux, where she came under the protection of the powerful revolutionary Jean-Lambert Tallien. In order to save her from the guillotine he took a leading part in the movement which brought about the fall of Robespierre in the month of Thermidor 1794. As Madame Tallien she became famous in revolutionary France as "Notre-Dame de Thermidor". During the reign of Napoleon she played a prominent and brilliant part in the Paris salons, and was able to maintain her position after the Restoration.

Teresa de Cabarrus, known as Madame Tallien (1773–1835)

Calderón de la Barca, one of the leading dramatists of the Spanish Siglo de Oro (Golden Age), came of a noble family. He studied theology at the universities of Alcalá and Salamanca, but abandoned his ecclesiastical career to devote himself to writing, in particular for the theatre. He took part in the campaign to repress a rebellion in Catalonia in 1640, and gave expression to his disappointment with military life in "El Alcalde de Zalamea". He became the most popular dramatist at the court of Philip IV. After being ordained as a priest he was appointed chaplain to the king.

D. PETRVS CALDERON DE LA BARCA

Pedro Calderón de la Barca (1600–81)

Calderón's dramatic work developed the themes and techniques of Lope de Vega (see below), but achieved wider scope and greater depth. His plays are notable for their philosophical content, their skilful plotting and their dramatic effectiveness. In his early work Calderón preferred comedy (e.g. "La Dama Duende"), but in his later allegorical plays he tackled theological and philosophical problems ("La Vida es Sueño", "El Mágico Prodigioso", etc.).

The author of "Don Quixote" was born in Alcalá de Henares (see Sights from A to Z, Alcalá de Henares), in the province of Madrid, the fourth of the seven children of an unsuccessful doctor. As a soldier he was severely wounded in 1571 in the Battle of Lepanto against the Turks, leaving him with a crippled left hand, and in 1575 he was taken prisoner in Algiers. After his ransom was at last paid in 1580 he found himself free but without any money. He received a royal grant of 100 ducats, but, unable to live by his writings, became a soldier in the Portuguese ser-

Miguel de Cervantes Saavedra (1547–1616)

vice and later set up as a merchant. His marriage in 1584 was unhappy, and his applications for a post in the Spanish colonies in South America were unsuccessful. He did, however, become commissioner of supplies in Andalusia for the Armada and in 1594 a tax collector in Granada. In 1597 a bank in which he had deposited government funds collapsed, and he spent some time in prison. In 1602 he again found himself in prison. During these years, particularly during his stays in prison, he worked on his great novel, the first part of which appeared in 1605. In spite of its success Cervantes, who lived in Valladolid from 1604, remained poor, the profit from the book being divided between the publisher and the printer. The second part of "Don Quixote" was completed in 1814 ; but in that year a spurious Part II was published, with insulting remarks about Cervantes. The second part was printed in 1616, but Cervantes did not live to see its success, dying of dropsy in April of that year.

Throughout his life Cervantes was plagued by misfortune: imprisonment, constant poverty, debts incurred during his time as a government employee. All the more admirable, therefore, is his literary achievement, the humour, the irony and above all the humanity of "Don Quixote". In this novel, conceived as a parody of the romances of chivalry which were widely popular at that time, he created a faithful picture of Spanish society, lamented the loss of ideals and recognised the decline of the Spanish empire which was already under way. In "Don Quixote", which reflects some of his own experiences, Cervantes showed himself a master story-teller; and in his genre tales, the "Noveles ejemplares", he set standards for the short story.

Ferdinand II
(1452–1616)
and Isabella I
(1451–1504)

The marriage in 1469 of Ferdinand, king of Sicily and heir to the throne of Aragon, with Isabella, heiress to the throne of Castile and León, brought about the union of two great Spanish kingdoms. After the death of Isabella's brother Henry IV in 1474 the new queen made her husband co-ruler with equal rights to herself. In the subsequent War of the Castilian Succession the two monarchs asserted their claims against those of Afonso V of Portugal. With the death of Ferdinand's father, John II, in 1479, the union of the kingdoms was complete. Ferdinand and Isabella concentrated their attention on Castile, where they set up a centralised administration and, with the support of the towns, established their authority as against the nobility. In 1478 Isabella reintroduced the Inquisition in Castile and León. With the conquest of Granada, the last Moorish stronghold, in 1492 the Reconquista was complete. In the same year Christopher Columbus, whose plans Isabella had supported, landed in America and paved the way for the Spanish *conquistadores*. It was the discovery of America that ensured Ferdinand and Isabella's place in history as the founders of the Spanish empire. In 1496 Pope Alexander VI granted them the honorific style of "Catholic Monarchs" (Reyes Católicos). In subsequent years both Naples and Navarre were conquered. When Isabella died in 1504 her son-in-law Philip I the Fair inherited the crown of Castile, but died only two years later, after which Ferdinand himself ruled on behalf of his daughter Juana la Loca (Joan the Mad) until his death. He was succeeded by his grandson Charles I (who became Holy Roman Emperor as Charles V).

Francisco de Goya was born in Fuentetodos in Aragon, the son of an artisan, although his mother was descended from the petty nobility. After twice trying unsuccessfully to be admitted to the Royal Academy, he began studying with Bayeu in Madrid. At the age of 24 he travelled to Italy. On his return he undertook various commissions and from 1775 belonged to a group of artists who supplied cartoons for the tapestries of the Real Fábrica de Tapices in Madrid. Painting in oils, he depicted mainly country scenes on large canvases in lively Rococo style. His reputation as a portraitist led to his being appointed First Royal Court Painter in 1799, although his portraits showed a merciless candour which frequently bordered on caricature, as can be seen particularly in his picture of the family of Charles IV (in the Prado). The popular uprising in Madrid in 1808 and the war of liberation against Napoleon were to have decisive effects on Goya's work. He became even more pessimistic in his outlook as a result of these events, and the works of his late creative phase are sombre and marked by a frightening and fantastic sense of horror. His etchings of this period in particular reveal his feelings. Goya emigrated to France in 1824 at the age of 78 and died in Bordeaux four years later. The Museo del Prado (see Sights from A to Z, Museo del Prado) has an outstanding collection of his work.

Francisco de Goya (1746–1828)

The painter Juan Gris (real name José Victoriano González) was a native of Madrid who achieved fame and reputation far from his native city. At the age of 19 he fled from the artistic provincialism of Madrid to Paris and took a studio in the Bateau-Lavoir in Montmartre, where Picasso also worked. He soon abandoned his decorative Art Nouveau style and joined the Cubist movement of Picasso and Braque. Like them, he experimented with collage, using such materials as newsprint and fragments of mirror glass. After the First World War he developed Cubism into "Synthetic Cubism". He was no longer concerned to depict the various aspects of the same subject, but instead "found" his subjects, creating his pictures from his inner conception of them. "Cézanne made a bottle into a cylinder: I make a cylinder into a bottle!", he declared. His early death interrupted a creative effort which strongly influenced later generations. There are a number of his works in the Centro de Arte Reina Sofía (see entry in Sights from A to Z).

Juan Gris (1887–1927)

Doña Maria Guerrero, as she was respectfully known, was the leading Spanish actress of the early part of the 20th century. She made her début in the Teatro Princesa in Madrid, now known as the Teatro Nacional Marla Guerrero (see entry in Sights from A to Z). Together with her husband, the aristocrat and actor Fernando Díaz de Mendoza, she directed the Teatro Español (see entry in Sights from A to Z), where she built up a considerable repertoire. Tours in Paris and South America brought her an international reputation. Her salon in the Teatro Español was a great rendezvous for the literary, artistic and theatrical world of Madrid.

María Guerrero (1868–1928)

Larra, one of the leading figures of the Spanish Romantic movement, was born in Madrid but spent his early years in France, where he came into contact with the French Romantics. In 1827 he began his literary

Mariano José de Larra (1809–37)

career in Madrid as a chronicler of life in the city, a dramatic critic and a political commentator. He wrote a number of plays in the Romantic mood of the day, but these had no success. The articles which he wrote under the pen-name of "Figaro", however, made him a celebrity in the literary and artistic world of Madrid. An unhappy love for a married woman and the constant frustrating pressure of the censorship on his literary work drove him to suicide before his 28th birthday. The Museo Romántico (see entry in Sights from A to Z) contains his only surviving portrait and the pistol with which he shot himself.

Félix Lope de
Vega y Carpío
(1562–1635)

The poet and dramatist Lope de Vega ranks as the creator of the Spanish *comedia* and the greatest playwright of the Spanish Golden Age. He was born in modest circumstances in Madrid, the son of an embroiderer, studied briefly in Salamanca and demonstrated his extraordinary literary talent at an early age in a series of poems and dramas. He took part in the disastrous expedition of the "Invincible Armada" in 1588, and in 1610 – after numerous amorous escapades and an unsettled life in Valencia, Toledo and Seville – settled down in Philip II's capital. After the death of his son and his wife Juana he was ordained as a priest. The house in which he lived is now a museum (see Sights from A to Z, Casa de Lope de Vega). His life continued to be ruled by passion and was enveloped in tragic events, which hastened his death. His funeral was attended by large numbers of citizens of Madrid in an impressive demonstration of mourning.

Lope de Vega, apostrophised in his lifetime as a "portent of nature" and a "phoenix of the mind", wrote more than 1500 comedies, some 500 of which have survived. He also wrote numerous short farces *(entremeses)*, religious plays *(autos sacramentales)* and many sonnets, romances and songs. In his theoretical work "Arte nuevo de hacer comedias" he set out the principles of his conception of theatre. Among his best-known plays are "Fuenteovejuna", "El Alcalde de Zalamea" and "Peribáñez".

Leandro
Fernández de
Moratín
(1760–1828)

Moratín was a dramatist whose plays promoted the ideas of the Enlightenment and the French-style classical drama (e.g. "La Comedia nueva o el Café", "El sí de las niñas"). As secretary to Cabarrús, a Spanish financier in Paris, he was able to travel widely in Europe. In Madrid he became a protégé of Charles IV's enlightened minister Manuel Godoy, who appointed him director of the Madrid theatres. After the War of Liberation (1808–12), having been a supporter of Joseph I, the king appointed by Napoleon, as well as a representative of the Enlightenment, he went into exile in France, living in Bordeaux, where he found a like-minded friend in Goya. Goya painted Moratín twice – once in his youth (Academia de San Fernando, Madrid) and again in his later years (Bilbao Museum).

José Ortega y
Gasset
(1883–1955)

As philosopher, essayist, critic, polemicist, member of parliament and professor Ortega y Gasset, a native of Madrid, exerted a powerful influence on the Spanish life of his day. After studying at Madrid, Leipzig, Berlin and Marburg he was a professor at Madrid University from 1911 to 1933, becoming the ideological and literary mentor of a whole generation. His essays "The Dehumanisation of Art" (1925) and "The Revolt of the Masses" (1930) brought him an international reputation; and as editor of the "Revista de Occidente" and leader of a group of intellectu-

als under the slogan "Al servicio de la República" he played an important part in bringing about the proclamation of the Second Republic in
1931. When the Spanish Civil War broke out in 1936 he went to France
and later to Argentina. After 1945 he returned for a time to Spain, and
died in Madrid.

Antonio Pérez, the highly gifted son of one of Philip II's secretaries,
studied at the universities of Alcalá, Louvain, Venice and Padua, and
while in Italy became familiar with the arts of diplomacy and politics, of
which he soon proved to be a master. Philip II called him back to Madrid
and appointed him his private secretary. The murder of his rival
Escobedo, in which he was involved, led to his fall. After spending
eleven years in prison he escaped to Zaragoza, where he took part in an
Aragonese rising against Philip. He fled to France to escape punishment
by the Spanish courts and the Inquisition, and died in Paris, poor, ill and
alone.

*Antonio Pérez
(c. 1540–1611)*

In the reign of Philip II, son of Charles V,
from 1556 to 1598, Spain reached its zenith
as a world power, ruling over large tracts of
Italy, the Netherlands, the American
colonies, the Philippines and Portugal.
During the Counter-Reformation Spain was
the leading power among the Catholic
countries. The intense rivalry between
Spain and England was for a short time
halted by Philip's marriage to Mary Tudor
(1554–58). In 1559, after the war with
France, Philip married Isabelle de Valois as
his third wife, and thereby exerted considerable influence over Spain's northern
neighbours until the accession of Henry IV.
In the naval battle of Lepanto in 1571 Don
John of Austria, Philip's half-brother,
defeated the Turkish fleet and ensured

*Philip II
(1527–98)*

Spain's hegemony in the Mediterranean. Nevertheless the inevitable
end of Spain's dominance as a world power began to be apparent even
during Philip's reign. From 1567 the Netherlands rebelled against
Spanish rule, and with the accession of Elizabeth I to the English throne
the old enmity came to the surface again. The defeat of the Spanish
Armada off the English coast in 1588 heralded Spain's decline as a naval
power.

In Spain itself Philip was able to consolidate the power of his royal
house, and moved the capital from Toledo to Madrid, near which he built
the palace/monastery of El Escorial (see entry in Sights from A to Z) as
a visible symbol of his rule. Both Protestants and Moors were pitilessly
pursued by the Inquisition, while Jews were expelled from Spain. These
measures, as well as continuing emigration to the colonies and the various wars which Philip waged, so weakened the country's economy that
even during Philip's reign a state of national bankruptcy had to be
declared on three occasions.

Picasso, a native of Málaga, ranks as the leading representative of
modern art, active as a painter, sculptor, graphic artist and ceramicist,
who dominated 20th century art for more than eight decades.

After early training by his father he studied at the academies of
Barcelona and Madrid (from 1896). After several stays in Paris he finally
left Spain for France in 1906. A charmingly melancholy note prevails in
his early work, which is divided, on the basis of the colours he used, into
his Blue and Rose Periods. With his key work, "Les Demoiselles
d'Avignon" (1907), he paved the way for his development, along with
George Braque, into Cubism, followed later by Juan Gris and Fernand

*Pablo Picasso
(1881–1973)*

Léger. While still occupied with cubic and geometric forms, he returned after the First World War to figural representation. He drew closer to the Surrealists; his use of forms became organic, and his pictures were full of action motifs and figures of vigorous plastic form. In the late twenties he became more interested in sculpture. Cycles of illustrations to ancient texts, works concerned with the Spanish Civil War, with scenes of destruction and maiming – "Guernica", painted after the German air raids on the Basque town (see Sights from A to Z, Centro de Arte Reina Sofía), is the prime example – bullfighting scenes and variations on the "artist and model" theme were now his main subjects. After the Second World War he devoted himself intensively to ceramics and also produced a great volume of graphic work. Thus when he died in the French town of Mougins in 1973 he left behind him a great body of work which displays his supreme creative power in his handling of the history of art, his own history and the most varied artistic materials and techniques. Therein lies the uniqueness of Picasso.

Enrique Jardiel
Poncela
(1901–52)

As a dramatist, journalist and humorist Jardiel Poncela was an imaginative proponent of Dadaist and Surrealist ideas. His plays, which enjoyed great success in Madrid, broke away from the traditions of popular comedy and showed a modern type of humour influenced by the silent film. Jardiel – as he was familiarly known in Madrid – worked for some time as a script-writer in Hollywood and later moved to Argentina. After the Spanish Civil War his comedies of the absurd fell out of favour with Madrid audiences, and he abandoned the theatre and died, embittered and forgotten.

In the 1950s and 1960s his plays and his special kind of humour enjoyed a comeback. Dramatists like Miguel Mihura, "Tono" and Alfonso Paso and the humorists associated with Alvaro de la Iglesia and the magazine "La Codorniz" would not be what they are but for Poncela.

Francisco de
Quevedo
(1580–1645)

The satirist, humanist, poet, courtier and diplomat Francisco de Quevedo is one of the great figures of the Spanish Baroque age. His family came from the Santander hills in northern Spain. He grew up in court circles, studied at the universities of Alcalá and Valladolid, where he received a thorough humanist education, and soon acquired a considerable reputation with his pamphlets and satirical writings. When Philip III moved the court from Valladolid to Madrid in 1606 the rising young writer went with it to the new capital, where he made the acquaintance of the powerful Duke of Osuna. When Osuna was appointed Viceroy of Sicily and later of Naples Quevedo went with him as his confidential political agent. The house in which he lived in Madrid now bears a commemorative tablet (see Sights from A to Z, Casa de Lope de Vega). When Philip IV came to the throne Osuna's star declined, and with it Quevedo's. A conflict with the king's all-powerful favourite the Duke of Olivares ended in Quevedo's arrest, and he languished in the prison of San Marcos in León until the Duke's fall in 1643 restored his freedom. He died a few years later, a sick and disappointed man. Quevedo's fame rests on his prose writings, in particular "El Buscón" and "Los Sueños", and he is seen as a forerunner of modern Spanish prose literature. He also wrote songs and classical sonnets of high quality.

José Gutiérrez
Solana
(1886–1945)

The painter José Gutiérrez Solana, one of Madrid's most famous citizens, came from Santander in northern Spain. At an early age he showed not only extraordinary talent as a painter but also considerable literary gifts. As a painter he developed a very individual style which has been classified as Expressionistic Realism. His paintings, in dark and muted tones, depict typical Rastro characters (see Sights from A to Z, El Rastro), bullfighters, prostitutes, tinkers, junk dealers and carnival figures. The Centro de Arte Reina Sofía (see entry in Sights from A to Z) has a number of his works, including the masterly group portrait, "La

Tertulia del Café Pornbo", which depicts the literary circle headed by Ramón Gómez de la Serna.

Tirso de Molina (real name Fray Gabriel Téllez) is one of the great trinity of 17th century Spanish dramatists (the others being Lope de Vega and Calderón). He became a member of the Mercedarian Order at an early age and lived for many years in their monastery in Madrid. As a playwright he saw himself as a disciple of Lope de Vega, and wrote more than 300 comedies, only a small proportion of which have survived. Among them is "Don Gil de las Calzas Verdes". This and other masterpieces made Tirso a great favourite with audiences at the Corral de ia Cruz and Príncipe theatres in Madrid.

Tirso was also the author of numerous religious dramas and of the first literary treatment of the Don Juan theme ("El Burlador de Sevilla", also known as "El Convidado de Piedra" (1630), which was to fire the imagination of later generations, from Molière and Mozart to Byron and E.T.A. Hoffmann.

Tirso de Molina
(1584–1648)

Consuelo Vello, known as "La Fornarina", was an actress whose beauty and intelligence shone in the theatres of Madrid during the early years of the 20th century, the "Belle Epoque". The daughter of a washerwoman and a Guardia Civil, she rose to international fame as a cabaret singer in Paris and Madrid. She died at an early age from the consequences of an operation. Her grave in the San Isidro cemetery still attracts many visitors.

Consuela Vello, La
Fornarina
(1884–1915)

Juan de Villanueva was one of the leading neo-classical architects of the 18th century. He began by training as a sculptor under his father and then worked with Giovanni Battista Sacchetti (1700 61) in Madrid as a draughtsman, becoming familiar with the Italian Baroque style. After a stay in Rome he began to work as an architect in Madrid. Among the buildings he designed were the Casita de Arriba in the Escorial (1773) and the Casita del Príncipe adjoining the palace of El Pardo. He was also responsible for the balcony and the neo-classical colonnade on the principal floor of the Casa de la Villa in Madrid (now the Town Hall: see Sights from A to Z, Plaza de la Villa). After a fire in 1790 he directed the rebuilding of the Plaza Mayor. His master work was the Prado (1787), originally built to house a museum of natural history.

Juan de
Villanueva
(1739–1811)

Madrid in Quotations

Félix Lope de Vega (1562–1639)

On the Manzanares:
You have a fine bridge which is hoping for a river.

Tirso de Molina (1584–1648)

They say it is difficult
to find in Madrid
a large empty house.
Countless are the nobles
who live there:
the whole of Castile goes to the court.

From "In Madrid there is a house"

A. Jouvin (17th century French traveller)

Madrid is a new-built town which has grown greatly since the kings of Spain have held their court there, on account of the purity and goodness of the air and the pleasant surroundings.

Giacomo Casanova (1725–98)

Casanova stayed in Madrid in 1767 and was an enthusiastic attender of masked balls: What I liked best about the spectacle was a wonderful and fantastic dance which was struck up at midnight. It was the famous fandango, of which I had often heard, but of which I had absolutely no idea. I had seen it danced on the stage in France and Italy, but the actors were careful not to use those voluptuous gestures which make it the most seductive in the world. It cannot be described. Each couple only dances three steps, but the gestures and the attitudes are the most lascivious imaginable. Everything is represented, from the desire to the final ecstasy; it is a very history of love. I could not conceive a woman refusing her partner anything after this dance, for it seemed made to stir up the senses. I was so excited at this Bacchanalian spectacle that I burst out into cries of delight. The masker who had taken me to his box told me that I should see the fandango danced by the Gitanas with good partners.

From his "Memoirs"

Victor Hugo (1802–85)

Compostella has its saint ... Madrid has the Manzanares.

Alexandre Dumas the Elder (1802–70)

When we awoke in the first grey light of morning and saw round us a vast desert landscape, a few white peaks rose above the violet ground mist. There lay the first object of our journey – Madrid! An hour later we passed through the handsome Alcalá Gate and found ourselves in the capital of Spain.

From "Journey to Spain"

Ramón de Mesonero Romanos (1803–82)

The people of Madrid are in general lively, bright and satirical. They are friendly. and are passionately concerned with fashion. They have a weakness for foreign customs and despise their own.

Alfred de Musset (1810–57)

Madrid, princess of Spain.

Mariano José de Larra (1809–97)

... If there is in Spain an industrial and commercial middle class, it is to be found not in Madrid but in Barcelona and Cádiz: here there are only an upper and a lower class ...

In Madrid there are no dances, no soirées. Everyone speaks, prays or behaves in his house as he will, along with four familiar friends: nothing more is required.

I walk along the Carrera de San Jerónimo, Calles Carretas, Príncipe and La Montera, and there, within this little span, I meet all my friends, who are similarly engaged. I talk to them all, buy cigars in a café, bow to a lady looking out of a window and return home to change.

From "Artículos costumbristas"

On the Prado Museum :
How sorry I am that you are not looking at Velázquez along with me. How great would be your delight, for the journey is worth while for his sake alone. The painters of all the various schools which surround him in the Prado, represented though they are by excellent examples of their work, appear mere botchers beside him. He is the greatest painter of all time. He has not astonished me: he has carried me away ...

Edouard Manet (1832–83)

From a letter to Fantin-Latour

... Then you come to the Puerta del Sol: what a magnificent sight! A spacious semicircular area surrounded by tall buildings, from which ten wide streets radiate. On each of these streets swarm people and carriages. Everything, as far as the eye can see, matches the scale of the square: the pavements, as broad as streets, the cafés, as big as city squares, the fountain basin, as large as a lake. And everywhere a dense, restless mass of people.

Edmondo de Amicis (1848–1908)

From "Spagna"

Madrid is a centre for the production of botched work, a great encampment of a people with nomadic instincts, a race of rascals.

Miguel de Unamuno Jugo (1864–1936)

From "La voluntad"

Madrid did not appeal to me. I took a long time to get used to its atmosphere – more the physical than the moral atmosphere. I did not like this harsh light, this glistening sun, the dust-filled air. Summer in particular was oppressive; I always liked Madrid's winter, until I became as chilly as an old tomcat.

Pío Baroja y Nessi (1872–1956)

From "La sensualidad pervertida"

... He left the village and came to Madrid. In Madrid his instinctive pessimism was reinforced; his will was totally dissolved in face of this spectacle of vanities and miseries ... What most repelled him was the frivolity, the foolishness and the instability of the literary world (the literary world of Madrid, that is).

Azorín (1874–1967)

Guadarrama, old friend,
Are you the grey and white mountain,
The mountain of my afternoons in Madrid
Which I saw bathed in blue?

Antonio Machado y Ruiz (1875–1939)

On the Sierra de Madrid:
We came up to La Morcuera as night was falling. The sun was setting as we drove through Miraflores. On the way up to the pass, a pink and grey landscape, yellow and silvery. Melancholy peace. On the pass, the black peaks of Peñalara and El Reventón and a pale transparent gold circle on the horizon. No one on the sierra. The valley, black. Magnificent air. Slight coolness.

Manuel Azaña y Ruiz (1880–1940)

On El Escorial:
We walked along the Herrería. A quiet sunny afternoon. Cold mountain air. On the way back, as darkness was falling, we stopped for a moment on the parapet of the Alamillos, above the Herta. Dense pinkish-red

sunset, without transparency; the blue vault of the sky. The monastery thrust forward into the garden like a colossus, in imposing nakedness.

From "Memoirs"

José Gutiérrez
Solana
(1886–1945)

On El Rastro, the flea market:
El Rastro is the busiest place in Madrid, the place where most work is done. In small cramped booths separated from one another by a few scraps of cloth we see all that we need – tools, beds, chests of drawers, rickety chairs ... Remnants of things that were once worth something, blankets, pictures and albums of faded photographs of people in the style of the thirties, of the Romantic period ...

From "Madrid: Escenas y Costumbres"

Corpus Barga
(1887–1957)

On the Royal Palace:
Seen from the west, the Royal Palace of Madrid has the aspect of a watchful fortress ready to defend the city but regardless of its own safety.

From "Los pasos contados"

Ernest
Hemingway
(1899–1961)

I saw Madrid come up over the plain, a compact white sky-line on the top of a little cliff away off across the sun-hardened country.

From "Fiesta"

Hans Christian
Andersen
(1805–75)

Madrid has nothing of the character of a Spanish town, still less of the capital of Spain. It became capital as a result of an idea that occurred to Philip II, and it has both frozen and sweated as a consequence of this royal will.

And yet it has one astonishing glory, the picture gallery ; it is a pearl, a treasure which is in itself worth the journey to Madrid ...

The wealth of masterpieces to be found here is surprising and overwhelming. Here you can see Raphael, Titian, Correggio, Paul Veronese, Rubens and above all Murillo and Velázquez. You would have to spend more than a year and a day here to discover all that the gallery offers and to appreciate all its treasures. Here I got to know Velázquez, a contemporary of Murillo's, for the first time. With what skill and genius he depicts the milk-pale infantas, of no real interest to us, in the ridiculous garb of their period! Thanks to the skill with which he has painted them and the gaudy setting, with the male and female dwarfs and the hungry dogs of characteristic ugliness, they become alive and eloquent and acquire a quality of beauty. The figures portrayed step out of their frame so strongly that one comes to credit the story that when some of these pictures were displayed in Velázquez's studio people in the adjoining room believed that the actual characters were in the studio.

From "In Spain"

Baedeker's "Spain
and Portugal"
(1906)

The gay and relaxed tone which prevails in cultivated society and the general politeness, rather hollow though it may be, appeals to visitors. They should take care, however, not to turn the conversation to more serious matters, and above all they should avoid any discussion of ecclesiastical or political matters. The sensitive and recently so deeply wounded national pride of Spaniards and their complete ignorance of conditions in other countries do not allow of quiet discussion of such questions. Visitors should therefore not go beyond the role of strangers with a friendly interest.

The lower classes are not free from national vanity, but they have also much common sense. In intercourse with them two things must be borne in mind: in the first place, when pursuing your own interests you should be quiet and determined but should avoid any brusqueness, which merely provokes opposition; and secondly, you should observe politeness and consideration when addressing even the most humble Spaniard, who nevertheless claims to be treated as a *caballero*. The feeling of equality has developed in Spain to an extent that excludes any obsequiousness and in the ordinary business of life, for example in the relationship of buyer and seller, can lead to disobligingness.

Although Madrid has such an abundant past it lacks a living tradition. Life in Madrid is lived in the present: in the year 1925 almost all the people of Madrid lived in accordance with the standards of 1925, in 1935 in accordance with the standards then prevailing. Even those of nostalgic disposition rapidly come to accept the fashions and customs of the present moment, disavow them though they may: their nostalgia is not genuinely felt, it is mere dreaming or idle chatter.

Pedro Laín Entralgo (b. 1908)

From "España como problema"

The men and women who make for Madrid at those hours are the real nightbirds, who go out in order to go out, who already show the lethargy of night life: the well-heeled patrons of the bars and cafés of the Gran Vía, with their perfumed and provocative women, who have dyed their hair black with one or two strands of white and wear fantastic fur coats.

Camilo José Cela (b. 1916)

From "La Colmena"

One cannot contemplate the size of Madrid nor the scale of life that prevails in it without some misgivings. Here is a city of nearly a million and a quarter inhabitants built in a wilderness and manufacturing next to nothing. Philip II chose the site for no other reason than that it was at the geographic centre of Spain, the point to which you would have to attach the string if you hung its cardboard replica horizontally from the ceiling. As a friend of mine once remarked, it was designed as the observation point in a centrally organised prison.

Gerald Brenan

From "The Face of Spain" (1950)

Suggested Tours

\The following suggestions are intended to help first-time visitors to Madrid to plan their sightseeing so as to make the best use of their time. Sights printed in **bold** are the subject of separate entries in the Sights from A to Z section of the guide, descriptions of other sights can be found by referring to the Index at the end of the volume.

If you have only a few hours in Madrid and want to see the principal sights the best plan is to take one of the many sightseeing tours on offer (see Practical Information, Sightseeing Tours).

One day

In good weather the pulsating central area of Madrid (the Centro), round the ★Puerta del Sol and the ★★Plaza Mayor can be seen on foot without undue exertion. If you prefer not to walk or want to see other characteristic quarters of Madrid such as the Retiro, Salamanca or Universidad districts you can use the city's well organised public transport (buses, Metro: see Practical Information, Public Transport) or take a taxi reasonably priced, and much preferable to driving your own car or a rented one.

Taking the **Atocha Station** or the ★★Centro de Arte Reina Sofía as your starting-point, you should head north along the tree-lined ★Paseo del Prado, past the ★Jardín Botánico and the world-famous ★★Museo del Prado, to Plaza Cánovas del Castillo and turn left into Carrera de San Jerónimo, passing the **Congreso de los Diputados** (Parliament), the grand Palace Hotel, a series of antique shops and an old-established confectioner's, the Casa Mira, to the ★Puerta del Sol. Alternatively, you can continue north from Plaza Cánovas del Castillo along the Paseo del Prado to ★Plaza de la Cibeles, one of the finest but also busiest of Madrid's squares.

Now turn left along Calle de Alcalá, which soon cuts across the ★Gran Vía, the city's main shopping street, and after passing the Baroque ★Real Academia de Bellas Artes comes to the ★Puerta del Sol, in the heart of Madrid. Here, in the old town, the numerous old-established shops (jewellers, drapers, music and craft shops, etc.) and cafés in and around Calle del Arenal, to the west, and Calle Mayor may tempt you to linger. Calle Mayor runs along the north side of the famous ★★Plaza Mayor, one of the oldest focal points of the city's life.

Continue west along Calle Mayor, passing the ★Plaza de la Villa, the Capitanía General and the **Catedral de la Almudena** (built between 1883 and 1995), which is dedicated to the city's patroness, the Virgen de la Almudena. Immediately north of it is the imposing ★★Palacio Real, in the ★Plaza de Oriente, opposite the recently reopened **Teatro Real**. A little way to the east, in a Renaissance palace, is the ★★Real Monasterio de las Descalzas Reales, which is well worth visiting for its treasures of art. From here it is a few minutes' walk back to the Plaza Mayor, where you can end the day in one of the typical Madrid cafés, restaurants, tascas and tabernas in the neighbourhood. For some suggestions see the entries on Food and Drink, Night Life and Restaurants in the Practical Information section of this guide.

The Plaza de Oriente, between the Palace and the Royal Opera, tempts visitors to rest and relax

Madrid's most exclusive shops are to be found north-east of the centre in the Salamanca district, between Calles Príncipe de Vergara and Serrano. Other good shopping areas are Preciados, Calle Mayor and Calle Arenal, round the Plaza Mayor, the avantgarde fashion quarter round Calle Almirante, Calle Princesa and the Rastro quarter (see ★El Rastro). For further information see Shopping and Souvenirs in the Practical Information section.

Shopping

Visitors who have still some energy left after their day's sightseeing can plunge into Madrid's famous night life. A very Spanish form of entertainment is a flamenco show – in popular and traditional form (with sevillanas dancing and a meal) *in tablaos,* in a more sophisticated form in *peñas* and other flamenco areas. Alternative possibilities are offered by a variety of "scene" establishments, discos, jazz bars, bars with South American music and night clubs. A typically Madrid outing is a tapa tour. See Food and Drink, Night Life and Restaurants in the Practical Information section.

Night life

After the varied programme of the first day the second day might be devoted to visiting one or more museums. One of the high points of a visit to Madrid is the Triángulo del Arte, the Triangle of Art, with its three great museums – the ★★**Museo Thyssen-Bornemisza**, housed in the Palacio Villahermosa, with a magnificent range of art from the 13th century to the present day; on the opposite side of Plaza Cánovas del Castillo the ★★**Museo del Prado**, with one of the world's finest collections of pictures; and the ★★**Centro de Arte Reina Sofía**, notable particularly for its collection of contemporary art, including Picasso's famous painting, "Guernica". The Centro de Arte is reached by going

Two days

41

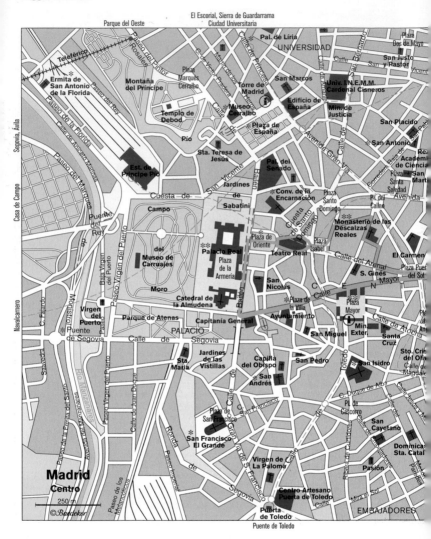

south along the ★**Paseo del Prado** to the recently renovated ★**Atocha Station**.

Other important museums are the ★★**Museo Arqueológico Nacional**, to the north in **Plaza de Colón** (Jardines del Descubrimiento), and the ★**Real Academia de Bellas Artes de San Fernando**, near the ★**Puerta del Sol**. For other museums, see the entry on Museums in the Practical Information section. For entertainment in the evening there is a choice

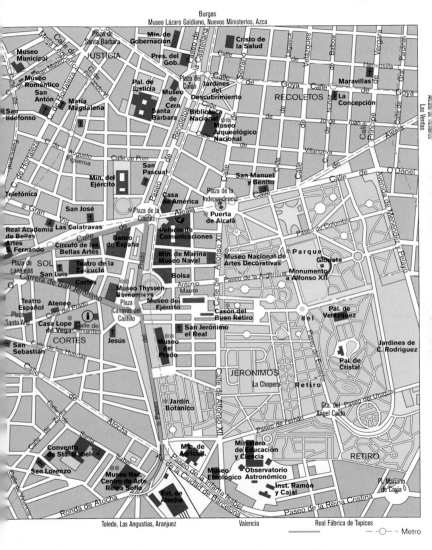

Burgos
Museo Lázaro Galdiano, Nuevos Ministerios, Azca

between a theatre, opera, ballet, concerts, a zarzuela show or visits to Madrid's typical bodegas, tascas, tabernas, bars and other night spots.

After two days mainly devoted to sights in the central area the third day might♦be spent rather farther afield – perhaps a visit to the Faro de Moncloa (see **Ciudad Universitaria**) for the wide view of the city it offers, or a trip to the ★**Casa de Campo** park, a traditional recreation area for Madrileños (which can be reached by cableway from the Paseo del

Three days

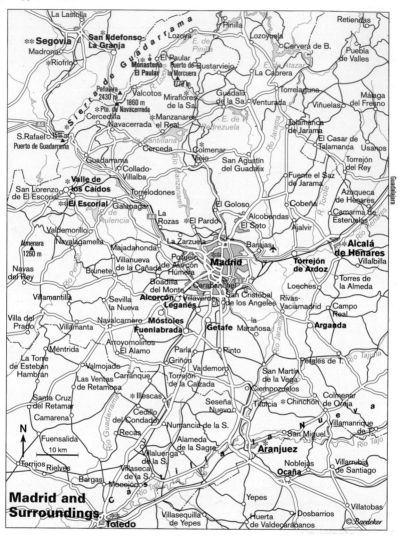

Madrid and Surroundings

Pintor Rosales). Popular with children are the **Parque Zoológico** and the Parque de Atracciones (both in the Casa de Campo).

The ★**Parque del Retiro**, particularly on Sundays, offers a variety of attractions – jugglers and other entertainers, street musicians, puppet shows, concerts – which draw large numbers of Madrileños and visitors. For bullfighting aficionados there is the arena, one of the most important in the world, in the outlying district of **Las Ventas**. Others may prefer to visit some of Madrid's numerous churches for example ★**San Antonio**

The Palace of Riofrío, near Segovia

de los Alemanes or ★**San Francisco el Grande**) and religious houses (the ★**Convento de la Encarnación** or the ★**Ermita de San Antonio de la Florida**).

Visitors with more time at their disposal can undertake a variety of attractive excursions (by rail, bus or hired car) into the surrounding area, which offers both the natural beauties of the mountains and interesting old towns. Since the people of Madrid are themselves enthusiastic excursionists, visitors will find charming hotels everywhere and excellent restaurants.

A longer stay

A must is a trip to the royal monastery of the ★★**Escorial**, 50 km (30 mi.) north-west of Madrid, and the Valle de los Caídos, with the gigantic monument to those who fell in the Spanish Civil War. Other possible excursions are to the former royal summer palace of ★**Aranjuez** (20 km (13 mi.) south), the old university town of ★**Alcalá de Henares** (30 km (20 mi.) west), the medieval town of ★Chinchón (52 km (32 mi.) south), the palaces of ★**La Granja** (78 km (48 mi.)) from Madrid on the northern slopes of the ★**Sierra de Guadarrama**) or **Riofrío**, the town of ★★**Segovia** in Old Castile (90 km (56 mi.) north-west) and ★★**Toledo**, with its many remains of Roman, Visigothic, Islamic, Jewish and Christian culture (70 km (43 mi.) south). These two towns, like the Escorial, are on UNESCO's list of world heritage sites.

**Sights
from A to Z**

Sights from A to Z

Alcalá de Henares

Excursion
30 km (20 mi.) E
of Madrid

The old town of Alcalá de Henares (pop. 164,000; alt. 587 m (1926 ft)) lies east of Madrid on the Río Henares (reached by car on N I, the road to Barcelona; by rail from the Atocha and Chamartín stations; by bus from Plaza de Castilla). The town, known to the Romans as Complutum and to the Moors as Al-Kal'a, was the birthplace of Cervantes and the seat of a university founded by Cardinal de Cisneros in 1498 at which Ignatius Loyola, St Thomas of Villanueva, Calderón, Lope de Vega, Quevedo and Tirso de Molina were students. The town was also notable for the polyglot Complutensian Bible (the New Testament in Latin, Greek, Hebrew and Chaldaean) which was published by the university between 1516 and 1520. With the transfer of the university to Madrid in 1838 Alcalá de Henares lost much of its previous importance. During the Civil War it suffered heavy destruction. The foundation of a new university in the town in 1973 brought an economic and cultural upswing.

Sights

★Colegio Mayor
de San Ildefonso

The central feature of the town is the handsome rectangular **Plaza de Cervantes**, with a statue of the famous writer. From here Calle Pedro Gumiel leads direct to the old university in Plaza de San Diego.

Of the main buildings of the university, built by Pedro Gumiel between 1498 and 1514, only the Great Hall survived the Civil War. The Plateresque main front (by Rodrigo Gil de Hontañón, 1543) is one of the finest in Spain (illustration, p. 177). The three inner courtyards were built between 1557 and 1662. In the first courtyard, the triple-galleried Patio de Santo Tomás y Villanueva, are a fountain, decorated with swans (the heraldic birds of Cardinal Cisneros) and a statue of the founder (1670). This leads into the Patio de Filósofos (rebuilt 1960) and beyond this the Patio Trilingüe (named after the three classical languages Greek, Hebrew and Latin). In this courtyard is the entrance to the Great Hall (Paraninfo), one of the few restored parts of the original building to remain almost unchanged. Adjoining the courtyard is the Hostería del Estudiante, which in spite of its name is not the students' refectory but an excellent restaurant (entrance at Calle Colegios 3).

There are regular tours of the university daily (mornings and afternoons).

Adjoining the university is the **Capilla de San Ildefonso**, in a style mingling Late Gothic, Mudéjar and Renaissance elements. In the chapel is the marble tomb (by Domenico Fancelli and Bartolomé Ordóñez) of Cardinal Cisneros (d. 1517).

There are other *colegios* belonging to the university in the central area of the town. The finest of these is the Colegio de Málaga, a little way south in Calle de los Colegios, which is notable for its beautiful inner courtyards and its brickwork. (The name *colegios* was applied both to the residences for students, grouped in their various nationalities, and to the "Latin schools" which prepared students for admission to university).

◀ *The Escorial, Philip II's monastery, palace and mausoleum, set against the majestic backdrop of the Sierra de Guadarrama*

The Patio de Santo Tomás y Villanueva, the first of the three inner courtyards of the University of Alcalá de Henares

In the arcaded Calle Mayor, which opens off Plaza de Cervantes, is the Museo Casa de Cervantes (No. 48), built in the style of the 16th century on the supposed site of Cervantes's birthplace. It contains mementoes of the author of "Don Quixote". Open Tue.–Fri. 10am–2pm, 4–7pm, Sat. and Sun. 10am–2pm.

Museo Casa de Cervantes

In **Plaza del Palacio** is the Archbishop's Palace, which was begun in the 13th century but owes its present form to extensive alteration and rebuilding in the 14th and 16th centuries. The end façades are Gothic, the main front Plateresque. From the massive Torreón de Tenorio the town walls extend to the Puerta de Madrid, continuing to the Puerta de Burgos.

Adjoining the palace are the church and convent of **Las Bernardas**, built between 1617 and 1626 by Sebastián de la Plaza. Notable features are the statue of St Bernard over the doorway, the church, on an oval plan with six chapels, and the Capilla Mayor, decorated with paintings by Angelo Nardi.

Other religious buildings round the Plaza del Palacio are the brick-built **Convento de la Madre de Dios** (1576), to the south, and, off the square, the **Oratorio de San Felipe Neri** (1698–1704). A little way to the south is the 16th century **Iglesia Magistral**, the town's principal church, with a tall bell-tower.

Surroundings

15 km (9 mi.) south-east is Nuevo Baztán, founded by Juan de Goyeneche in 1709–1713 as a pottery- and glass-manufacturing town, complete with a palace, a parade ground, a market square and the

Nuevo Baztán

parish church of San Francisco Javier. It was designed by the famous architect José Churriguera, who was also responsible for the retable in the church.

Almudena Cathedral

See Catedral de la Almudena

★Aranjuez

Excursion
47 km (29 mi.) S
of Madrid

The former royal summer residence of Aranjuez (pop. 37,700; alt. 492 m (1614 ft)) lies to the south of Madrid on the Río Tajo (Tagus). The surrounding area is a supplier of fruit and vegetables to Madrid. The town's attraction lies not only in the palace and its gardens but in its regular grid of streets, fine avenues, bridges, churches, squares and house-fronts of brick and white stone, forming a harmonious whole.

Access

Aranjuez can be reached by car on N IV, by rail from Atocha Station and by bus from Estación Sur, Calle de Canarias 17. For romantics and railway buffs there is the Tren de la Fresa ("Strawberry Train "; see Practical Information, Excursions).

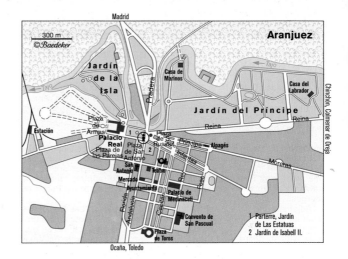

Sights

★Palacio Real

Open Tue.–Sun.
10am–6pm,
winter 5.15pm

The Palacio Real (Royal Palace), built for Philip II by Juan Bautista de Toledo, was begun in 1560. After Toledo's death in 1567 the work was carried on by Juan de Herrera, who put his own unmistakable stamp of classical severity on the building. The palace was destroyed by two fires in 1660 and 1665, but Philip V had it rebuilt almost unchanged. In the reign of the Bourbon ruler Charles III, who enlarged and altered the palace on the rationalist principles of the Enlightenment, Francesco Sabatini added two side wings, forming a spacious parade ground in front of the palace. The main front of the palace reflects Herrera's Renaissance style, though it also displays the Baroque influence of his successors.

The Royal Palace of Aranjuez

The **interior** contains valuable carpets, furniture, porcelain, clocks, pictures and other objets d'art appropriate to the rank of its inhabitants. Particularly notable features are the grand staircase designed by Giacomo Bonavia, the Royal Chapel by Sabatini, the Throne Room, hung with velvet, and – the high point of the visit – the Porcelain Room (Sala de China). This, the first creation of the porcelain manufactory brought by the king from Capodimonte to Madrid (Buen Retiro), is clad with porcelain delicately painted with Chinese scenes.

Other fine rooms are the Arabian Saloon, the Hall of the Two Sisters (modelled on the Alhambra in Granada) and the Sala de Papeles Chinos with its delicate rice-paper paintings. The pictures in the palace were the work of Giordano, Mengs, Bayeu and Maella.

The ★**gardens** of Aranjuez are justly famous. They surround the palace and extend along the banks of the Tagus, shading the riverside with their ancient trees.

To the south of the Plaza de San Rusiñol is the Jardín de Isabel II, a favourite resort of the Bourbon kings.

Jardín de Isabel II

On the east side of the palace is the French-style Parterre, laid out by Philip V in 1726. Within this area is the Jardín de las Estatuas, which dates from the time of Philip II, with busts of Roman emperors and figures of gods and heroes.

Parterre

The Jardín de la Isla, on an artificial island in the Tagus, is the oldest part of the Aranjuez gardens. It was laid out by Isabella the Catholic in an area which had previously been a vegetable garden and extended in the reign of Philip II. A very beautiful avenue of plane trees runs along the banks of the Tagus.

Jardín de la Isla

The largest and most beautiful of the gardens is the Jardín del Príncipe, to the north-east of the palace. It was laid out for Charles III in 1763 by the French landscape architect Boutelou, who had earlier designed the

Jardín del Príncipe

51

Parterre. Apart from a number of fountains and some exotic plants the main attraction of the gardens is the Casa del Labrador (Countryman's Cottage) at the eastern tip of the garden, at the end of the Calle de la Reina. This little palace, with a main block flanked by two side wings, was built for Charles IV in 1803 by Isidro González Velázquez. The façade is decorated with statues of ancient heroes. The principal features of the interior, which is sumptuously appointed in Louis XVI and Empire styles, are the Grand Staircase, the Billiard Room, the Gallery of Statues, the Grand Saloon, Queen Maria Luisa's Hall and the Platinum Cabinet.

★Casa de Marinos

The Casa de Marinos (Seamen's House), in a horseshoe bend in the Tagus within the Jardín del Príncipe, houses six royal barges, the finest of which are Charles IV's barge, with painting by Maella, Alfonso XII's mahogany boat and Philip V's felucca, a gift from Venetian nobles.

Surroundings

★Chinchón

Plaza Mayor, Chinchón

20 km (13 mi.) northeast of Aranjuez on M 305 is the little Castilian town of Chinchón (pop. 4000), which is famed for its aniseed brandy. The central feature of the town is its handsome Plaza Mayor, surrounded by three- and four-storey buildings with open galleries, occupied by small cafés, restaurants and shops. During the summer bullfights (see Baedeker Special, p. 162) are held in the square, as they have been since the 16th century, as well as theatrical productions and other events. From the Iglesia de la Asunción (1537–1626), on higher ground, there is a fine view of the little town. Goya, whose brother was priest here, bequeathed his painting of the Assumption to the church. The castle above the town, seat of the Counts of Chinchón, dates from the 15th century. In 1706, during the War of the Spanish Succession, it suffered heavy destruction.

Armería

See Palacio Real

Ateneo Artístico, Científico y Literario   H 10

For a century after its foundation in 1820 the Ateneo was the centre of Madrid's and Spain's intellectual and political life. Here men of letters, philosophers and politicians met to discuss the latest literary, artistic, political and scientific developments. During the reign of Ferdinand VII and again during Primo de Rivera's dictatorship it was forced to close its doors. Its finest days were in the time of the Republic.

After the Civil War it resisted, so far as it was able, the Franco dictatorship. Since 1975 it has sought to recover its former leading position in the life of the capital and has become the venue of numerous cultural events – readings by authors, lectures, film shows, etc. Its library and reading room are open only to members.

Location
Calle del Prado 21

Metro
Sevilla

Buses
9, 15

The garden of Atocha Station, frequented not only by passengers

Atocha Station   J/K 11/12

The Atocha Station (Estación de Atocha) or South Station lies opposite the Centro de Arte Reina Sofía (see entry). "One day, on February 9th 1851, there appeared near the Atocha Monastery a monster breathing smoke and emitting fire, with whistles which were heard over half Madrid" – as a guide to Madrid described the opening of the railway line from Madrid to Aranjuez. The present station, built in 1889–91 to the design of Alberto del Palacio Elissague, is an imposing brick building with a large metal and glass dome, modelled on London's St Pancras Station (built 1866). This was the departure point for the southern suburbs of Madrid and for Andalusia and Extremadura: hence its alternative name of Estación del Mediodía (South Station).

In 1992, when the Spanish high-speed train AVE began a daily service to the World's Fair in Seville, the station was given a face-lift. Under the

Location
Glorieta de
Carlos V

Metro
Atocha, Atocha-
Renfe

Buses
6, 14, 19, 26, 27,
32, 37, 45, C

53

direction of the Spanish architect Rafael Moneo the old concourse was transformed into a post-modern vestibule, the predominant elements in which are grey marble, glass and high-tech. Where the railway lines ended there is now a botanic garden watered by a misty spray from a thousand jets. Passengers and visitors sit in the shade of palms with a view of a waterlily pond. Trains now come into another part of the station, which is now used only by the modern high-class trains, the AVEs and the Talgos, lesser services being relegated to Chamartín Station (see Practical Information, Rail Stations). There is one exception: at weekends the Tren de la Fresa ("Strawberry Train") still departs from Atocha Station for Aranjuez (see entry, and Practical Information, Excursions). Access to the Cercanías (local lines) and the Atocha-Renfe Metro station is from a simple brick-built rotunda designed by Moneo to match the style of the old station.

Auditorio Nacional de Música   A–C 6–10

Location
Calle Príncipe de
Vergara 146

Metro
Cruz del Rayo,
Prosperidad

Buses
29, 52

This modern concert hall, designed by José María García de Paredes and opened in 1989, is the home of the Spanish National Orchestra. Hall A, the Auditorio Principal, has seating for 2280, Hall B (for chamber music) for 707. The equipment and acoustics are up to international standards.

Behind the Auditorio, in the busy Calle Príncipe de Vergara, is the new multi-media City Museum (see Museo de la Ciudad).

Azca Quarter   H/J 1/2

Location
E of Calle Orense

Metro
Nuevos
Ministerios,
Santiago
Bernabéu

Buses
5, 14, 27, 40, 43, C

Half-way along the Paseo de la Castellana (see entry), between Calles General Perón, Raimundo Fernández Villaverde and Orense, is the Urbanización Azca (Alta Zona de la Castellana), a complex of offices and shops with a pedestrian precinct and public gardens (1954–64; architect Antonio Perpiñá). A symbol of the progressive beliefs of recent years, it is known as Madrid's Little Manhattan. It is surrounded by a number of striking skyscrapers.

On the southern edge of the Azca quarter is the **Torre BBV** (1971–81), a 102.7 m (337 ft) high tower block, now russet-coloured from the effects of wind and weather, built for the Banco Bilbao-Vizcaya by Francisco Javier Saénz de Oiza.

Above the Azca quarter soars the dazzlingly white **Torre de Picasso**, built between 1977 and 1988 by the Japanese architect Minoru Yamasaki, who had previously designed the World Trade Center in New York. With a height of 157 m (515 ft) and 44 floors, it is the tallest building in Spain – at any rate if television towers such as the Torrespaña to the east of the city (220 m (722 ft)) and the Torre de Coliserola in Barcelona (288 m (945 ft)) are left out of account.

On the northern edge of the Azca quarter is the 113 m (371 ft) high **Torre de Europa** (1974–87; architect Miguel Oriol e Ybarra), notable for its curving façades and the external sculpture by José María Cruz Novillo.

Immediately north of the Azca quarter, at the corner of Plaza de Joan Miró, is the **Palacio de Exposiciones y Congresos**, an exhibition and conference centre (1964–70; architect P. Pintado). The huge ceramic mural was designed by Joan Miró. On the opposite side of the street is the **Estadio Santiago Bernabéu**, home ground of Madrid's famous football team, Real Madrid. Since their foundations are higher, the two leaning towers of the Puerta de Europa, also known as the Torres Kio, reach higher into Madrid's skyline (see Paseo de la Castellana).

Botanic Gardens

See Jardín Botánico

The cableway in the Casa de Campo offers fine views of western Madrid as well as of the park

Casa de Campo

A–C 6–10

The Casa de Campo, a traditional resort and recreation area of the Madrileños, lies to the west of the city. Its holm-oaks, pines, planes, poplars and shrubs of all kinds cover an area of 1700 ha (4200 acres). Its origins go back to the time of Philip II, who established a large royal hunting preserve near the Alcázar and built a hunting lodge, the Casa de Campo (it lies in the eastern part of the park and is now occupied by the municipal police authority). As a royal estate, closed to the public, it continued to be extended by purchases of adjoining land until the 19th century. It became a public park in 1931, under the Second Republic.

Metro
Lago, Batán

Buses
33, 65

The park offers a wide range of facilities for sport and other leisure activities – an artificial **lake** with canoes for hire, a swimming pool, tennis courts, riding, basket-ball courts and football pitches, an amusement park with numerous rides (the Parque de Atracciones; open Apr.–Sep. Tue.–Sun. from 12 noon; Metro: Batán) and a zoo (see Parque Zoológico). Also within the park are trade fair grounds and an auditorium for rock concerts, the Rockódromo.

It is worth while taking a trip in the cableway (★**Teleférico**) which runs over the park from the Paseo del Pintor Rosales (Metro: Argüelles) for the sake of the views of the park and the surrounding parts of Madrid. The stables of the Venta del Batán bullring are not open to the public.

Casa Longoria, one of Madrid's few Art Nouveau buildings

Although the encroachment of building development on the edges of the woodland has to some extent been controlled, the main problem of the Casa de Campo is now the damage caused by exhaust gases and the great masses of people who frequent it In the late nineties much of the northern (and largest) part of the park was closed to motor traffic; but the area round the Zoo and the Lago is still invaded by more than 40,000 cars every week. This too is the area where most of the park's visitors (around 500,000 a week) congregate and where the sandy hills and the vegetation suffer from the huge numbers of people and the hordes of mountain bikers. During the Civil War the Casa de Campo, lying as it was in the front line, suffered heavy devastation and thereafter was replanted mainly with pines. As a result of a large-scale reafforestation programme, with money coming from the city and the European Union, however, holm oaks and other native species are now gaining ground.

Casa Longoria   H 7

Address
Fernando VI 6
Metro
Alonso Martínez
Bus
37

The Chueca district of Madrid, whose other sights include the Museo Municipal, the Museo Romántico and the Teatro Nacional María Guerrero (see entries), also has one of the city's few examples of Art Nouveau architecture, whose best known Spanish exponent was Antoni Gaudí. This is the Casa Longoria, which stands at the corner of Calle Fernando VI and Calle Pelayo. It was built in 1902 by the Catalan architect José Grases Riera for a banker. It is now occupied by the Sociedad de Autores (Society of Authors). Apart from its strikingly ornate façade its most notable feature is a staircase developed out of a circular form.

★Casa de Lope de Vega   H 10

The house once occupied by Lope de Vega lies in a narrow street in the Barrio de los Literarios or de las Musas (the men of letter's or the Muses' quarter), between Plaza de Santa Ana (see Teatro Español), Atocha and Plaza de las Cortes. The great dramatist and poet (see Famous People), founder of the 17th century Spanish comedia, settled here in 1610. The house now contains a small museum which gives an impression of everyday life in the Madrid of the Golden Age.

On a house at the corner of Calle Lope de Vega and Calle de Quevedo is a tablet recording that the writer Francisco de Quevedo (1580–1645) lived here. His rival Góngora (1561–1627) is also believed to have lived in this area around 1619.

Nearby, at the intersection of Calle de Cervantes and Calle del León, there stood until its demolition in the 19th century a house occupied by Cervantes, who died there on April 23rd 1616.

Address
Calle de
Cervantes 11

Metro
Antón Martín

Buses
9, 14

Open Tue.–Fri.
9.30am–2pm,
Sat. 10am–1pm

Casa de la Villa

See Plaza de la Villa

★Casón del Buen Retiro   J 10

The Casón art gallery, like the nearby Army Museum (see Museo del Ejército) and Retiro Park (see Parque del Retiro), formed part of the former royal residence, the Real Sitio del Buen Retiro, built by the Habsburg rulers in the 17th century. Designed by Alonso Carbonell (1638), with ceiling frescoes by Luca Giordano, it was the royal ballroom. In the 19th century it was thoroughly restored and extended in the neoclassical style of the Prado, and the west front was rebuilt by Ricardo Velázquez Bosco in 1886 after suffering storm damage. Thereafter it housed in succession a Topographical Cabinet, a riding school, a sports hall and finally a Museum of Reproductions. It is now an annexe of the Prado Museum (see Museo del Prado), containing works by 19th century Spanish masters in the then prevailing styles – Historicism, Romanticism, Impressionism – with the exception of Goya's works, which are shown in the Prado itself.

Location
Calle Alfonso XII
28

Metro
Retiro, Banco de
España

Buses
10, 14, 19, 27

Open Tue.–Sat.
9am–7pm, Sun.
and pub. hols.
9am–2pm

The **historical painting** which was so popular in the 19th century is represented by works by Francisco Pradillo ("Joan the Mad"), Antonio Gisbert ("Execution of Torrijos"), Antonio Muñoz Degrain ("The Lovers of Teruel") and Rosales ("The Testament of Isabella the Catholic").

Among the best known **Realists** are the portrait painters Carlos Luis de Ribera, Federico Madrazo, Director of the Prado 1860–68 and First Court Painter ("Carolina Coronado", "Federico Flores"), Antonio María Esquivel, Leonardo Alenza and Vicente López ("Goya at 80","Court Organist Félix López").

Among the **Impressionists** are the very gifted Mariano Fortuny (1838–74; "Banks of the Guadaira", "Landscape", "The Painter's Children in the Japanese Saloon"), Eduardo Rosales ("Nude"), Aureliano Beruete, Darío Regoyos, Joaquín Mir and Joaquín Sorolla.

Other notable painters are the **Catalans** Santiago Rusiñol (1861–1931), Ramón Casas (1866–1932) and Isidro Nonell (1873–1911).

Catedral de la Almudena

E 9

Location
Plaza de la
Armería

Metro
Ópera

Buses
3, 25, 33, 39, 48

A figure of Christ in the Almudena Cathedral

The Almudena Cathedral is one of Madrid's oldest churches, dating from the 9th century; but in the course of later centuries it suffered much alteration and enlargement. In the time of Lope de Vega (16th/17th centuries: see Famous People) a rich and handsome church stood on this site, near the Alcázar, but in 1870, for some unknown reason, this was pulled down, and in 1883 the foundation stone of a large new neo-Gothic church designed by Marqués de Cubas was laid on the same site. Work on its construction proceeded at a snail's pace, and only really got going in the 1940s, to plans which had been altered in some respects by Fernando Chueca Goitia. In 1960 the neo-classical façade facing the Royal Palace (see Palacio Real) was completed. In 1993 the church was consecrated as the cathedral of the Madrid diocese, and in 1995 it was finally completed. The interior is in a relatively sober neo-Gothic style; much of the furnishings came from older Madrid churches.

Opening hours

The cathedral is open to the public Mon.–Sat. 10am–1.30pm, 6–7.30pm, Sun. 10am–2.30pm, 6–7.30pm.

★★Centro de Arte Reina Sofía

H 11

Location
Calle Santa Isabel
52

Metro
Atocha

Buses
10, 14, 27, 37, 45

Open Mon. and
Wed.–Sat.
10am–9pm, Sun.
10am–2.30pm

The Museo Nacional Centro de Arte Reina Sofía is Madrid's museum of contemporary art. It occupies the former Hospital General de San Carlos, a massive Late Baroque building consisting of four wings enclosing a courtyard laid out as a garden. It was built in the 18th century by José de Hermosilla and the Italian architect Francesco Sabatini, who was also responsible for the design of the Royal Palace (see Palacio Real). It served as a hospital until 1965; then, after renovation from 1980 onwards (architects José Luis Iñiguez de Onzoño and Antonio Vázquez de Castro), it was opened in 1986 as an Art Centre and in 1990 was given the status of a National Museum.

There are two glass lifts for visitors on the main front (and a third lift for goods). The Centre, with six floors, has a total floor space of 54,600 sq. m (588,000 sq. ft), providing accommodation for the Spanish Museum of Contemporary Art, periodic special exhibitions, a cafeteria, a well-stocked bookshop, a library, a cinema for film and video shows and administrative offices.

The core of the Centre is the collection of the Museo Español de Arte Contemporáneo on the second floor, which offers a general survey of Spanish art from the end of the 19th century to the present day. Particularly well represented are the three giants of the Spanish avant-garde, Picasso, Miró and Dalí. Other artists include Juan Gris, Martín Chirino, Isidro Nonell, Eduardo Chillida, Pancho Cossío, Gargallo, Palazuelo, Antonio Tápies, Manuel Millares, Equipo 57, Equipo Crónica, Zuloaga, Gutiérrez, Solana and Rafael Canogar. Foreign modernist schools are represented by Bacon, Alechinsky, Fontana, Dubuffet, Magritte, Kounellis, Pistoletto, Flavin, Newman, Judd and Schnabel.

The Centre's main attraction is "**Guernica**", Picasso's famous painting in tones of black and white, giving expression to his revulsion at the bombing of the little Basque town of Guernica by the German Condor Legion in April 1937 in support of Franco's side in the Spanish Civil War.
The picture – Picasso's contribution to the Spanish pavilion in the Paris Universal Exhibition of 1937 – is a powerful indictment of the terrorism of war and fascism. Picasso bequeathed it to the democratic state of Spain, and under the terms of his will it remained outside Spain during the Franco dictatorship and was shown in New York's Museum of Modern Art. It was brought back to Spain in 1981.

Picasso's indictment of the horrors of war, "Guernica", has lost none of its actuality

Chinchón

See Aranjuez, Surroundings

Círculo de Bellas Artes   H 9

The Círculo de Bellas Artes, an association for the promotion of the fine arts founded in the late 19th century, occupies a building erected in 1919 by Antonio Palacios, who was also the architect of the Head Post Office (Palacio de Comunicaciones: see Plaza de las Cibeles). On the ground floor is the Café del Círculo, also known as La Pecera (open daily 9am–1am, Sat. 3am; sculpture by Moisés Huertas, "Recumbent Woman").

The Círculo also has exhibition and function rooms, theatres, studios

Location
Calle de Alcalá
44/Marqués de
Casa Riera 2

Metro
Banco de España,
Sevilla

and a cinema. It is a popular venue for a variety of festivals, rock concerts, Shrovetide balls, etc.

Ciudad Universitaria   A–D 1–4

Metro
Ciudad
Universitaria

Buses
46, 62, 82, 83, A,
D, G

The University City lies to the north-west of Madrid on N IV, the road to La Coruña. In 1927, during the reign of Alfonso XII, it was moved to the site of the royal gardens of La Moncloa, replacing the Universidad Central in Calle San Bernardo, founded in 1836 after the closure of the renowned University of Alcalá de Henares (see entry). The architect of the University City was Modesto López Otero. During the Civil War the University City and the nearby Parque del Oeste (see entry) were the scene of bitter fighting, during which many buildings were destroyed. The rebuilding and extension of the university began in the 1940s, and as a result it shows a considerable variety of architectural styles. In recent years the university buildings on both sides of the Avenida de Puerta de Hierro, extending to the Puerta de Hierro (see entry), have increased immeasurably in number. Among them are a number of buildings not occupied by the university, including the large complex round the Moncloa Palace (originally 18th century; occupied by the Regent Maria Cristina, 1833–1840, and Queen Isabella II, 1843–68; now government offices) and a low building adjoining the Faculty of Architecture (Avenida de Juan de Herrera 2; by Jaime López Asiaín and Angel Díaz, 1969), formerly housing the Museum of Contemporary Art (see Centro de Arte Reina Sofía) and now occupied by the Museo de Reproducciones Artísticas (and also used for special exhibitions of contemporary art).

The Faro de Moncloa, one of Madrid's few viewpoints

Between the Cuartel del Ejército del Aire and the Puerta de Hierro

Buildings between the Cuartel del Ejército del Aire, the massive complex of the Ministry of Aviation in Plaza de la Moncloa, and the Puerta de Hierro (see entry) at the north end of the University City:

Arco de la Victoria (Victory Arch, Avenida del Arco de Victoria; by Modesto López Otero, 1956); beyond this the Faro de Moncloa, a 92 m (302 ft) high outlook tower (by Salvador Pérez Arroyo, 1991; open Tue.–Sun. 11am–1.45pm, 5.30–8pm); Facultad de Ciencias (Faculty of Science, Calle Paraninfo; by Miguel de Santos Nicolás and Eduardo Torroja, 1936); Hospital Clínico de San Carlos (Calle Isaac Peral; by Manuel Sánchez Arcas and Eduardo Torroja, 1932–36); Facultad de Medicina and Escuela de

Estomatología (Faculty of Medicine and Dental School), Plaza de Ramón y Cajal; by Miguel de los Santos Nicolás, 1935–45); Facultad de Farmacia (Faculty of Pharmacy, Plaza de Ramón y Cajal; by Agustín Aguirre and Mariano Garrigues, 1935); Facultad de Filosofía y Letras (Faculty of Philosophy and Letters, Plaza de Menéndez Pelayo; Building A by Agustín Aguirre, 1932–33; Building B, also by Aguirre, 1962); Museo de América and Iglesia de Santo Tomás de Aquino (see Museo de América; Avenida del Arco de Victoria/Avenida de los Reyes Católicos; by Luis Moya Blanco and Luis Martínez Feduchi); Dependencias de la Facultad de Ciencias Políticas y Sociología (Faculty of Politics and Sociology, Avenida de Puerta de Hierro; by Miguel Fisac, 1953).

To the south-west, along the orbital motorway M 30, a number of interesting buildings have been erected since the foundation in 1972 of UNED, the Open University. Among them is the Library (by José Ignacio Linazaroso, 1994), a huge but elegant brick-built structure with the book-stacks set round a central light shaft.

The Palacio de las Cortes, now named the Congreso de los Diputados, is the seat of the Spanish Parliament

Congreso de los Diputados H 9

The Palacio de las Cortes has been since 1978 the seat of the Congreso de los Diputados, the lower house of the Spanish Parliament. A stately building with a neo-classical portico, it stands on the Carrera de San Jerónimo, looking on to the charming Plaza de las Cortes and the showy façade of the Palace Hotel. It was built in 1843–50 (architect Pascual y Colomer) on the site of a former monastery; a post-modern annexe extending along the Carrera de San Jerónimo was built in 1986–90 (architects María Rubert de Ventos, Oriol Clos and Josep Parcerisa). Flanking the main entrance, which is used only on ceremonial occa-

Location
Plaza de las Cortes

Metro
Banco de España

Bus
9

sions, are two bronze lions cast from cannon captured in the Moroccan war which ended in 1860.

History The Spanish Cortes have had an eventful history. In the late mediaeval period the Curia Regia, the royal council consisting of representatives of the nobility and higher clergy, was transformed by the addition of representatives of the third estate and renamed the Cortes. At first their main function was to approve the granting of money to the king, but they soon gained the right of participation in political matters. In the 16th and 17th centuries the centralising policies of the Spanish state led to a steady decline in the Cortes' importance. Charles V was still dependent on the Cortes for the execution of his military plans, but Philip V summoned them only to confirm formally his decisions. The Spanish Liberals of the early 19th century harked back to the mediaeval model of the Cortes when they held the first National Assembly at Cádiz in 1812 and proclaimed Spain's first constitution. At that time Spain was occupied by French troops and the Spanish king, Ferdinand VII, was a prisoner in French hands. When Ferdinand returned to Spain he annulled the constitution and dissolved the Cortes. After a brief constitutional interlude in 1820–23 he ruled without a constitution until his death in 1833. In the course of the 19th century Spain had a series of different constitutions – in 1834, 1837, 1869, 1873 (the first republican constitution, which never came into force) and 1876. The 1876 constitution was abrogated by General Primo de Rivera's coup d'état in 1923, and the fall of the dictator brought with it the fall of the monarchy. The Republic proclaimed in 1931 introduced a constitution which was among the most progressive of its time. The present Spanish constitution was adopted by the Congreso de los Diputados on October 31st 1978 and approved in a national referendum on December 6th of that year. It makes Spain a parliamentary democracy. The Parliament consists of the

The Convento de la Encarnación, now a museum

Cortes Generales – the Congreso de los Diputados and the Senate. The Congreso is elected every four years on a mixture of direct and proportional representation and has around 300 members, depending on the number of seats won by specific candidates over and above the number of seats to which the parties are entitled by the number of votes cast for them.

On Fridays from 6pm visitors can apply at an office in Calle Zorilla (behind the Congreso), on presentation of their passport or identity document, for a ticket for admission to a sitting of the Congreso in the following week. Only the first 19 applicants are admitted.

★Convento de la Encarnación
E 9

Juan Gómez de Mora, a pupil of Herrera and architect of the Plaza Mayor (see entry), built the Augustinian Convent of the Incarnation for Margaret of Austria, Philip III's wife (foundation stone laid 1611, consecrated 1616). It was originally an annexe of the royal Alcázar, with which it was connected by a long corridor. After a fire the church was rebuilt by Ventura Rodríguez in 1767, with a refashioned interior. There is a remarkable contrast between the plain façade, in a style characteristic of the Habsburg rulers and reminiscent of the Escorial, and the overcharged Baroque style of the interior. In 1965 part of the convent was opened to the public as a museum, with numerous 17th century paintings and church furnishings and a collection of relics. Notable among the relics is an ampulla containing the blood of St Pantaleon, which liquefies annually on his feast day, July 27th.

As they enter the first room visitors are enveloped in the austere and yet gracious atmosphere of a 17th century convent. The panelled doors, the exposed beams of the ceiling and the portraits of Habsburg monarchs recall the world of Lope de Vega's *comedias*. A landscape by Peter van der Meulen, "Entrega en el Bidassoa", commemorates the double marriage which linked the royal houses of France and Spain, between Ana, Philip III's daughter, and Louis XIII of France and between Isabelle, daughter of the French king Henry IV, and Philip IV. Among the pictures on display are works by 17th century Spanish masters (Juan Carreño, Bartolomé Román, Carducho, Antonio de Pereda). Works by some of the leading religious sculptors of the 17th century – Gregorio Hernández (Fernández), José de Mora, Pedro de Mena – give some impression of this typically Spanish art.

The choir has stalls dating from the foundation of the convent and paintings by Bartolomé Roldán; the walls are clad with Talavera tiles.

Location
Plaza de la Encarnación 1

Metro
Ópera, Santo Domingo

Buses
25, 33, 39

Open Tue.–Sun.
10.30am–1.30pm,
4–5.30pm,
morning only Fri.

Convento de las Trinitarias
H 10

Near Plaza de Santa Ana, in the quiet Calle de Lope de Vega (see Casa de Lope de Vega and Teatro Español) in the Barrio de los Literarios, is the Convento de las Trinitarias. Flanking the convent church, with its three-arched entrance and oval windows, are two plain two-storey buildings with balconies. The convent was founded in 1612, but the present building dates only from 1673. Designed by Marcos López, it is a showpiece of 17th century Madrid architecture. In an earlier church on this site Cervantes was buried in 1616 – an event commemorated by a neo-Plateresque gravestone, although the position of his grave is not known. The same fate has befallen the graves of Calderón and Velázquez (see Plaza de Oriente). Lope de Vega's grave is also empty: until the 18th century his remains rested in the Iglesia de San Martín, at the corner of Calle Atocha and Calle San Sebastián, now a National Monument, which still preserves the memory of the great Baroque writer.

A daughter of Cervantes, who lived in the nearby Calle Cervantes, took

Location
Calle Lope de Vega 18

Metro
Antón Martín

Buses
10, 14, 27, 34, 37

the veil in the Trinitarias, and the daughter of Lope de Vega, who had a house in the same street (see Casa de Lope de Vega), was also a nun here, under the name of Sor Marcela.

Cuartel del Conde-Duque
E 7

Location
Calle Conde-Duque 9

Metro
Ventura
Rodríguez, San
Bernardo,
Noviciado

Buses
1, 2, 44, C

The Barracks of the Count-Duke (Conde-Duque de Olivares, Philip IV's minister) were built in 1720 to the design of Philip V's architect Pedro Ribera. They reflected the new military policy of the Bourbon rulers, who wanted to have troops permanently stationed in the capital. With its unusually large scale the complex, laid out round three inner courtyards, formed a unity with the adjoining Palacio de Liria and its gardens. It was originally occupied by the royal bodyguard, later by cavalry and finally by a military academy. For 150 years the barracks defended the north-western approach to the capital.

The long ranges of plain brick buildings have rather forbidding aspect. Only the handsome main entrance recalls the architect who created the Hospicio de San Fernando (see Museo Municipal) and the Toledo Bridge (see Puente de Toledo). After many years' restoration work the barracks now house the Centro Cultural Conde-Duque, used mainly for exhibitions, readings by authors and lectures (open Tue.–Sat. 10am–2pm, 5.30–9pm, Sun. and pub. hols. 10.30am–2.30pm). Here too are the City Archives, the Municipal Library, the Music Archives and the Newspaper Archives, the Hemeroteca Municipal (open Mon.–Fri. 9am–9pm; to obtain a reader's ticket you must produce a passport or other identity document and three passport photographs).

Descalzas Reales

See Monasterio de las Descalzas Reales

There are more than 50 figures in Goya's painting of "St Anthony's Miracle" in the dome of the Ermita de San Antonio de la Florida

★Ermita de San Antonio de la Florida   C 7

The chapel of San Antonio de la Florida, situated on the banks of the Manzanares, has always been a popular place of pilgrimage with the people of Madrid, and is still the scene of a great annual festival in honour of St Anthony of Padua. It is also famed as the place of burial of the great Spanish painter Francisco de Goya (see Famous People) and as the Museo Panteón de Goya, containing some of his finest work.

In 120 days, between August and December 1798, Goya, then Charles IV's court painter, decorated the dome of this modest neo-classical building (architect Francisco Fontana) with frescoes of a miracle performed by St Anthony at the trial of an innocent father. The theme gave him the opportunity of depicting scenes from the everyday life of Madrid in a composition of great boldness and revolutionary painting technique. The frescoes, painted at the same time as his famous etchings, the "Caprichos", mark a turning-point in the art of Goya, who is rightly honoured as a precursor of modern painting. In order to protect the frescoes a duplicate version of the chapel now used for worship – was built in 1928 alongside the original, which is now a National Monument.

Location
Paseo de la
Florida

Metro
Príncipe Pío

Buses
41, 46, 75

Open Tue.–Fri.
10am–2pm,
4–8pm, Sat. and
Sun. 10am–2pm;
closed pub. hols.

El Escorial

The little town of San Lorenzo de El Escorial (alt. 1028 m (3373 ft); pop. 9000), known for short as El Escorial, lies north-west of Madrid on the southern slopes of the Sierra de Guadarrama (see entry). A royal summer residence, it became during the summer months the central point of the whole Spanish empire. The gigantic complex of the Escorial monastery/palace, with its treasures of art, now a UNESCO World Heritage site, is one of the most-visited sights in Spain.

Excursion
56 km (35 mi.)
NW

By car: on N VI to exit 2 (Guadarrama and El Escorial), then M 600; or N VI to Las Rozas turn-off, then C 505. By rail: from any Cercanías station (line C 8a). By bus: line 661 (Herranza company) from Moncloa, Paseo Moret 7.

Access

★★Monasterio de San Lorenzo de El Escorial

After the battle of Saint-Quentin on August 10th 1557, in which the Spanish army defeated the troops of Henry IV of France, Philip II vowed to found a monastery in honour of St Lawrence, whose feast-day it was. After careful preparations, including the consultation of astrologers, the little town of San Lorenzo was chosen as the site of a huge complex which should be at the same time a monastery, a church, a palace, a mausoleum, a library and a museum, as well as a monument to Philip II and his reign. Construction began on April 23rd 1563 and the building was completed, in presence of the king, who had supervised the whole operation, on September 13th 1584. The architects were Juan Bautista de Toledo, who died in 1567, and Juan de Herrera. The interior decoration was the work of many Spanish painters and mainly Italian masters, among them the painters Pellegrino Tibaldi and Luca Giordano and the sculptors Pompeo and Leone Leoni.

From the outside the Escorial looks more like a fortress or a barracks than a monastery. Its architecture, influenced by the classical style of the 16th century, marks the beginnings of Spanish Baroque. Built in whitish-grey marble, its ground-plan is a rectangle measuring 161 m (528 ft) by 204 m (997 ft). The core of the complex is the church with its twin towers and 90 m (295 ft) high dome. On the west side of the church is the Patio de los Reyes (Courtyard of the Kings), on the south side the Cloister

Open
spring/summer
Tue.–Sun.
10am–6pm;
autumn/winter
Tue.–Sun.
10am–5pm

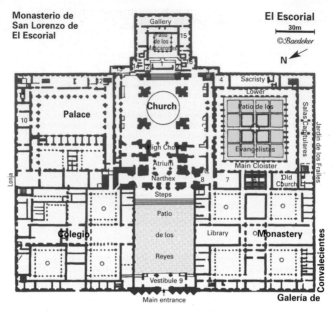

Monasterio de
San Lorenzo de
El Escorial

El Escorial
30m
©Baedeker

1 High Altar, in Presbytery	4 Antesacristia	9 Up to Library	13 Sala de Batallas
2 Royal oratories	5 Altar de la Sagradga Forma	10 Entrance to Palace	14 Apartments of Infanta Isabel Clara Eugenia
3 Steps to Choir; entrance to Pantheon	6 Grand Staircase	11 Palace staircase (to Bourbon range)	15 Throne Room
	7 Sala de la Trinidad	12 Up to 16th c. apartments (museums)	16 Oratory of Phillip II
	8 Sala de la Secretos		

(Patio de los Evangelistas), with the sacristy and the chapterhouses, on the east and north sides the royal palace. Altogether the Escorial has 16 courtyards, 2673 windows, 1250 doors, 86 staircases and 88 fountains; the corridors have a total length of 16 km (10 mi.).

On the west side of the complex is the **Puerta Principal**, the main entrance. Above the doorway are St Lawrence's gridiron, the Habsburg coat of arms and a statue of St Lawrence by Juan Bautista Monegro.

The main doorway leads into the **Patio de los Reyes**, the Courtyard of the Kings. It is dominated by the façade of the church, with its statues of the Old Testament kings from which the courtyard takes its name, and the two massive bell-towers.

The **church**, with its frescoes by Luca Giordano, is notable for its austerity and monumentality. A cold light filters into the church from the dome over the crossing, casting a glow on the precious materials of the 30 m (100 m) high retable. Seventeen steps lead up to Herrera's four-tier altar of jasper and red marble, with paintings by the Italian artists Zucaro and Tibaldi and statues of fathers of the church and the evangelists by Pompeo and Leone Leoni.

These two sculptors also created the bronze funerary monuments of

Spain's two most important rulers in niches in the presbytery. On the Evangel (right) side is a gilded bronze statue of Charles V looking towards the altar, with his wife Isabella, his daughter María and his sisters Eleonora and María kneeling behind him; on the Epistle (left) side is a kneeling figure of Philip II with his three wives – Anne of Austria, Isabelle de Valois and María of Portugal – and his son Don Carlos.

Immediately below the church is the **Panteón de los Reyes** (Pantheon of the Kings), the burialplace of the Spanish monarchs, an octagonal domed structure designed by Horroro, enlarged by Juan Gómez de Mora and completed in 1654. The Baroque

High altar of the Escorial church

taste of the time is reflected in the interior decoration of black marble and gilded bronze (by the Italian master Giovanni Battista Crescenti). On the left are all the Spanish kings since Charles V (with a few exceptions) and Isabella II in identical granite sarcophagi. On the right are the Queen Mothers and Isabella II's husband Francisco de Assís.

Below the Sacristy and the Chapter Houses is the **Panteón de los Infantes,** mausoleum of Spanish princes and princesses and queens whose children did not become kings. In the fifth chamber is the tomb of Don John of Austria (by Giuseppe Galeotto; designed by Ponzano).

In the south aisle of the church is the entrance to the **Sacristy** (not open to the public), which has ceiling paintings by Nicolás Granello and Fabrizio Castello. On the walls are a number of notable pictures, including works by Titian, Ribera, Giordano and Claudio Coello. Coello's "Adoration of the Host by Charles II" (1684) hangs over a recess in which the Host is reserved.

On the south side of the church is the Lower Cloister (frescoes by Tibaldi), which runs round the outside of the **Patio de los Evangelistas**. The patio takes its name from the fountain with figures of the four Evangelists (by Herrera) in the centre.

Along the south side of the Lower Cloister are the **Salas Capitulares** (Chapter Houses), the vaulted ceilings of which have frescoes by Fabrizio Castello and Nicolás Granello. In the Vicar's Room are paintings by Titian, Ribera, Velázquez, El Greco and other artists, and the Prior's Room has works by Titian, Tintoretto, Veronese and Moretto da Brescia. Also on display are vestments, a portable altar belonging to Charles V and liturgical utensils.

Philip II's library – a symbolic union of knowledge, faith and power – was decorated with appropriate magnificence

Adjoining the Chapter Houses is the **Iglesia Antigua** (Old Church), which was used for worship during the construction of the Escorial. It contains a notable painting of "The Martyrdom of St Lawrence". (Admission only with special permission).

The **Escalera Principal** (Grand Staircase) has two symmetrical flights leading to the upper floor. It is believed to have been designed by Gian Battista Castello, Il Bergamasco. On the vaulting is a painting of the battle of Saint-Quentin by Luca Giordano; on the walls are portraits, including representations of Juan Bautista de Toledo and Juan de Herrera.

On the second floor of the rooms on the south side of the Patio de los Reyes is the **Library**. The main hall, with magnificent frescoes by Tibaldi ("The Foundations of Knowledge"), contains more than 30,000 volumes. In show-cases are displayed some of the Library's finest incunabula, as well as the Codex Aureus (1093), which is ascribed to the German Emperor Conrad II, a manuscript of Alfonso the Wise's "Hymns to the Virgin", manuscripts of St Teresa of Avila and Hebrew and Arabic works.

Palacio Real

The Palacio Real (Royal Palace) extends over two wings of the Escorial complex. On the north side of the church is the administrative palace, with the royal offices.

The most impressive part of the palace is the range of **Bourbon rooms**. A staircase remodelled by Villanueva in the 18th century leads up to the state apartments of Charles IV and Maria Luisa of Parma on the third floor. The rooms are furnished with valuable 18th century furniture and porcelain. The most striking features, however, are the 338 tapestries from the Santa Bárbara manufactory in Madrid and from Flemish man-

In this fresco Philip I, sought to set his campaigns for predominance in Europe in the tradition of the Reconquista

ufactories. They include scenes of everyday life (some from cartoons by Goya) and hunting scenes by Teniers, Wouwerman, Bayeu and Maella.

At the north-east corner of the administrative palace is the **Hall of Battles** (55 m (180 ft) long and 7 m (23 ft) high), with frescoes by Nicolás Granello, Fabrizio Castello, Orazio Cambiasso and L. Tavarone. Philip II set the most important battles of the Reconquista opposite the victories of his reign: thus the battle of La Higueruela in 1431 (on the long wall; copy of a 15th century drawing from the Alcázar in Segovia) hangs opposite episodes from the battle of Saint-Quentin, the Portuguese campaign and the fighting against England in the Azores (on the end walls and between the balconies).

Beyond the Hall of Battles are the **private apartments of Philip II**, which adjoin the choir of the church and lie round the Patio de los Mascarones (Hall of the Masks). The most interesting rooms are Philip II's Alcove, from which he had direct access to the church and in which he died in 1598; "Philip II's Cell", with Hieronymus Bosch's "Hay-Wagon" (possibly a copy) and eleven watercolours ascribed to Albrecht Dürer; the Throne Room; and the apartments of the Infanta Isabel Clara Eugenia.

In the centre of the north front is the entrance to the **Nuevos Museos** (New Museums), which bring together pictures and applied art from all parts of the Escorial complex. They consist of an architectural museum and an art gallery.

The architectural museum is housed in the eastern basement rooms of the administrative palace (entrance beyond the El Greco Room: see below). It illustrates the history of the construction of the Escorial with the help of prints, models, instruments and original plans.

The art gallery, which displays a large collection of important pictures,

South front of the Escorial, with the Gallery of the Convalescents, where sick monks could recover, and the pool in the kitchen garden

is on the lower floor of the "summer palace" (within Philip II's private apartments).

In the first room of the gallery is a painted wooden sculpture of St Michael and the Dragon by Luisa Roldán. In the second room is El Greco's "Martyrdom of St Maurice and the Theban Legion", which was commissioned by Philip II for the altar in the church, though he finally decided on a painting by Romolo Cincinnatos. Only a selection of other artists represented in the gallery can be mentioned here. In the first room are pictures of the 16th century Venetian school, including works by Luca Cambiasso, Titian, Tintoretto and Veronese (attributed); the second room has works by 16th and 17th century Flemish painters, including Martin de Vos, Pieter Aertsen, Rubens, van Dyck and Giordano; the third shows works by Michiel van Coxie; and rooms 4, 5 and 6, which look out on to the Courtyard of the Masks, display works by Italian, Spanish and Dutch painters, including Andrea di Lione, Juan van der Hamen and Guercino.

In room 7, formerly the indoor walk of the summer palace, are pictures by Veronese, Tintoretto, Federico Zuccaro, Juan Fernández de Navarrete and Federico Barocci, a copy by Coxie of Rogier van der Weyden's "Descent from the Cross" (the original of which is in the Prado) and van der Weyden's "Calvary". Rooms 8 and 9 (Philip II's summer bedroom) is devoted to 17th century Spanish painting (José de Ribera, Luca Giordano, Alonso Cano, etc.).

Jardines del Príncipe

To the south-east of the monastery are the Jardines del Príncipe (Prince's Gardens), with tree-lined avenues and huge centuries-old individual trees. In the lower part of the gardens is the Casita del Príncipe, a small palace built in 1773 for the Prince of the Asturias, the future Charles IV. The palace, furnished in the style of the period, is open to visitors.

Casita del Infante

The Casita del Infante, to the south-west of the Escorial, is a smaller

The Valle de los Caídos, a grandiose memorial to the dead of the Spanish Civil War

counterpart to the Casita del Príncipe, built as a retreat for the Infante Gabriel, Charles IV's brother.

On a low hill 3 km (2 mi.) south of the Escorial are a number of stone blocks from which Philip II is said to have watched the construction of the monastery: hence the name Philip II's Seat. From here there is a magnificent view of the Escorial against the backdrop of the Sierra de Guadarrama (see entry)'

The Silla de Felipe II can be reached on a road to the west of the town, passing the golf course, from which point the road is signposted.

Silla de Felipe II

Valle de los Caídos

In the mountains 6 km (4 mi.) north of the Escorial as the crow flies is the Monumento Nacional de Santa Cruz del Valle de los Caídos, known for short as the Valle de los Caídos, the Valley of the Fallen, erected by General Franco between 1940 and 1958 as a monument to those who died in the Civil War, on both sides – though it was built on this remote and difficult site by prisoners of war from the defeated Republican forces. The entrance to the site is several kilometres below the monument itself, which is reached by car on a country road, M 600. The 150 m (490 ft) high concrete cross which towers above the basilica can be seen from a long way off on N VI.

Location
13 km (8 mi.) N

Open Tue.–Sun.
10am–6pm

In front of the basilica is a huge forecourt (3.6 ha (9 acres)) from which there are wide views of the beautiful mountain landscape. Above the entrance to the basilica, which was blasted out of the rock, is a gigantic Pietà by Juan de Avalos. Beyond this is a smaller – but still impressively large – hall with a vault which re-echoes even a whisper and compels visitors to silence. This in turn leads into the immense nave of the church (262 m (860 ft) long), the walls of which are hung with copies of Brussels tapestries. At the heart of the church, under the

42 m (138 ft) high, mosaic-decorated crossing, is the altar. Under a gravestone in front of the altar is buried Primo de Rivera, founder of the Falange, and a similar slab to the rear of the altar marks the tomb of General Franco. To the right of the altar, in urns set into the vaulting of the Capilla de los Caídos, are the ashes of 40,000 men and women who fell in the Civil War (not open to the public). To the right on leaving the basilica is a funicular running up to the foot of the cross, from which there is a breathtaking view of the foothills and the Sierra de Guadarrama (see entry)

Estadio Santiago Bernabéu   J 1

Location
Concha Espina 1

Metro
Lima

Buses
14, 43

Madrid is one of the few cities in Europe with two football teams of international standing, Real Madrid (established 1902; about 67,000 members) and Atlético de Madrid (established 1903; about 30,000 members). In spite of their names Real (Royal) Madrid was originally the club of "red" Madrid, while Atlético Aviación, as it was originally known, was the club of the Franquist pilots who bombed Madrid so unmercifully during the Civil War. Real Madrid's triumphal years were between 1955 and 1960, when, with players like di Stefano and Gento, it won the Europa Cup five times running. At a time when the democratic governments of Europe were turning a cold shoulder to Franco's Spain the Real Madrid team was enthusiastically received everywhere. In our own day its supporters, the Madridistas, are proud of their club, which is seen as the "classier" of the two, and the Real players regard it as an honour to wear the team's all-white jersey.

The Santiago Bernabéu Stadium, named after the club's founder and long-time chairman, is situated on the Paseo de la Castellana (see entry) in one of the best and most expensive districts in northern Madrid. The construction of the stadium began in 1944 (architects Manuel Muñoz Monasterio and Luis Alemany Soler), and was inaugurated in 1947 with a match against the Lisbon team Os Belenenses. It then had a capacity of 125,000 spectators, but since it was modernised for the 1982 world championship it now has seating for only 90,800. In recent years the club, seven times winner of the Europa Cup, has fallen short of its earlier successes, and is deeply in debt. Accordingly there are plans to pull down its present stadium and build a new one in the Orthaleza district, 10 km (6 mi.) north. High-rise apartment blocks would then be built on the expensive site – conveniently, Lorenzo Sanz, Real's powerful chairman, is a property magnate. But negotiations seem at present to be bogged down, for the authorities, concerned about the very heavy traffic the plan would generate, would prefer the site to be developed as a park – and this would of course mean a considerable loss of income for the club.

Estadio Vicente Calderón   D 13

Location
Ribera del
Manzanares

Metro
Pirámides

Buses
17, 36, 50

Madrid's second football club, Atlético de Madrid, was established in 1903 as an offshoot of Atletic de Bilbao. In contrast to Real Madrid, it is thought of as the ordinary man's club – although its most celebrated fan is Crown Prince Felipe. The Vicente Calderón Stadium, with a capacity of 70,000, is situated on the banks of the Manzanares to the south of Madrid, near the working-class quarters of the city. The orbital motorway M 30 runs under the stadium.

Encounters between Madrid's two rival teams are, of course, great sporting events; but the rivalry between the two chairmen, who rule their clubs like absolute monarchs, is also headline material. Jesús Gil y Gil, Atlético's chairman, a wealthy building contractor and scandal-prone mayor of Marbella, is much given to abuse of people he has no

View over the Grand Cascade to the garden front of the Palace of La Granja

time for, which leads to his frequently being banned from entering the stadiums. He achieved a great coup in 1990 when he signed on the German player Berndt Schuster, who had been released by Real Madrid, and Atlético, for so long Madrid's No. 2 team, began to outpoint Real, who had been more than twenty times champion.

★La Granja de San Ildefonso

The little town of La Granja de San Ildefonso lies at an altitude of 1200 m (3900 ft) at the foot of Mt Peñalara in the Sierra de Guadarrama (see entry), 11 km (7 mi.) from Segovia (see entry). It originally grew up round a grange (farm) belonging to the monastery of El Parral in Segovia. After the War of the Spanish Succession the Bourbon ruler Philip V resolved to build a palace on the model of Versailles here, which should also incorporate a church and a tomb. Construction of the palace, designed by the Madrid architect Teodoro Ardemans, with four wings enclosing a central courtyard and corner towers, began in 1721. Between 1727 and 1734 the palace was enlarged by the addition of two large three-winged extensions looking on to the gardens designed by the Italian architects Andrea Procaccini and Sempronio Subisati. In 1762, during the reign of Charles III, accommodation for the court, with subsidiary and office buildings, was added to the complex, together with the Real Fábrica de Cristales de La Granja, the Royal Glass Factory (see Baedeker Special, p. 76, and below).

Excursion
78 km (48 mi.) N

Sights

The palace is approached from the rear front, which is dominated by the imposing palace church. In the church is the marble tomb of Philip V and his wife Isabella Farnese.

Palace

73

La Granja de San Ildefonso

Open Tue.–Sat.
10am–1pm,
3–5pm, Sun. and
pub. hols.
10am–2pm

The main front of the palace, 155 m (510 ft) long, looks on to the gardens. It was built in 1734 to the design of Sacchetti and Juvara, who were also responsible for the Royal Palace in Madrid (see Palacio Real). With its tall door-windows, round columns, pilasters, caryatids, coats of arms and decorative suits of armour in marble, granite and pink Sepúlveda sandstone, it shows the influence of French and Italian architecture.

A conducted tour of the palace (which was badly damaged by a fire in 1919) includes a Japanese Cabinet, the king's Reception Room and the Throne Room, with furnishings and mementoes of the Bourbon rulers. There is also a Tapestry

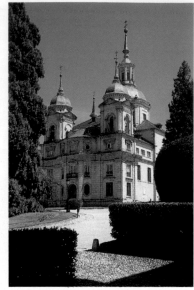

The palace church, La Granja

Museum, with outstanding examples of Flemish, Spanish and French tapestries.

Open daily
10am–6.30pm,
summer 7pm

The magnificent **gardens** of the palace, below the main front, are approached by way of the Grand Cascade with its eleven steps. With an area of 140 ha (380 acres) (and thus exceeding in size the gardens of Versailles), they were originally designed by a French landscape architect named Marchand and were laid out in 1722 by two other Frenchmen, Etienne Boutelou and René Carlier. They are notable for the variety of form of the flower-beds, the carefully trimmed bushes, hedges and avenues of trees and the numerous decorated fountains and sculpture, most of them (by René Fremin and Jean Fermy) representing mythological figures.

The **fountains** are not driven by circulating pumps, so that they work only when the 18th century system of pipes bringing water from a reservoir above the eastern part of the gardens in the sierra is working. Some of the fountains are usually brought into operation from Easter week until October on Wednesdays, Saturdays and Sundays at 5.30pm, provided that there is enough water in the reservoir; but they are to be seen in their full glory during the festival in honour of the town's patron saint San Luis on August 25th, an occasion which attracts thousands of visitors. Other occasions for the full display (water supplies permitting) are Easter week, May 30th and July 25th.

Centro Nacional
del Vidrio

Open Tue.– Sun.
11am–8pm
spring/summer;
11am–7pm
autumn/winter

In the newer part of the glass factory glass for everyday use is still produced. The old factory has been excellently restored as an example of early industrial architecture and now houses the Centro Nacional del Vidrio, the National Glass Centre. There is an exhibition on the history of glass-blowing, and the tradition is still continued in the production of craft glassware. There is a museum which puts on interesting special exhibitions and also has a permanent collection of old glass, and a shop selling items of blown glassware.

The Centro Nacional is at Paseo del Pocillo 1, a short walk from the palace. See Baedeker Special, p. 76.

★Gran Vía   E–H 8/9

The Gran Vía, which runs from Calle de Alcalá to the Plaza de España (see entry), is Madrid's principal traffic artery and east–west connection. It is also the city's main shopping street and the very epitome of its metropolitan spirit. With its office blocks, banks, department stores, cafés, cinemas, Metro stations and underground car parks, it is a display window, a meeting-place, a promenade, a place to see and be seen, the centre of the city's commercial life and a traffic hub. Under the influence of the heavy traffic and the proliferation of fast-food outlets the Gran Vía has certainly lost something of its originality and style. In particular the street's pulsating night life moved away into the surrounding districts during the 1980s.

Metro
Banco de España,
Gran Vía, Callao,
Santo Domingo,
Plaza de España

Buses
1, 2, 46, 74, 146, 149

The plan to drive a broad thoroughfare through central Madrid to link the city's eastern and western districts originated in the 19th century, but the realisation of this ambitious project, which involved the demolition of 14 older streets and countless narrow lanes in the old town, as well as over 300 buildings over a length of 1.5 km (just under a mile), began only in 1910. The first section was built by 1920. It still preserves the atmosphere of the 19th century, and in such buildings as the Metrópolis with its monumental figure of an angel (corner of Calle de Alcalá), the Gran Peña (Gran Vía 2), the Ybarra building (No. 8) and the building at the corner of Calle Clavel is vaguely reminiscent of Paris. The massive Telefónica building (1929), Europe's first skyscraper, marked the advent of a new architectural style. From the Red de San Luis to the Plaza del Castillo and from there to the Plaza de España the Gran Vía has a marked American air. At the west end the silhouette of the Carrión building, with the Capitol cinema, stands out like the prow of ship against the sea of light of a Madrid sunset. On both sides of the street are the buildings of the 1920s and 1930s which give Madrid's "Broadway" its distinctive character.●

The **Telefónica** building (Gran Vía 28), originally the headquarters of the state telephone corporation which was privatised in 1997, is now a hotel. Built in 1925–29 to the design of Ignacio de Cárdenas and Louis S. Weeks, it was for many years Madrid's tallest and most popular building. Its 14 floors reach to a height of 81 m (266 ft) and has a total floor area of 1600 sq. m (17,223 sq. ft). Its neighbour at No. 32 is the former department store Madrid-Paris (now SEPU), which was designed by a French architect. On the opposite side are the former Palacio de la Música (No. 35; by Secundino Zuazu, 1924–29), long since taken over by a cinema, and the Avenida cinema, adjoining Plaza del Callao. The square is dominated by the massive façade of the Palacio de la Prensa (Gran Vía 46; by Pedro Muguruza, 1924), now also a cinema. In the Carrión building (No. 41), at the corner of Calle de Jacometrezo, is the Capitol cinema (by Louis Martínez Feduchi and Vicente Eced, 1931–33), with a charming Art Nouveau interior – perhaps the most authentically styled building on the Gran Vía.

This is the starting-point of the third section of the Gran Vía, which also reflects the spirit of the architectural avantgarde of the 1930s and is undoubtedly the most "American" stretch of the street. Buildings such as the Rialto cinema, an imitation of New York's Roxy and Paramount cinemas, the former head office of the Banco Español de la Edificación (Gran Vía 60), with Victorio Macho's gigantic statue, the building at the corner of Calle San Bernando and the Coliseum, with its rationalist façade (Gran Vía 78; by Pedro Muguruza and Casto Fernández Shaw, 1931–33) bear witness to the enthusiasm of contemporaries for modern American architecture.

Painting with Coloured Threads

Only half an hour's walk from the Prado, in an inconspicuous brick building at Calle Fuenterrabía 2, is an institution with a long tradition behind it: the Real Fábrica de Tapices (Royal Tapestry Manufactory). It was founded by the Bourbon ruler Philip V in 1721 because the Spanish Netherlands had become independent seven years before and Spain was thus cut off from supplies of the Dutch tapestries and fabrics which were then in great favour. The first artistic director of the manufactory was Jakob van der Goten, a Flemish tapestry weaver from Antwerp. In 1744 he became independent, and the manufactory is still in the hands of his descendants, now in the ninth generation.

The preparation of designs for tapestries was originally one of the more tiresome duties of the Court Painter, painted cartoons from pictures by Flemish artists or older tapestries. This changed when Anton Raphael Mengs, Charles III's German court painter, took over the artistic direction of the manufactory. He engaged young and previously unknown artists to paint cartoons, and they realised that this was the opportunity they had hitherto lacked to show their skills. Among them was the young and until then unsuccessful Francisco de Goya (born 1746). A new creative phase now began for the manufactory: between 1776 and 1780 it produced more than 120 new cartoons, the finest of which can now be seen in the Prado Museum. The subjects of the tapestries also changed. While in the past the dominant themes had been Christian and courtly scenes, scenes from everyday life in Madrid now became popular. They depicted popular festivals, weddings, bullfights, ball games and card-playing, picnics

Tapestry-knotter at work

and dances, conveying a sense of enjoyment of the pleasures of life in a carefree Rococo atmosphere.

The war of liberation interrupted the development of the tapestry manufactory, whose premises were used as a barracks for French troops. Under Ferdinand VII, Isabella II and Alfonso XII the production of new tapestries took second place to the weaving and repair of old ones. Then in the 20th century there was a revival, with such artists as Sert, Picasso and Dalí creating cartoons.

The manufactory is still producing tapestries, but in recent years it has been fighting for survival. The number of tapestry workers has fallen from 186 in 1975 to no more than 40. Over the 280 years of the manufactory's existence there has been very little change in its way of working. The only real change is that the natural dyes, whose composition was for centuries a family secret, gave place in the mid 20th century to non-fade chemical dyes. The craftsmen usually work standing with the tapestry suspended from a high wooden frame. The pattern is traced on to the warp threads, with a reduced-size copy serving as a check on the colours. The workers dye their own wool, and the composition of the colours and the selection of the right yarns call for high skill. A single silk thread, which is made up of many finer threads, may have anything up to fifteen shades of colour. The tapestries are created knot by knot or thread by thread. It takes between one and four months, depending on whether the tapestry is knotted or woven, to produce a square metre, at a cost ranging between £6000 and £8000 Carpets are quicker and cheaper to produce, but even they cost at least £500 per square metre. The manufactory's main customers are the royal family, private collectors and wealthy business organisations.

In addition to the production of new tapestries, the manufactory has an additional source of income in the restoration of old ones. This work is done by women sitting at long tables, who show great skill in cutting out damaged places, inserting new warp threads and making good the damage. But even the considerable demand for this work it is not sufficient to ensure the existence of the tapestry manufactory. Negotiations have been going on for some years about the possibility of financial aid or the take-over of the manufactory by the state as part of Spain's cultural heritage, since it is one of the last factories still using old traditional techniques. It is well worth a visit (see Sights from A to Z, Real Fábrica de Tapices). Work is at present in progress on the renovation of the building to make it wind- and watertight.

"Painting with coloured threads" was

also practised at La Granja – not with organic materials but with glass. The Real Fábrica de Cristales (Royal Crystal Factory) is a similarly traditional institution, its origins going back to a small glass factory established by Ventura Sit and Carlos Sac in 1727. The mirrors they produced were in great demand among the ladies of the court, and Philip V's attention was soon drawn to the factory. Having already shown his interest in promoting Spanish industry in the foundation of the tapestry manufactory, he now declared the glass factory an institution of national importance and promoted its development, as did his successor Charles III. Glass-makers and glass artists were brought to La Granja from all over Europe, and the factory was moved to Madrid and given the status of Royal Glass Factory. The glassware it produced soon established its reputation, and it was able to compete with the large European glass factories. In the 19th century it passed into private hands, but finally closed down in 1969.

Built at the end of the 18th century by the court architect José Días Gamones, the factory has recently been renovated and is now open to the public (see Sights from A to Z, La Granja). It is an interesting example of early industrial architecture, built in granite with a brick facing on its vaulting and dome. It now houses the Fundación Centro Nacional del Vidrio (National Glass Centre), founded in 1982. This includes a museum of technology which illustrates the history of glass manufacture and art, with old equipment, machinery and tools and collections of beautiful glassware from La Granja and other European countries which demonstrate the high quality of La Granja glassware. Some very recent examples show that this craft is still very much alive. Periodic special exhibitions, a school of glass art, and a documentation and research centre ensure that the knowledge and skills of glass manufacture will be preserved and developed for the future.

The buildings in the Plaza de España (see entry), with its two sky-scrapers, the Edificio Español and the Torre de Madrid, which both date from the 1950s and until the eighties were the incarnation of modern Madrid, mark the end of the Gran Vía.

Beyond this is a district centred on the Princesa–Argüelles axis. Typical features of this area are the Cuartel del Conde-Duque and the Palacio de Liria (see entries), giant hotels and the student population.

Guadalajara

Guadalajara (alt. 641 m (2103 ft); pop. 57,000), chief town of its province, lies above the left bank of the Río Henares, some 20 km (13 mi.) east of Alcalá de Henares. It can be reached from Madrid by car (N II, the Barcelona road), train or bus. Its name is derived from the Moorish Wad el-Hajara ("river of stones"). The powerful Mendoza family, which gained possession of the town in the 14th century, left an enduring mark on its development. At nearby Brihuega the Battle of Guadalajara between Republican and Italian troops was fought in March 1937.

Location
56 km (35 mi.) NE

Sights

This palace of honey-coloured limestone was built for the Mendoza family between 1461 and 1480 by the French-born architect Juan Guas. With its mingling of Late Gothic and Mudéjar elements, it is one of his finest works. Here, after being taken prisoner in the battle of Pavia (1525), the French king François I was given a sumptuous reception; and here Philip II married the 15-year-old Isabelle de Valois as his third wife. During the Civil War, in 1936, the palace was largely destroyed, but was later rebuilt. It has a façade studded with sharply facetted stones, a style introduced in the Italian Renaissance and imported into Spain, and a projecting gallery with intricately carved columns. It encloses a beautiful two-storey patio in Isabelline style.

★Palacio del
Duque del
Infantado

The palace houses an outstation of the Museo de Bellas Artes, mainly devoted to paintings of the 15th–17th centuries.

The church of Santa María de la Fuente was built in the 14th century on the site of a mosque. Its architecture shows Arab features, for example its minaret-like tower and two doorways in purest Arab style. It contains 15th century tombs.

Santa María de la
Fuente

The church of San Ginés (begun in 1557) contains tombs of the Infantado and Tendilla families. The high altar has 16th century bas-reliefs.

San Ginés

The Convento de la Piedad (now occupied by an institute) was founded around 1530 by Doña Brianda de Mendoza. The finest part of the building is the cloister with its Plateresque doorways and double arcading. The foundress is commemorated by an alabaster tomb.

Convento de la
Piedad

Hipódromo de la Zarzuela

The Hipódromo de la Zarzuela, to the west of the Manzanares, near the wooded areas of El Pardo and Puerta de Hierro (reached by way of Avenida del Padre Huidobro, the La Coruña road), is regularly the venue of horse races and riding events. It is an interesting example of 1930s

Excursion
7 km (4½ mi.) NW

Buses
83, I

◀ *The starting-point of the Gran Vía, which with its imposing architecture can stand comparison with the boulevards of other great cities*

Façade of the Palacio del Duque del Infantado, Guadalajara

architecture (architects Carlos Arniches and Martín Domínguez; main stand by Eduardo Torroja). The racecourse, with an area of 111 ha (274 acres), is decidedly rundown and needs new owners who will restore to the summer "Noches del Hipódromo" their former appeal for the *gente guapa* ("beautiful people", but particularly the wealthy) of Madrid and the rest of the world.

Inmaculada Concepción de Mercedarias Descalzas   H 8

Location
Calle de Luis de Góngora 5

Metro
Chueca

Buses
3, 7, 37, 40, 149

The convent of the Inmaculada Concepción de Mercedarias Descalzas, known for short as Las Góngoras after its founder Don Juan de Góngora, is a typical example of Madrid architecture of the second half of the 17th century. The church is well preserved, and its nave and short transept are given spaciousness and light by the dominating dome. The convent is open to the public when not in use for worship.

The surrounding streets and squares – Gravina, Libertad, Fernando VI, San Lucás, San Mateo, Plaza de la Villa de París (see entry) and Plaza de las Salesas – are evidence of the changes brought about in the pattern of 17th century Madrid by the middle-class expansion of the city in the reign of Isabella II.

Instituto Valencia de Don Juan   J 5

Location
Fortuny 43

Metro
Colón, Alonso Martínez, Rubén Darío

The Moorish-style villa of the art collector Guillermo de Osma and his wife, Countess of Valencia de Don Juan, is one of Madrid's most attractive museums, and one that is usually not overcrowded.

The collection, founded in 1916, covers a wide range – weapons, miniatures, Flemish tapestries, coins, autograph manuscripts, textiles and jewellery. There is a particularly fine display of porcelain of the

Moorish period in Spain and in the Mudéjar style. The pictures include an El Greco and a number of early Goya drawings.

The museum can be seen only by appointment (tel. 913081848). It is closed from July 1st to September 15th.

Jardín Botánico   J 10/11

Madrid's Botanic Gardens were founded by the enlightened Bourbon king Charles III as part of his ambitious plans for the development of the eastern part of the city. Along with the Scientific Museum, the Prado and the Observatory in the Parque del Retiro (see entry), it was intended to foster the diffusion and the study of the natural sciences. The park was designed by Juan de Villanueva. It is enclosed by railings, with two entrances in neo-classical style. Its three terraces are respectively in Romantic, Isabelline and neo-classical style.

Laid out by the botanist Gómez d'Ortega, the Botanic Gardens were opened in 1781, and with their acquisition of plants and seeds from America and the Philippines gained an international reputation. In the library are 6000 drawings of the flora of New Granada, brought from South America by the famous botanist Celestino Mutis. The manuscript collection includes books and documents of the 15th–18th centuries.

On the **Cuesta de Moyano**, which leads to the Paseo del Prado (see entry), are numerous bookshops.

Location
Plaza de Murillo

Metro
Atocha

Buses
10, 14, 19, 27, 32, 37, 45

Open Daily
10am–9pm;
winter 6pm

Bookshops on the Cuesta de Moyano, where you can find valuable first editions, old schoolbooks and the latest fiction

Mercado de San Miguel   F 10

Location
Plaza de San
Miguel

Metro
Puerta del Sol

Bus
3

The lively Mercado de San Miguel, just off Calle Mayor near the Plaza Mayor (see entry), is an example of 19th century urban development. This colourful market has been established here since 1835, on the site of the eastern gate in Madrid's second ring of walls.

The present iron structure, with its stalls in an orderly arrangement on two floors, was built between 1911 and 1916 (architect Alfonso Dubé y Díez), replacing the hugger-mugger of the old market square. The market hall has recently been given protection against heat and cold by the addition of glass walls.

Ministerio de Hacienda   G 9

Location
Alcalá 11

Metro
Puerta del Sol

Buses
5, 15, 20, 50, 51,
52, 53

The Ministry of Finance is housed in the old royal Custom House (Antigua Aduana), situated near the Puerta del Sol (see entry). The building is a typical example of the architecture of the time of Charles III, and along with the adjoining Goyaneche Palace (see Real Academia de Bellas Artes de San Fernando) gives the first part of Calle de Alcalá a severe Italianising character. In this building, completed in 1769, the king's favourite architect, Francesco Sabatini, who had followed him from Italy to Spain, followed the model of Italian Renaissance palaces. In 1928–29 the palace was enlarged and given a new façade (by Pedro de Ribera, 1710) from the Palacio de Torrecilla.

★★Monasterio de las Descalzas Reales   F 9

Location
Plaza de las
Descalzas Reales 3

Metro
Sol, Callao

Buses
1, 2, 6, 20, 46, 52,
53, 74

Open Tue.–Thu.
10.30am–12.30pm,
4–5.45pm, Fri.
11am–1.30pm,
Sun. and pub.
hols. 11am–
1.30pm

The church and convent of the Descalzas Reales, the Royal Discalced (Barefoot) Sisters, lies in the square of that name near the busy Puerta del Sol and the Gran Vía (see entries). The nuns occupy a Renaissance palace which belonged to the Emperor Charles V's treasurer, Alonso Gutiérrez.

Charles V's daughter Johanna, who had married Crown Prince Juan Manuel of Portugal, returned to Madrid as a young widow and founded the order of Descalzas Reales in the house in which she had been born. The palace was converted for the purpose by Antonio Sillero and Juan Bautista de Toledo (who was also involved in the building of the Escorial) between 1556 and 1564. The imposing façade of red brick and granite – the traditional mixture – is one of the city's few surviving examples of 16th century architecture. Parts of the convent, now reoccupied by nuns, have been open to the public since 1986. The sumptuously appointed interior with its many works of art can be seen in the course of a conducted tour (only in Spanish) which takes visitors into the world of the Renaissance princes. The visit also gives an impression of the monastic life-style of the Habsburg princesses who took the veil here and had no further part in the political life of the court.

The two-storey façade of the **church** is built into the walls of the convent. The interior was remodelled in neo-classical style by Villanueva in the 18th century. On the wall of the presbytery is Johanna's burial chapel (by Giacomo da Trezzo, 1574; marble statue by Pompeo Leoni).

The convent is entered by a doorway to the left of the church. This opens into a hall (information) in which the convent's coach was kept; the wooden ceiling dates from 1540. From here a Plateresque door leads

Within the walls of the convent of the Descalzas Reales lived many princesses of the house of Habsburg

into the convent proper. The **cloister**, now glassed over, was originally the inner courtyard of the palace. Round the walls are numerous altars and chapels presented by former inmates of the convent.

The **Grand Staircase** on the north side of the cloister belongs to the oldest part of the convent, though it was remodelled in sumptuous Baroque style in 1684 by Anna Dorothea, daughter of the German Emperor Rudolf II. One wall is occupied by a "Calvary" by Antonio de Pereda, and the facing wall has ornamental frescoes in the Italian tradition. They depict Philip IV, with his second wife Maria Anna of Austria, Princess Margarita and Prince Philip Prosperus, in a *trompe-l'oeil* loggia, as if looking down on visitors from a balcony. The portraits are attributed to Claudio Coello, who was involved along with Antonio de Pereda in the decoration of the convent.

In the corridor on the upper floor there are numerous richly orna-mented altars and chapels, also presented by inmates of the convent and their families, as well as a much revered recumbent figure of Christ by Gaspar Becerra.

In the rooms and passages of the convent visitors encounter the **Habsburgs** everywhere. Doña Juana, the foundress, and the Empress María, Maximilian's widow, collected the portraits of their family, which now cover the walls of the Salón de Reyes and the hall known as El Candilón.

The popularity of tapestries at that period is illustrated in the **Gran Sala de Tapices** (the former dormitory of the nuns). It displays the major part of the 14-piece series of tapestries, the "Triumph of the Eucharist", on cartoons by Rubens, commissioned by Philip II's daughter Isabel Clara Eugenia and made in Brussels in 1625—28.

The convent also has an interesting collection of **relics**.

Of particular charm are the small **chapels**, clad with Talavera tiles, containing works of art and other valuable objects commemorating their former occupants.

The chapel of Anna Dorothea of Habsburg contains a collection of Baroque bronzes and sculpture and has stained glass on Biblical themes by Herrera de Barnuevo.

In the Capilla de la Dormición are a ceiling painting of the Assumption by Luca Giordano and a portrait (attributed to Rubens) of Anna Dorothea.

The Capilla del Milagro (Chapel of the Miracle), named after the wonderworking image of the Madonna which now stands on the high altar of the church, was created by Juan José de Austria, Philip IV's illegitimate son, for his illegitimate daughter Margarita la Cruz. The frescoes are by Dionisio Mantovano (perspective painting) and Francisco Ricci. The four figures of saints on the altar were the work of Luisa Roldán, Charles II's court sculptress.

The **Museum Hall** contains an overwhelming collection of works of art: Flemish panel paintings which belonged to the Empress Isabella, Charles V's wife, works by such masters as Hans Memling, Adriaen Isenbrant, Dirk Bouts, and Rogier van der Weyden and pictures by Spanish painters like Francisco de Zurbarán, Bartolomé Esteban Murillo and Juseppe Ribera. High points of the collection are Titian's "Tribute Money" and Brueghel the Elder's "Adoration of the Three Kings".

Monasterio de la Encarnación

See Convento de la Encarnación

Montaña del Príncipe Pío   D 7/8

Location
Paseo del Pintor
Rosales

Metro
Plaza de España,
Ventura Rodríguez

Bus
74

The Montaña del Principe Pío was a large country estate extending to the Prado which came into the possession of the crown in 1792. During the war of liberation (1808–13) the palace which stood on the hill suffered severe destruction. It was near here that the shootings of May 3rd 1808, the subject of Goya's famous picture in the Prado, took place. Around 1860 were built the barracks, the Cuartel de la Montaña, Cuartel de la Montaña which played a major part at the outbreak of the Civil War. The battle on July 18th 1936, when the people of Madrid stormed the barracks held by the rebellious military forces, marked the beginning of the three-year-long defence and siege of the Republican capital – a conflict which entered the history books as the "battle for Madrid".

Park The top of the hill is now occupied by one of Madrid's most beautiful parks. From here there are magnificent views of the Royal Palace, the church of San Francisco el Grande, the Casa de Campo, the Rosaleda rose garden, the Parque del Oeste and the distant Sierra de Guadarrama.

The **Templo de Debod** originally stood in the Nubian village of Debod, which was due to be drowned by the construction of the Aswan High Dam. The temple, like other monuments, was removed from its site, and in 1968 was presented to Spain by the Egyptian government in gratitude for the Spanish contribution to the rescue effort.

The temple thus brought from the banks of the Nile to the Manzanares was built in the 4th century BC and was dedicated to the god Amun. Two of its three gate-towers, as well as reliefs on the inside and rear of the rectangular structure, were preserved. In the temple is a small collection of archaeological finds.

The Templo de Debod, a Nubian temple in the heart of Madrid

Museo de América   C/D 4

The Museum of America immediately adjoins the University (see Ciudad Universitaria), offering a fine view of the Sierra de Guadarrama (see entry). It was installed in 1965 in rooms round the cloister of the church of Santo Tomás de Aquino.

The collection, which was begun by Charles III, contains a mass of material on Spanish colonial history, from the discovery of America by Columbus in 1492 to the 19th century. It illustrates not only the lost native cultures but also the Spanish influence on the conquered territories. The museum is particularly strong on the art of the old cultures of Colombia, Mexico and Peru, but it also shows the development of the Spanish colonies, giving attention to their way of life and customs.

Among the museum's most notable exhibits are the "Treasure of the Quimbayas", a famous collection of 62 objects of pure gold (total weight 16 kg) from an exterminated Indian tribe, a gift from the Colombian government in 1892; the Tro Cortesian Codex, one of the three Mayan folding books that have survived; a calendar of the 260-day Mayan year (*c.* 1200), which belonged to the conquistador Hernán Cortés (1485–1547); stone sculpture of the Aztecs, the Mayas and the Incas; obsidian masks from Mexico; and pottery and vases.

Address
Av. Reyes
Católicos 6

Metro
Moncloa

Buses
62, G

Open Tue.–Sat.
10am–3pm, Sun.
and pub. hols.
10am–2.30pm

Museo de Antigüedades

See Real Academia de la Historia

★★Museo Arqueológico Nacional   · J 8

The National Archaeological Museum is Madrid's most important museum after the Museo del Prado (see entry). It was founded by

Location
Serrano 13

Museo Arqueológico Nacional

Metro
Colón, Serrano

Buses
9, 14, 19, 27, 45,
51, 150

Open Tue.–Sat.
9.30am– 8.30pm,
Sun. and pub. hols.
9.30am– 2.30pm

Isabella II in 1867 and installed in the same building as the National Library (see below) in 1895.

The best place to start a tour of the museum, which covers the history of Spain from prehistory to the 19th century, is in the garden in front of the entrance. Here can be seen a faithful reproduction of the famous Altamira cave, discovered in 1879 near Santander in the province of Cantabria, which contains rock paintings and drawings dating from the Palaeolithic period, some 15,000 years ago.

The basement of the museum is devoted to **prehistory** down to the Bronze Age (c. 500 BC). Rooms 1 to 9 display material from mainland Spain, Rooms 10 to 12 from the Balearics, the Canaries and the Western Sahara, Rooms 13 to 16 from Egypt and Nubia, together with geometric and Corinthian pottery. Rooms 15 and 16 contain Attic and other Greek pottery, Rooms 17 and 18 Campanian material and Etruscan art.

Room 19 is devoted to **Iberian archaeology**, with displays of art objects, jewellery, pottery and everyday objects (8th–6th centuries BC). There are examples of Iberian art from Sagrajas (Badajoz), Aliseda (Cáceres), Lebrija (Seville), Jávea (Alicante) and Abengibre (Alicante). Room 20 is dominated by three major pieces of Iberian sculpture – the "Lady of Elche", a limestone bust which is believed to date from the 5th century BC; the seated figure of the "Lady of Baza" (4th century BC); and the "Lady of Cerro de los Santos" (4th century BC).

Roman art in the province of Hispania (established after the Roman conquest of the Iberian peninsula in the second Punic War in 219 BC) is displayed in Rooms 21 to 26: bronze portraits, statues of emperors and gods, portrait busts, sarcophagi, mosaics, everyday objects of bronze, pottery and glass, etc. Of particular interest are the statue of Livia (1st century BC) and the beautiful mosaics, notably the "Months and

Iberian sculpture: the "Lady of Elche" and ...   ... the "Lady of Baza"

Seasons" from Hellín (Albacete; 3rd/4th century), the "Labours of Hercules" from Liria (Valencia) and the "Triumph of Bacchus" from Zaragoza.

Rooms 27 to 29 display **Visigothic art**, including architectural fragments, models of Visigothic basilicas, bronze implements and utensils, stoneware and jewellery. The treasure of Guarrazar (Toledo) is the centrepiece of Room 29: this collection of votive crowns with their associated gold chains and crosses, precious stones and crystal from the royal church in Toledo (see entry) bears witness to the skill of 7th century Visigothic goldsmiths.

The **Islamic art** of Andalusia from the 8th to the 15th century is displayed in Rooms 30 and 31: bronze articles, pottery, ivories, architectural fragments, etc. Particularly notable items include pottery from Medina az-Zahara (Córdoba), a precious ivory casket which belonged to Caliph Al-Hakam (10th century), fragments from the Aljafería Palace in Zaragoza, Almoravid and Almohad stucco-work, pottery from Málaga and metalwork from Granada.

Rooms 31A to 33 are devoted to the religious art of the **Christian Middle Ages**. Among the masterpieces of Spanish Romanesque art displayed here are the ivory-coloured crucifix of Don Fernando and Doña Sancha from the church of San Isidoro in León (11th century), the lid of Anfus Perez's sarcophagus from Sahagún (León), the Apostle Column by Master Mateo from Santiago de Compostela (first half of 12th century) and the Madonna and Child from Sahagún.

Gothic art is represented by the tombs of Doña Inés Rodríguez de Villalobos, Dona Berenguela and Abbot Aparicio (14th century), panel paintings (a retablo from San Martín de Tours; 15th century), enamels, ivories, jewellery and chalices. In Rooms 34 and 35 (13th–16th centuries) are displayed fine artesonado ceilings from the palace of the Dukes of Maqueda (see Toledo) and the Trinitarian convent in Seville.

The royal collection of Italian **Renaissance** bronzes and 16th century Talavera ceramics is displayed in Room 37. Room 38 contains Baccarat crystal and Spanish glass, Room 39 silverware and Alcora ceramics and Room 40 Buen Retiro porcelain.

The ★**Biblioteca Nacional** (National Library), founded by Philip V in 1711, is one of the major libraries of Europe. The building, consisting of four wings laid out round (originally) four inner courtyards, with an octagonal reading room in the centre, was erected between 1866 and 1894 to the design of Francisco Jareño y Alarcón. It was completed under the direction of Antonio Ruiz de Salces, who made some changes to the original plans, moving the National Library to the front part of the building and the National Archaeological Museum to the rear.

The National Library has some 2½ million printed volumes, over 300,000 prints and 18,000 drawings, incunabula, music scores, manuscripts, maps and the largest Cervantes collection (over 13,000 titles, including 800 editions of "Don Quixote" and over 3000 brochures). The entrance is at Paseo de Recoletos 20.

Museo de Carruajes

D 9

The Carriage Museum, housed in a pavilion (opened 1967) in the Campo del Moro, behind the Palacio Real (see entry), has a notable collection of carriages and litters. The entrance is in the Paseo Virgen del Puerto, part of a popular 18th century promenade. The oldest item in the collection is Charles V's litter (16th century). Other exhibits include Joan the Mad's

Location
Campo del Moro

Metro
Puente de
Segovia, Príncipe
Pío, Ópera

Buses
5, 25, 33, 39, 41,
500, C

coach and the sumptuous official coaches used by 19th century members of the Cortes.

The museum is at present in course of restoration, and the new opening hours are not yet known: up-to-date information can be obtained from tourist information offices (see Practical Information, Information).

★Museo Cerralbo   E 8

Location
Ventura Rodríguez
17

Metro
Plaza de España,
Ventura Rodríguez

Buses
1, 2, 44, 74, C

Open Tue.–Sun.
10am–2pm;
closed pub. hols.
and Aug.

The Museo Cerralbo lies near the Plaza de España (see entry) and Paseo del Pintor Rosales. Its original owner, Enrique de Aguilera y Gamboa, Marquis of Cerralbo (1845–1922), bequeathed his palace and the art treasures it contained to the state in 1922.

The museum, opened in 1924, displays a varied collection, including archaeological material of the Iberian, Punic and Roman periods, Meissen, Buen Retiro, Sèvres and Wedgwood porcelain, weapons, tapestries and furniture of various periods. Among the pictures are works by such great masters as El Greco ("St Francis in Ecstasy", in the chapel), Zurbarán ("Immaculata", in the gallery), Alonso Cano, Ribera ("Jacob watching his sheep", an old copy of the original, now lost), Herrera el Mozo ("Ecce Homo" and "Via Crucis"), Valdés Leal, Carreño, Tintoretto, Tiepolo and Goya. The Dutch, Flemish and French schools are also represented.

Museo de la Ciudad   L 3

Location
Príncipe de
Vergara 140

Metro
Cruz del Rayo

Next door to the Auditorio Nacional de Música (see entry) is Madrid's new multi-media City Museum. The ground and first floors are used for special exhibitions; the second floor deals with the city's infrastructure (the Metro and gas and electricity systems); the third floor illustrates the history of Madrid from its origins to the 18th century with the help of models and pictures; and the fourth floor is devoted to the 19th and 20th centuries, with numerous interesting models of the city and individual buildings and photographs of the most recently built.

The museum is open Mon.–Fri. 10am–2pm, 5–7pm, Sat. and Sun. 10am–2pm.

Museo del Ejército   J 9

Location
Méndez Núñez 1

Metro
Banco de España

Buses
10, 14, 19, 27, 34,
37, 45

Open Tue.–Sun.
10am–4pm

The Army Museum was founded by Manuel Godoy, Charles IV's minister, in 1803. After the Armería in the Royal Palace (see Palacio Real) it is Spain's largest collection of arms and armour, with some 27,000 exhibits. It has been housed since 1939 in the oldest surviving part of the palace of Buen Retiro (1632). It illustrates Spain's military history and displays the whole range of its artillery, cavalry and infantry weaponry. The oldest exhibit is the sword of the Cid, the Castilian hero whose deeds are celebrated in a famous medieval epic poem. In the Arab Room can be seen the velvet cloak and sword of the last Moorish king of Granada.

There are proposals to transfer the museum to the Alcázar in Toledo (see entry) and make its present accommodation available to the Prado Museum. Plans for this move were considered in the time of Primo de Rivera and Franco, and were taken up again in 1996; but the necessary renovation of the Alcázar is still hanging fire.

Museo Naval

See Practical Information, Museums.

Museo de Escultura al Aire Libre   J/K 5

Madrid's open-air museum of abstract sculpture lies below the reinforced concrete flyover which carries Calles Juan Bravo and Eduardo
Dato over the busy Paseo de la Castellana. The site has been used since
1971 for the display of work by Spanish sculptors belonging to the
school of Geometric Abstraction.

Location
Paseo de la
Castellana 38

Metro
Rubén Darío,
Núñez de Balboa

The range of work begins with two avantgarde sculptors of the 1920s
and 1930s, Julio González and Alberto Sánchez. Among leading contemporary sculptors represented are Andrés Alfaro, Martín Chirino, José
María Subirachs, Amadeo Gabino and Pablo Serrano (on the terrace
opposite Calle Eduardo Dato). Two particularly notable works are
Eduardo Chillida's "Stranded Water-Nymph" and Joan Miró's "Mère
Ubu".

Buses
14, 27, 45

★Museo Lázaro Galdiano   K 5

The publisher and businessman José Lázaro Galdiano, an art-lover,
bequeathed his rich art collection and his mansion, Parque Florido, to
the state in 1947, and the museum which bears his name was opened to
the public in 1951. This huge collection of some 9000 items ranging in
date from antiquity to the 19th century occupies more than 35 rooms on
the four floors of the house.

Location
Serrano 122

Metro
Av. de América,
Núñez de Balboa

Buses
9, 12, 16, 19, 51, 61

The ground floor is devoted to the decorative arts from antiquity to the
19th century. The collection is particularly strong on mediaeval and
Renaissance art, including enamels, gold- and silversmiths' work,
carved ivories; jewellery from ancient times to the 19th century; armour;
Celtic weapons; Gothic ivories; Baroque crystal dishes; Italian terracot-
tas; tapestries and small bronzes.

Open Tue.–Sun.
10am– 2pm;
closed Mon. and
pub. hols.

On the first and second floors is the museum's large **collection of paint-
ings**. The Spanish school is well represented, with works by Coello,
Antolínsky, Carreño, Pereda, Herrera the Elder, Madrazo, López,
Zacarías, González Velázquez, Mor, Berruguete, El Greco, Ribera,
Zurbarán and Murillo.

In Room XXX are a number of pictures by Goya.

The collection of Dutch, Flemish and German painting includes works
by David, Joos van Cleve, Hieronymus Bosch, Brueghel, van Dyck,
Rubens, Cranach, Gossaert, Koffermanns, Memling, de Vos, Quentin,
Massys, Schaffner and Pourbus.

English painting is represented by Reynolds, Romney, Gainsborough,
Hoppner and Constable.

The third floor is devoted to **decorative art** – textiles, weapons, fans,
medals, coins, etc.

★Museo Municipal   G 7

Opposite the rather ponderous building (second half of 19th century)
once occupied by the Tribunal de Cuentos del Reino (the Court of Audits)
is the former Hospicio de San Fernando, which since 1926 has housed
the Municipal Library and Museum. The façade, by Pedro de Ribera
(1683–1742), is one of the finest examples of Baroque architecture in
Madrid.

Location
Fuencarral 78

Metro
Tribunal

The museum illustrates the development of Madrid from prehistoric
times to the 19th century, with models, plans, prints, views of the city
and pictures. Items of particular interest are the oldest plan of Madrid

Buses
3, 40, 149

Museo del Prado

Open Tue.–Fri.
9.30am–8pm, Sat.
and Sun.
10am–2pm;
closed pub. hols.

(by Pedro Texeira, 1656), a model of the Alcázar in the time of Juan Gómez de Mora and a model of the town by León Gil del Palacio (1830). Other notable exhibits are Roman pottery, mediaeval manuscripts, tapestries, goldsmith's work and porcelain.

Among the pictures are works by Pedro Berruguete, a late 15th century "Madonna and Child", a portrait head of Philip II by Pompeo Leoni and Goya's famous "Allegory of May 3rd 1808" (1809/10).

On the ground floor of the museum is a small but interesting bookshop (closed 2–4.30pm).

Behind the museum, in the Jardín del Arquitecto Ribera, is a Baroque fountain with water spouting from the mouths of dolphins, the **Fuente de la Fama** or Fountain of Fame (by Ribera, 1731).

Museo Nacional Centro de Arte Reina Sofía

See Centro de Arte Reina Sofía

★★Museo del Prado   J 10

Location
Paseo del Prado

Metro
Atocha

Buses
10, 14, 27, 34, 37,
45, M 6

Open Tue.–Fri.
9am–7pm, Sat.
and Sun.
10am–2pm;
closed Jan. 1st,
Good Friday, May
1st and Dec. 25th

No other museum offers such a magnificent conspectus of Spanish painting from the 12th to the 19th century as the Prado, the undoubted highlight of a visit to Madrid.

In origin the Prado was a royal art collection assembled by both Habsburg rulers (particularly the Emperor Charles V, Philip II and Philip IV) and Bourbons (Philip V, Charles III and Charles IV). The building which it now occupies was built in 1785, in the reign of Charles III, by Juan de Villanueva. It was originally designed to house a museum of natural history, but in 1819, during the reign of Ferdinand VII, it was reopened as the home of the royal art collections. In neo-classical style, the building consists of a central section with Doric columns and two extensive wings. The sumptuous façade has a total length of more than 200 m (650 ft). Since the museum has long suffered from a chronic shortage of space, it has been extended on several occasions. An international competition for a further extension was held in 1996, but this produced no result. In 1998 the roof, which had been leaking, was renewed, and this gave the museum ten new exhibition rooms on the attic floor. Negotiations are now in progress for clearing some neighbouring buildings and making them available to the Prado.

The Prado possesses over 8000 **paintings**, of which some 2300 are on show in 130 rooms on its three floors. It also has a large collection of sculpture (see below). It is not possible to give any full description of this vast collection; and besides the modernisation work in progress means that some rooms have been temporarily closed and many pictures have been temporarily moved. There is a plan in the Prado which enables visi-

The ornate façade of the former Hospicio de San Fernando is a ▶
typical example of Baroque ornament

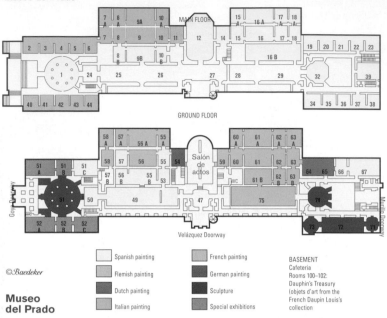

©*Baedeker*

**Museo
del Prado**

tors to locate individual works of art, and there are a free leaflet with a
general plan of the gallery and a "Guide to the Prado" which lists all
works of art and artists but does not give the location of the pictures.
Visitors can also engage a private guide.

The most important works of **ancient sculpture** in the Prado's collection
(some 80 out of 220) have been on show again since 1998 in Rooms 67,
71, 72, 73 and 74).

The following description is confined mainly to the principal works of
Spanish painting – without any intention of disparaging other masterpieces of European painting in the Prado. To enable individual works to
be located their inventory numbers are given in parentheses.

Romanesque painting

The oldest pictures in the Prado are 13th century frescoes preserved on
a linen backing – though, strictly speaking, they cannot be described as
Spanish painting, since a Spanish national style developed only after the
union of the kingdoms of Aragon and Castile at the end of the 15th century. The painting of the early and high mediaeval periods is marked by
different regional schools which show many Moorish and Byzantine features. The early 13th century hunting scenes and representations of animals which decorate the walls of the Mozarabic chapel of San Baudelio
de Berlanga (province of Soria) reveal clear influence of Moorish decorative styles in their figural austerity and the contoured style of the light-
coloured figures set against a deep red ground. Similar influences can
be seen in the ivories and ceramics of the same period. The early 12th
century cycle of frescoes on Biblical themes (Christ in a mandorla, the
Evangelists, angels, apostles, the story of Creation, the Fall, the offerings

In the Museo del Prado

of Cain and Abel, the Washing of the Feet) from the Ermita de la Cruz in Maderuelo (province of Segovia) shows a monumental decorative style, with similar summarily drawn figures, in which attitudes and gestures are frequently clumsy but which is remarkable for its archaic but vivid expressive force. Altogether these Romanesque fresco cycles are a good example of the co-existence and intermingling on the Iberian peninsula of Christian conceptions and Mozarabic decorative art.

Faced with the Moorish culture, hostile to representations of figures, Christian iconography could assert itself only gradually during the Reconquista. Moorish decorative styles remained popular in central Spain until the end of the 14th century. Even the few Christian pictures, such as the 14th century Castilian retablo with a monumental frontal figure of St Christopher, a small-scale "Descent from the Cross" and several scenes from the lives of St Peter and St Emilianus (No. 3150), still show simpler linear forms which are purely Romanesque.

Gothic painting

It was only around 1400 that Spanish painting gained fresh impulses from international Gothic, brought in by paintings imported into Spain and artists who came to Spain from western Europe. At first French and Italian influences were predominant, but in the course of the 15th century these gave place to Flemish influence, which finally led to the emergence of a Hispano-Flemish style.

The "Altarpiece of Archbishop Sancho de Rojas" (No. 1321), by an unknown master of the first quarter of the 15th century, shows Sienese stylistic influence, probably as a result of the work of the Tuscan master Gherardo Starnina in Toledo. The central panel shows the Virgin and Child surrounded by angel musicians and flanked on the left by two Dominican saints recommending the archbishop to the Virgin, from whom he receives his mitre, and on the right by the kneeling figure of

King Ferdinand I of Aragon, who is crowned by the Infant Christ – a religious and political demonstration of the legitimacy of the king's succession to the throne which he had won in battle in 1412. The figures, in their delicately patterned flowing garments, are almost immaterial, reflecting the sensitive feeling for form and colour of the Sienese painting of the period.

The "Virgin and St Francis" polyptych by **Nicolás Francés** (1430–68; No. 2545) shows the influence of French and Italian Gothic. The left-hand panel has lively scenes from the life of St Francis, depicted as a continuing narrative in a series of separate incidents separated by tracery. This marked feeling for scenic presentation, with a rich palette of colours and spatial imagination, had a powerful influence on painting in Spain.

The most vigorous exponents of the international Gothic style were **Jaume Huguet** and the **Masters of Arguis and Sigüenza**. The fragment of a "Prophet" (No. 2683) by Jaume Huguet (c. 1415–92) shows his terse style, with a tendency towards gentle melancholy, in the prophet's face. The Aragonese Master of Arguis displays the elegant courtly variant of international Gothic, with its delight in narrative, in the "Retablo of St Michael" (No. 1332; c. 1450). The Master of Sigüenza – so called after his panel paintings in Sigüenza Cathedral but now identified as Juan de Peralta – offers another example of the lively interplay of lines characteristic of international Gothic in his "St John the Baptist and St Katherine" altarpiece (No. 1336).

The most enduring influences on Spanish painting, however, came from the painters of the Netherlands, in particular Jan van Eyck, who visited the Iberian peninsula in 1428/29. In the second half of the 15th century some notable works were produced in the Hispano-Flemish style.

The outstanding representative of the Hispano-Flemish style was **Bartolomé Bermejo** (before 1450–1498), a native of Córdoba, who was probably responsible for introducing the technique of oil-painting developed by the van Eyck brothers in Flanders into Aragon. His principal work was the St Dominic Altar in Daroca, the central panel of which, depicting St Dominic of Silos, is in the Prado (No. 1323). Under the terms of his commission this monumental work was to be painted in oils, using the finest pigments, the valuable blue made from lapis lazuli dust; it was to be a work by the master's own hand, for the production of which he was allowed a period of 26 months and would receive the considerable fee of 2300 or 3000 sueldos. The result of this contract was a magnificent retablo (1474–77) notable for its sharp naturalistic detail but in an austere style remote from common humanity which gives the saint a statuesque, hieratic aspect. On the elaborately carved throne are female figures clad in coloured garments symbolising the seven cardinal and theological virtues – faith, hope, charity, justice, fortitude, prudence and temperance.

Bermejo: "St Dominic"

In Castile Flemish influence was most powerfully reflected in the work of **Fernando Gallego** (1467–1507), which in turn influenced his contemporaries. It is not known whether Gallego learnt the new technique at first hand in the Netherlands or from Flemish works imported into Spain: at any rate his work clearly shows the influence of Bouts and van der Weyden, as well as Witz and Schongauer. His precise, clear, rather hard style can be seen in his "Pietà" in the Prado (No. 2998), for example in the stiff attitude of Christ's body and the much creased garment of the Virgin. Gallego's paintings are notable for their luminous colours, particularly in the darker tones. His figures have Castilian faces, but the finely tiered landscape backgrounds are Flemish.

Another work, "Christ enthroned, blessing" (No. 2647), the central panel of an altar dedicated to St Lawrence (after 1492), shows a Late Gothic delight in decoration, for example in the rich tracery above the throne and the strictly symmetrical disposition of the figures, large and small. On Christ's left is a personification of the Church, with the symbols of the Evangelists Mark (a lion) and John (an eagle), on his right the Synagogue, with the symbols of Luke (an ox) and Matthew (an angel) – the whole composition giving expression to Christianity's claim to world domination.

Two major representatives of the Hispano-Flemish style of the second half of the 15th century are the **Master of Sopetrán**, with an "Annunciation" (No. 2576) and a "Founder in Prayer" (No. 2576) from the Benedictine monastery of Sopetrán, both strongly influenced by Rogier van der Weyden, and the **Master of La Sisla** (from the Hieronymite monastery of that name), with six panels of scenes from the lives of Christ and the Virgin (Nos. 1254–59); the "Death of the Virgin" (No. 1259) is an almost exact copy of a copperplate by the German painter Martin Schongauer.

Other notable examples of Hispano-Flemish painting are the anonymous "Virgin of the Catholic Monarchs" (No. 1260; c. 1490) and "Sacra Conversazione" (No. 1335; c. 1500). The former, from the royal chapel of Santo Tomás in Avila, depicts St Thomas recommending to the Virgin King Ferdinand of Aragon, praying, accompanied by his son and Grand Inquisitor Torquemada, on the left and Queen Isabella of Castile, praying, with her daughter and a chronicler, on the right. The painting is notable for its detailed and accurate reproduction of reality in fresh and lively colours. The "Sacra Conversazione" , attributed to a Valencian master, depicts the Virgin and Child, flanked by St Bernard and St Benedict, receiving a donor, a knight of the Order of Montesa. The picture charms by the delicacy of its draughtsmanship, the light-and-shadow effect of the colours and the expression of the inner experience of the figures.

With **Juan de Flandes** (d. 1519), who had been trained as a painter in Ghent and worked for Queen Isabella from 1496 onwards, Renaissance art came to Spain. His skill in spatial composition, his lively and realistic depiction of figures and his strong contrasting colours can be seen in his four altarpieces (Nos. 2935–38), the "Raising of Lazarus", the "Prayer in the Garden", the "Ascension" and the "Descent of the Holy Ghost".

Renaissance painting

The Castilian **Pedro Berruguete** (c. 1450 to before 1504), more than any other contemporary Spanish painter, achieved a synthesis of the various Flemish and Italian stylistic traditions, developing a Spanish national style entirely in tune with the age of the Catholic Monarchs. His many years of work at the ducal court in Urbino had made him familiar with the achievements of Italian Renaissance art. After the duke's death he returned to Spain in 1482, working in Toledo and later in Avila. In

Berruguete: "Auto-da-fé"

Morales: "Virgin and Child"

1497–98 he created a number of panel paintings for the monastery of Santo Tomás in Avila, a favourite foundation of the Catholic Monarchs, which are now in the Prado. Among them is the "Auto-da-fé of St Dominic" (No. 618), part of a polyptych dedicated to St Dominic. This was based on actual events: a tribunal of the Inquisition was then sitting in Santo Tomás, presided over by the Spanish founder of the Dominican order, St Dominic Guzmán (1170–1221), and the painting depicts the public proclamation of its judgment. The Inquisition had been founded by Pope Gregory IX in 1231/1232 to detect and punish heretics, and was run by the Franciscans and Dominicans. In Spain a Grand Inquisitor was appointed in 1478, during the Christian campaign to recover the Iberian peninsula from the Moors, to watch strictly over the rule of the faith.

Berruguete's picture gives an exact depiction of the execution of a judgment of the Inquisition – the proclamation of the judgment, the execution of the sentence on the offenders, wearing pointed hats and white wraps, their death at the stake (with the "grace" accorded to them of being strangled before being exposed to the flames). Berruguete presents the scene in a clearly defined sequence, with three platforms or galleries on which the events take place. The different levels are linked by numbers of lively and active figures, giving the scene great vividness and truth to reality. This is true also of the paintings (Nos. 611–614) depicting scenes from the life of the Dominican preacher and inquisitor Peter Martyr (1202–52). The "Virgin and Child" (No. 2709) conveys a sense of the deeply felt relationship between mother and child. Berruguete's paintings show a sure handing of spatial problems, perspective and the disposition of figures. His figures radiate dignity and humanity.

In the first half of the 16th century, however, the High Renaissance styles of Leonardo da Vinci, Raphael and Michelangelo had little impact in Spain. Only the next development, Italian Mannerism, with its sometimes unnatural sense of form and colour, led to an increased emotional expressiveness which appealed to Spanish painters. In an intensely

Catholic country like Spain a faith which could be emotionally experienced became the main theme of painting.

"St Catherine of Alexandria" (No. 2902), by **Fernando Yáñez de la Almedina** (active 1505–36), is a figure of touching maiden innocence, with her attributes, the sword and wheel with which she was tortured, the crown as a symbol of her princely descent and the palm-branch and book of a martyr. The figure of the saint, plastically modelled with the help of chiaroscuro, was long regarded as the very image of classic beauty.

The paintings of **Luis de Morales** (c. 1500–1586) – "Madonna and Child" (No. 2656), "Ecce Homo" (No. 2770), "St Stephen" (No. 948a) – give expression to deep inner emotion. Although his work had little appeal for the court it met the spiritual needs of ordinary people. The mystical features in his painting earned him the style of El Divino. Contrasting with his deeply Catholic style, however, is his cool range of colours.

Juan de Juanes (Vicente Juan Masip, c. 1523–1579) also appealed to the pious feelings of his contemporaries. His "Last Supper" (No. 846), although following in the footsteps of Raphael and Leonardo da Vinci, has a remarkable theatricality in the setting of the scene, the affectedness of the figures and the rather tasteless colours. There is a similar sentimentality of expression in his "Visitation" (No. 851) and other altarpieces.

Pedro Machuca (end of 15th c. to 1550), who trained as a painter in Italy, shows the influence of Roman Mannerism. His "Descent from the Cross" (No. 3017) of 1547 is a dramatic composition built up from diagonal and vertical lines of movement with strong chiaroscuro contrasts. Machuca also gained reputation as architect of Charles V's palace in Granada.

The Flemish-trained portrait painter **Alonso Sánchez Coello** (1531/32–88), as court painter to Philip II, followed the model of his teacher Anthonis Mor. His portraits of the royal family are frequently painted in three-quarters view against a neutral background. His portraits of Philip II (No. 1036; attributed), his son Don Carlos (No. 1136) and his daughter, the Infanta Isabel Clara Eugenia (No. 1137) are realistic presentations of real people, who in spite of the aloof air required by protocol and the stiff garments are given human traits by the sensual colouring. The double portrait of the two young infantas, Isabel and her sister Catarina (No. 1138), points the contrast between the artificial courtly attitudes of the two little girls as princesses and their childlike expressions.

The high point of Spanish Mannerism (the late phase of Renaissance art) is the work of **El Greco** (Domenikos Theotokopoulos, 1541–1614). A native of Crete, he was trained in Italy and came to Spain in 1577, perhaps to escape from the competition in Rome and Venice and in the hope of taking part in the decoration of the Escorial. His painting, however, did not appeal to Philip II. He then settled in Toledo (see entry) and rapidly gained a reputation, devoting himself mainly to portraits and religious themes. The "Trinity" (No. 824) was his first commissioned work in Toledo. The strong Italian influence on his work can be seen at the first glance. Christ's body, weighing heavily on God the Father's lap, has still – under the influence of Michelangelo – a plastically formed corporeality (compare Michelangelo's Pietà in the Duomo in Florence), which in El Greco's later work increasingly gave place to weightlessness. In the abstract theme of the Trinity, difficult as it is to represent, the body of Christ directs the eye to the human suffering of the Son of God. The

El Greco: "Nobleman" (detail)

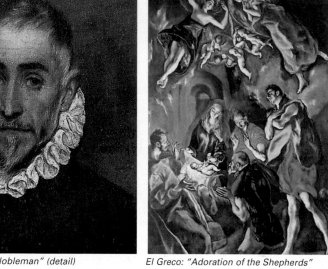

El Greco: "Adoration of the Shepherds"

theme has a long tradition in art. It again became popular in painting in the time of the Counter-Reformation. The Father's pain at the suffering which he himself has imposed on his Son appealed to the late 16th century's religious feeling of desolation.

The "Resurrection" (No. 825) was part, along with two other exceptionally tall panel paintings, of a commission from María de Aragón, lady-in-waiting to the queen. It was painted in 1596, in El Greco's mature style. In a transfiguring light Christ floats weightlessly upward, holding the banner of victory. Only one of the guards is unmoved by the event: he sleeps on. Some of the others start back in horror; others are lost in amazement. The soldiers who, mindful of their duty, have drawn their swords and seek to hold back the risen Christ with them are an invention of El Greco's.

El Greco's enthusiasm in the depiction of religious themes, at times applying a heavy impasto, at times almost transparent brush-strokes, led to an unnatural elongation of the figures, which seem to be detached from the earthly world – a development of the *maniera greca,* the Greco-Byzantine stylistic tradition which was one of the sources of the Mannerist style. Flickering light, sharp changes of colour, lines of movement running counter to one another all combine to give El Greco's pictures a dynamism which amounts to ecstasy.

The "Easter Miracle" (No. 828) is a further example of his ecstatic style, in a carefully worked out composition which builds up the scene of the Descent of the Holy Ghost in a series of layers – of figures, space and colours – so that the eye is directed towards the Virgin and the dove of the Holy Ghost hovering above her. The bodies of the apostles in the upper part of the background are disposed in an almost horizontal undulating line which separates the disturbing terrestrial events in the foreground from the celestial happenings above. The various levels of the picture are brought together to form a unity with the help of a triangular composition between Mary in the centre and the two other figures at the edges.

El Greco's approach to painting, a mixture of trance and rational consideration, shows him to be fully in line with the ideas of the Counter-Reformation. He had the reputation in Toledo of a learned man and a humanist.

In his late style, exemplified by his "Adoration of the Shepherds" (No. 2988), which was intended for his burial chapel, El Greco again confined himself to clearly directed shaft of light. From the child in the manger the Light of the World streams out, binding men together in its clarity and warmth.

El Greco was an excellent portraitist who concentrated almost exclusively on the faces of his sitters. They frequently have features of no particular distinction and are shown bathed in bright light against a dark background, acquiring individuality and humanity only by their penetrating glances. The "Nobleman with his Hand on his Breast" (No. 809) is believed to be a portrait of Juan de Silva, a knight of the Order of Santiago and governor of the Philippines. The portraits of the lawyer Jerónimo de Cevallos (No. 812) and the "Old Nobleman" (No. 806) are other examples of El Greco's work as a portraitist, painted with free brush-strokes.

Baroque painting

When El Greco died in 1614 a new development in painting towards a naturalistic chiaroccuro style, which had originated in Italy, had reached Spain. With the help of strong light effects individualities were given increased emphasis, and sometimes theatrically exaggerated. At the beginning of the 17th century, under the influence of Caravaggio in Italy, Spanish painters turned away from Mannerism and returned to a more ordered type of composition, with a clarity and directness of formal language of which there were indications in the artists who worked on the Escorial.

Vicente Carducho (1576/78–1638), who had worked on the Escorial and risen to become court painter, was also the author of a work on the theory of painting, "Conversations on Painting" (1633). In addition to a number of historical paintings (Nos. 636–637) for the Imperial Hall in the Buen Retiro Palace he painted a series of pictures for the cloister of the Carthusian monastery of El Paular (Nos. 639 and 639a, 2227, 2501 and 2502, 2956, 3062), including "The Death of the Venerable Odón de Novara" (1632), with a self-portrait in the nearer of the two kneeling figures on the left of the picture. Since there were no existing portraits of the characters involved in the series, Carducho had to rely on his own creativity for their likenesses. The arrangement of the figures, which was frequently complicated, was achieved with masterly skill. Caravaggiesque naturalism is combined with emotional appeal and celestial events are drawn into everyday terrestrial reality.

Fray Juan Bautista Maino (1581–1649) also worked at the Spanish court, where he was Philip IV's drawing master. An Early Baroque painter under Italian influence, Maino painted pictures with a delight in narration of almost hyper-realistic quality, with precise observation of the surfaces, forms and volumes of objects, combined with a cold but luminous use of colour and light. His "Adoration of the Kings" (No. 856) and "Adoration of the Shepherds" (No. 3227), both of 1612, are good examples of his style. His historical painting "The Conquest of Bahía in Brazil" (No. 885), recording an event in 1625 when Don Fabrique de Toledo reconquered the fortress of Bahía from the Dutch, dates from 1634. On the right of the picture, in a tapestry, Philip IV appears between Don Fabrique and the goddess of victory, with allegorical figures of Heresy, Wrath and War as corpses at their feet, while on the right is a scene depicting the wounded being cared for by the local population.

The scene charms with its narrative spontaneity, its clear representation of the figures and its unified composition, formed by the volume of the bodies, the areas of colour and the diagonal line which structures it.

Maino's still lifes also achieve a high level of reality.

Felipe Ramírez, who was active in the first thirty years of the 17th century, painted still lifes (No. 2802) of extreme economy and clarity. **Juan de Arellano** (1614–76) painted still lifes with flowers (Nos. 592–597, 3138, 3139) after Dutch and Italian models. The large and colourful bunches of flowers against a dark background, with their fallen and withered blooms, are a kind of *memento mori,* a symbol of the vanity and transitoriness of all earthly things.

Francisco Ribalta (1551/55–1628), of Catalan origin, was trained in Madrid and worked as a painter in Valencia.

Maino: "Adoration of the Shepherds"

He combined emotional religiosity with marked naturalism. His versions of mystical themes like "Christ embracing St Bernard" (No.2804) and "St Francis consoled by an Angel" (No. 1062) show familiarity with the chiaroscuro technique copied from Caravaggio which gives an increased character of reality to the scenes.

The Valencian painter **José Ribera** (1591–1652), known as Lo Spagnoletto, went to Italy as a young man and worked in Naples. He never returned to Spain, though he maintained active contacts with it. Some of his pictures were bought by Philip IV for the Escorial. Even though working abroad Ribera retained the typically Spanish concern, despite all religiosity, for the observation of everyday reality and the individuality of each human being. Thus his "Archimedes" (No. 1121), signed and dated to 1630, is an impressive portrait of an elderly man who looks like a contemporary Neapolitan. This is not an idealisation or glorification of a great scientist but a depiction of a man's individual personality and humanity. This can also be said of his likeness of "St Andrew" (No. 1078) as an old fisherman and numerous other portraits of saints and Biblical or mythological figures.

In his early period Ribera painted a number of highly dramatic and sometimes gruesome pictures in dark colours. His "Tityus" (No. 1113), dated 1632, which is darkened by the use of bitumen in the paint, depicts the fettered giant with his liver being torn out by a vulture, a punishment ordered by Zeus for his attempted rape of Leto, Apollo's mother. Another sinner, "Ixion" (No. 1114), is shown bound to a fiery wheel because he had attempted to seduce Hera. Ribera's dramatic power and passionately religious feelings are displayed in Biblical themes, for example in his "Martyrdom of St Philip" (No. 1101) of about 1639. The centre of the elaborate composition is a system of coordinates formed by the beam up to which the martyr's body, lying diagonally, is being drawn. The dramatic interplay between the horizontal, the vertical and the diagonal is still further enhanced by the contrasts between light and dark. Philip's pain-stricken face contrasts with the look on the faces of the eagerly watching spectators. Ribera's picture has a double aspect: on the one hand it depicts a group of ordinary people in the harbour of

Naples, on the other it presents with great sensitivity a tragic individual fate. In the "Trinity" (No. 1069), of about 1635, the composition is based on curving diagonals, representing the supernatural forces which bear Christ's body. The majestic figure of God the Father forms a sharp contrast to the broken body of the divine Son of Man.

In the work of his mature period Ribera's palette takes on brighter tones as a result of his contact with Venetian painting. In this period he produced a series of large-scale naturalistic compositions, such as "Jacob's Dream" (No. 1117), a fine study of sleep in which, instead of the traditional ladder up to heaven, a diffuse cloud of light illuminates the picture and symbolises the angelic vision of the sleeping Jacob.

Cano: "Christ supported by an Angel"

The painter, sculptor and architect **Alonso Cano** (1601–67) was trained as a painter in Granada and did most of his work there. He also worked for a time, along with Velázquez, at the royal court in Madrid. A "Madonna and Child" (No. 627), painted about 1646–50, depicts a type of female figure with delicate features and large eyes which is characteristic of Cano's work. His naturalism was learned from Caravaggio, the sensuality, elegance and dignity of his figures came from Rubens and van Dyck. His "Dead Christ supported by an Angel" (No. 629), of about 1645, a theme which is fairly rare in 15th century Flemish and Italian painting is treated by Cano with thick brush-strokes and an effective interplay of light and shadow. His "Miracle of the Well" (No. 2806) is a finely balanced composition in brilliant Venetian-style colours and acute realism depicting the thanksgiving of St Isidore, whose son had fallen into a well and been saved by an angel.

Francisco de Herrera the Elder (c. 1576–1656) lived and worked mainly in Seville. His painting style developed from his original Mannerism into a realism expressed in narrative scenes, as in "St Bonaventura receiving the Franciscan Habit" (No. 2441a), of about 1628. As Velázquez's first teacher and the teacher of his own son Francisco, Herrera prepared the way for the great achievements of Spanish painting in the mid 17th century.

Although in the 17th century Spain suffered a decline in its standing as a European power, following the loss of its domination of the sea to England and the revolt of the Netherlands, it achieved a late flowering in art and literature known as the Siglo de Oro (Golden Age). The greatness of Cervantes, Lope de Vega and Calderón in literature was matched by that of the painters Zurbarán, Velázquez and Murillo. **Francisco de Zurbarán**

Zurbarán: "St Casilda"

(1598–1664), of the same age as Velázquez but of a very different temperament, abandoned the Baroque in favour of a serene, almost matter-of-fact style, so that both figures and objects, frequently shown isolated against a dark background, are given a severely ascetic spiritualisation and a sense of timeless repose. This is particularly evident in his religious paintings, for example in "St Peter Nolasco's Vision of the Heavenly Jerusalem" (No. 1236) and "St Peter appearing to St Pedro Nolasco" (No. 1237). Both of these pictures were painted in 1629 for the Mercedarian Order, which had been founded by St Peter Nolasco in 1233 to purchase the freedom of Christian prisoners in Africa. His canonisation in 1628 was the occasion for Zurbarán's commission, and as there was no iconographical tradition to fall back on the painter was free to create his own version of the saint's life.

"St Casilda" (No. 1239), of 1640, is presented as an aristocratic figure in a magnificent 17th century Andalusian dress. The daughter of an 11th century emir in Toledo, she secretly took bread to starving Christian prisoners, but when the matter was investigated the bread turned into roses. The figure, set against a neutral dark background, is given a strongly plastic effect by the light coming from one side.

In 1634 Zurbarán produced ten panel paintings depicting the "Labours of Hercules" (Nos. 1241–50) which originally hung above the windows in the Hall of Kings in the Buen Retiro palace and accordingly were given strong bottom lighting. Traditionally paintings of the Labours of Hercules were designed for the glorification of the victory of a righteous ruler over his enemies.

In Zurbarán's still lifes (No. 2803) – in sharp contrast to the over-abundance of contemporary Dutch and Flemish work – the individual objects are shown lined up in the foreground, equidistant from one another, in a balanced rhythm of varying height and size, reducing the depth of the picture. Everyday objects are thus given an unsuspected poetry and a mysterious charm.

The historical painting "The Defence of Cádiz against the English" (No. 658) of 1634, depicting an event in 1625, was commissioned for the Royal Palace. It has the air of a scene in a play, with Governor Fernando Girón as the star actor.

The most highly esteemed painter at the royal court in Madrid in the 17th century was Diego Rodríguez de Silva y **Velázquez** (1599–1660). He came from Seville, where he was trained in the studio of Herrera the Elder and Francisco Pacheco Del Rio, whose daughter he married in 1618. At first Velázquez painted still lifes, genre pieces and religious scenes, including an "Adoration of the Kings" (No. 1166) of 1619. He then attracted King Philip IV's attention as a portrait-painter, and from 1623 to the end of his life was court painter, working almost exclusively for the royal family. In the art collections of the royal palaces he had the opportunity of studying a great range of old and contemporary masters but in the end, undistracted by contemporary trends – Rubens, Rembrandt and Bernini were all active at the same time –followed his own artistic course. Velázquez's brilliant artistic and social rise culminated in his diplomatic missions for the king on two visits to Italy in 1629 and 1649 and his admission to the Order of Santiago, normally open only to the high nobility.

Of predominant importance in Velázquez's work was his skill in portraiture, which enabled him to convey a

Velázquez: "Infante Baltasar Carlos"

sitter's individual psyche through the realistic representation of his outer man without stressing his social standing and without decorative adjuncts, whether he is depicting members of the royal family, historical figures or ladies of the court. His half-length portrait of Philip IV (No. 1182) shows the young king without the attributes of a ruler, simply dressed in garments of black silk and in an attitude which betrays both his dignity as a king and an inner insecurity. The full-length portrait of the Infante Don Carlos (No. 1188) depicts the king's brother, a sensitive, art-loving man who died young in 1632, with an air of melancholy. Simplicity, elegance and carelessness (note the finger-tips holding his right-hand glove) mark the figure of the Infante, whose silhouette with its dissolving shadows stands out against the dark corner of the picture, illuminated by the bright light falling on his head and hands. The equestrian figure of the Infante Baltasar Carlos (No. 1160), heir to the Spanish throne, who died at the age of 17, shows him as a six-year-old boy in the pose of a future king against the backdrop of the Sierra de Guadarrama (see entry), alluding symbolically in his mastery of the horse to hid role as the ruler of an empire. Velázquez's portrait shows with great psychological insight the tension between childishness (the horse as the analogy of a rocking-horse) and the power of a ruler (the boy's imperial pose).

Velázquez's masterpiece is **"Las Meniñas"** ("The Ladies of the Court") or "The Family of Philip IV" (No. 1174), painted in 1656, which combines different elements – a court group portrait, a self-portrait of the painter and an interior painting – into a magnificent unity, while preserving the spontaneity and intimacy of an everyday scene in the royal palace. In the centre of the scene is the little Infanta Margarita (later Empress of Austria; d. 1673), who has come, with her suite, to watch Velázquez (on left, at the easel) painting. One of her ladies-in-waiting, Maria Augustina

Sarmiento, kneels as she offers the infanta a drink, while others suddenly look up, and only the young dwarf continues to tease the sleeping dog in the right-hand corner of the scene, as the king and queen, already noticed by the female dwarf and another lady-in-waiting, Isabel de Velasco, enter the room, coming from the foreground, from the same direction as the observer, as can be seen in the mirror on the rear wall of the room, so that the major-domo, José Nieto, pauses for a moment before disappearing through the door in the background. In his picture Velázquez records for posterity, in a tour de force never before achieved, a passing moment of reality, with an impressionistic brush-stroke and a highly effective use of light and colour. The picture still retains a secret, for we do not known whom or what Velázquez is painting on the easel, which is turned away from the spectator. The presence of the king and queen in the studio is an honour for the painter, but this in no way interferes with his creative freedom.

Numerous other portraits, particularly those of court dwarfs and court jesters, bear witness to Velázquez's ability to catch the individuality of his sitters and at the same time achieve a psychological tension between objective representation and subjective insight, while still preserving respect and sympathy for his figures. The court jester "Calabacillas" (No. 1205), in spite of his deformity, has an almost relaxed and happy look on his face; the dwarf "Sebastián de Morra" (No. 1202) is given a sharp and penetrating eye; the jester "Don John of Austria" (No. 1200) believes himself, in his dream world, to be the victor in the battle of Lepanto and is surrounded by a variety of weapons; the fool "Don Diego de Acedo", known as El Primo (No. 1201), sits with his deformed body amid heavy folio volumes, suggesting literary ambitions. The illustrious names mocked these poor creatures, who spent their lives exposed to scorn and derision for the amusement of courtly society.

Of Velázquez's few works on themes taken from antiquity – there was practically no tradition of mythological pictures in Spain – the Prado possesses three important examples. "Los Borrachos" ("The Drinkers"), also known as the "Triumph of Bacchus" (No. 1170), painted in 1616, the year before his first visit to Italy, shows in a starkly naturalistic style a party of jolly drinkers with the drunk wine god Bacchus in a rural setting. In "Vulcan's Smithy" (No. 1171), painted in Rome, the gods are depicted without any form of idealisation. In spite of Velázquez's increased interest in the naked body as a result of his study of antiquity in Italy his figures have an entirely credible reality. The hard sweaty work in the smithy comes to a stop when Apollo surprises Vulcan and his companions with the news of the adultery of Venus, Vulcan's wife, with Mars, to which the deceived husband reacts with disbelief, shock and anger.

In "The Weavers" or "The Story of Arachne" (No. 1173), painted about 1657, Velázquez depicts Minerva, the inventor and goddess of weaving, and her arrogant challenger Arachne the carpet-weaver, whom she later turns into a spider (see Ovid's "Metamorphoses"), along with women workers from the Royal Tapestry Manufactory in Madrid. Their busy activity, in the foreground of the picture, is conveyed with brilliant directness through impressionistic light and colour effects.

One of the peaks of Velázquez's work as a historical painter is his "Surrender of Breda" (No. 1172), painted before 1635. In his representation of this event, which took place in 1625, he concentrates on the meeting between the victors and the defeated at the handing over of the keys of the town by its commandant Justinus of Nassau to the Genoese/Spanish general Ambrogio Spinola. As Nassau prepares to kneel before his victor Spinola goes up to him in an almost friendly and personal way, as a sign of respect for the defeated commander – the *grandeza* which was part of the Spanish conception of honour. The troops on both sides are symmetrically disposed: on one side the Dutch forces, with the gunpowder smoke and the broken positions which bear witness to their defeat, on the other the Spaniards, drawn up in order with lances held high in token of victory.

In sharp contrast to the serious psychological realism of Velázquez was the serene, gentle, charming style of **Bartolomé Esteban Murillo** (baptised 1618–1682), whose subjects were mostly religious. A native of Seville, he achieved fame there with his pictures of the Holy Family, the Good Shepherd and the visions and miracles of saints, with glowing light and colour which gave his subjects a transfiguring or a touching effect.

In the naturalistic and realistic style of Murillo's early period the influence of Caravaggio predominated, with sharply contrasting light and shadow. The "Adoration of the Shepherds" (No. 961) and "Holy Family" (No. 960), both dating from about 1650, are characteristic of his simple, pious genre scenes.

His profound religious feeling is given expression particularly in his Madonnas. "The Virgin appearing to St Bernard" (No. 978) shows the irruption of the inconceivable into everyday reality as a perfectly natural occurrence. The "Immaculate Conception" (Nos. 972, 974), with its soft lines and colours, depicts the charm and grace of the Virgin that looks forward to the age of Rococo. The "Virgin of the Rosary" (No. 975) combines female beauty and youthful charm that owes something to Raphael's Madonnas.

Murillo liked to paint children – street urchins, children eating grapes, the boy Jesus or the young John the Baptist. Only this last type is represented in the Prado. To Murillo the child was a symbol of an unquestioning, comforting trust in God – a conception which in the 19th century trivialised his pictures into pious illustrations in prayer-books.

In his two-part painting of the "Legend of the Foundation of the Church of Santa Maria Maggiore in Rome" (Nos. 994, 995) Murillo again shows himself as the depicter of human situations In his representation of the Virgin's appearance in a dream to a Roman patrician, who then, along with his wife, tells the astonished Pope Liberius that she had prescribed the site and ground-plan for a church dedicated to her at a place where there had been a miraculous fall of snow in August. (August 5th is now the feast-day of St Mary of the Snows).

Although overshadowed by painters of European standing such as Zurbarán, Velázquez and Murillo, there are a number of other important High Baroque works by Spanish artists, particularly those of the Madrid school, in the second half of the 17th century. In the reign of Charles II **Juan Carreño de Miranda** (1614–85) made his name as court painter with showy portraits under the influence of van Dyck – an influence seen particularly in the full-length portrait of the "Duque de Pastrana" (No. 650), whose dark and impressive figure is brought out by he delicate, almost gloomy use of colour. The picture of Petr Ivanovich Potemkin, the Russian ambassador to Spain, is a typical state portrait of a nobleman. There are also portraits of the royal family, of Charles II (No. 642) and Maria Anna of Austria (No. 644) and of court jesters.

Claudio Coello (1642–93), the son of a Portuguese bronzefounder, is the principal representative of the Baroque style popular in the second half of the 17th century. His work is characterised by magnificent spatial prospects and a dynamism produced by diagonal compositions and rich sensual colouring.

The "Triumph of St Augustine" (No. 664), in which the saint is depicted in flowing garments striving heavenwards, shows the influence of Rubens. "The Virgin revered by St Louis of France" (No. 661) and "The Virgin among the Theological Virtues" (No. 660) belong to the type of the Sacra Conversazione.

Francisco Herrera the Younger (1622–85), who was trained in Italy, has a lively Baroque style, seen, for example, in his "Triumph of St Hermenegild" (No. 833). Hermenegild, canonised in 1586, was the son of the Visigothic king Leovigild. He renounced his Arian faith and rebelled against his father, who imprisoned him and had him beheaded in Tarragona in 585, according to church tradition because he had refused to receive communion from an Arian bishop.

Juan de Valdés Leal (1622–90), who worked in Seville, offered a contrast to Murillo with violent and fantastic compositions of highly subjective expressive power. Examples of his work are "The 12-year-old Jesus in the Temple" (No. 1161), "Martyrs of the Hieronymite Order" (No. 2582) and "St Jerome" (No. 2593).

Rococo and Neo-Classicism

In the 18th century the early Bourbon rulers' lack of interest in Spanish art led to a general stagnation, compensated for by the import of works from France. Only in the second half of the century did Spanish artists come to the fore.

Luis Paret Alcázar (1746–1798/99) was the leading representative of Spanish Rococo painting, whose work shows the influence of Venetian and French models (Boucher). He painted social occasions like his "Masked Ball" (No. 2875) and "Las Parejas Reales" ("The Royal Couples"; No. 1044), flower pictures (Nos. 1042, 1043) and scenes of court ceremonial like "Charles III dining in presence of his Court" (No. 2422). His pictures, with a fairly thick impasto, show the elegance and refinement of the Rococo period.

Francisco Bayeu (1734–95) was a fresco painter much employed in the royal service. His "Fall of the Giants" or "Olympus" (No. 604), a fresco still at the sketch stage, is filled with movement and light. His brother Ramón Bayeu (1746–93) worked from 1775 along with Goya as a cartoon-painter for the Royal Tapestry Manufactory, producing, among other things, a series of genre scenes (Nos. 2451 ff.).

Still-life painting was given new impulses by **Luis Eugenio Meléndez** (1716–80), who is represented in the Prado by numerous works from the Palace of Aranjuez (see entry). A typical example of his *bodegones* (still lifes; Nos. 902–919, 924, 927, 929–938) is No. 902 (1772), which shows a piece of salmon, a lemon and three jars. Thanks to the painter's virtuoso style, with strong light contrasts, these simple objects have an almost palpable reality. Meléndez has a very delicate feeling for the materiality of the objects, from the pink flesh of the salmon by way of the brilliant yellow of the lemon and the varying textures of the copper, brass and pottery jars to the worn wood of the table. The strongly plastic naturalistic representation follows in the tradition of Zurbarán.

Mariano Salvador Maella (1739–1819) trained in the Madrid Academy of Art and studied Italian art in Rome, where he came under the influence of Anton Raphael Mengs. As *pintor del rey* (First Court Painter) he was a rival of Goya at the court in Madrid. His work, which includes seascapes (Nos. 874, 874) and depictions of the seasons (Nos. 2497–2500), shows a mingling of Rococo and neo-classicism.

One of the most gifted artists in the story of Spanish, and indeed European, art was **Francisco de Goya y Lucientes** (1746–1828). As painter, draughtsman and etcher he left a large, complex and profound oeuvre, of which only the briefest account can be given here. His range extended from the serene and gay Rococo world depicted in the cartoons he painted in his early period for the Royal Tapestry Manufactory to the morbid "black" paintings he produced in his country house, the Quinta del Sordo ("Deaf Man's House"), in his final phase. Something of his personality can be seen in his "Self-Portrait" (No. 723) of 1815. Goya

Goya: "King Charles IV and his Family"

was then 69 and had for many years been deaf (having lost his hearing in 1792) and a widower. His face is not that of an old man, but it shows bitterness and disappointment on his personal circumstances and the political and social situation in Spain. As a liberal intellectual he could not accept the authoritarian and conservative policy followed by King Ferdinand VII after the war of liberation from the French. He withdrew into "internal exile" and, tormented by angst and depression, painted on the walls of his country house his oppressive vision of humanity fallen into chaos. At the age of 77 he left Spain and, after a relatively peaceful phase, died at a great age in Bordeaux.

Of Goya's 120 or so works in the Prado. only a few masterpieces can be mentioned here. The cartoons he painted in his early period for tapestries to decorate the royal palaces of El Escorial and El Pardo (see entries) are notable for their depiction of the carefree Rococo atmosphere, for example in "The Parasol" (No. 773) and "Blind Man's Buff" (No. 804). The

Goya: "The Milk Girl of Bordeaux"

pleasures of the people are shown in "The Vintage – Autumn" (No. 795) in fresh and carefully graded colour – a scene from the life of ordinary country folk as the court liked to imagine it.

Goya's portraits are much more subtly differentiated. He painted his sitters with unsparing candour, sometimes bordering on caricature. In "The Family of the Duke of Osuna" (No. 739), which is dated 1788, he seeks to achieve a faithful likeness, while creating a triangular composition which gives unity to the family group and giving careful attention to the colouring, in light harmonious tones with delicate shading. **"King Charles IV and his Family"** (No. 726; 1800/01), on the other hand, amounts to a severe criticism of the monarchy. In the unimaginative lining-up of the royal family the domineering Queen Maria Luisa takes the central place, looking severely out of the picture past the spectator. Beside her stands the king, with a rather vacant look. On either side are other members of the family, with bored expressions. In the dark background can be seen Goya himself. The royal family evidently were not upset by this rather unflattering portrait: they were more concerned with the brilliant jewellery and precious fabrics which Goya has painted with such glittering colour.

The delicacy and transparency of fine fabrics is also an essential element in the portrait of "The Maja Clothed" (No. 741), while its counterpart "The Maja Naked" (No. 742) is a sensual and erotic, but ideal female nude. (The *maja* – a girl of the people – is sometimes said, quite wrongly, to be a likeness of the Duchess of Alba). Goya's late portraits have an impressionistic, sketchy look: an example of this is the "Milk Girl of Bordeaux" (No. 2899), painted in 1827.

In the field of historical painting Goya's pictures of the heroic fight of the people of Madrid against the French occupiers on May 3rd 1808 (No. 749; illustration, p. 26) marked an epoch. Goya painted these pictures six years later, in 1814, for the Spanish government. The picture of the shooting of the rebels at night in particular is of enormous dramatic power, underlining the desperate anger and the impotence of the oppressed people of Madrid against the brutality of the victors, as universal human modes of behaviour in extreme situations which lead to a loss of humanity.

Goya's pessimistic view of mankind – the inability of men to maintain peace and happiness for any length of time – finds its most powerful expression in the *pinturas negras* or "black pictures" (Nos. 754–767). In these visions of horror Goya formulates with immense imaginative power a criticism of human life, displaying a world that has got out of joint, with men and women who are mere travesties of themselves. In his subjectivity and expressiveness Goya anticipates the art of the 20th century.

Museo Romántico   G 7

Location
San Mateo 13

Metro
Alonso Martínez,
Tribunal

Buses
3, 7, 37, 40, 48

Open Tue.–Sat.
9am– 2.45pm,
Sun. 10am–1pm;
closed pub. hols.
and Aug.

In one of the narrow streets built during the extension of the city in the 19th century is the Romantic Museum. The core of the museum, which is housed in a late 18th century palace, is the collection of the Marqués de la Vega-Inclán (1858–1942), which he presented to the city in 1920. The palace and its furnishings and the works of art displayed – including pictures by Murillo, Zurbarán, Mengs, Goya and Sorolla – give an impression of aristocratic and upper middle-class life in the reign of Isabella II and of the period from Ferdinand VII's return to the throne after the country's liberation from French rule (1814) and Isabella's overthrow by General Prim's military coup in 1868. Among the exhibits are two pistols, with one of which the Romantic writer Mariano José de Larra (see Famous People) is said to have shot himself in 1837.

★Museo Sorolla

The villa built by the artist Joaquín Sorolla in 1911 houses some 100 works by the Valencian Impressionists, little known in Europe, of the years 1890–1920. Also of interest are the grand drawing-room, a rustic-style kitchen, the dining room (with a decorative frieze of oranges and lemons) and the artist's studio.
Open Tue.–Sat. 10am–3pm, Sun. 10am– 2pm.

Location
General Martínez
Campos 37

Metro
Rubén Darío,
Iglesia

★★Museo Thyssen-Bornemisza

The Villahermosa Palace, built in the first half of the 19th century to the design of Silvestre Pérez and Antonio López Aguado, now houses the art collection of Baron Hans-Heinrich von Thyssen-Bornemisza, the second largest private collection in the world. The collection, originally in Lugano (Switzerland), was first moved to Madrid on loan and was purchased by the Spanish government in 1992. The Villahermosa Palace was converted for its new purpose by Rafael Moneo and is now an extension to the nearby Prado Museum (see Museo del Prado).

Address
Paseo del Prado 8

Metro
Sevilla

Buses
9, 10, 14, 27, 34,
45

Open Tue.–Sun.
10am–7pm

The foundation of the collection were laid in the 1920s by Baron Heinrich von Thyssen-Bornemisza (1875–1947) with classic works of European painting. His son, also a keen collector, added modern works to the collection from the 1960s onwards. It now consists of some 800 works, mainly paintings, which are displayed on the museum's three floors, arranged in chronological order and by schools. They range in date from the 13th to the 20th century, and the modern part of the collection fills a major gap, since the European schools of painting and American painting of the 18th and 19th centuries were not particularly well represented in Madrid's museums.

The tour of the gallery begins on the **second floor** (Planta segunda) with masters of the Early Renaissance, Renaissance and Baroque. Among the main attractions are Duccio di Buoninsegna's "Christ and the Samaritan Woman", Jan van Eyck's "Annunciation", Johann Koerbecke's "Assumption" and the outstanding collection of portraits, including Domenico Ghirlandaio's "Giovanna Tornabuoni", Hans Memling's "Young Man" and Hans Holbein the Younger's "Henry VIII". Other notable artists represented are Zurbarán ("St Casilda"), Carpaccio ("A Young Knight in a Landscape"), Titian ("Doge Francesco Vernier"), Dürer ("The Twelve-Year-Old Jesus among the Scribes"), Lucas Cranach the Elder ("Nymph of the Spring"), Hans Baldung Grien ("Portrait of a Lady"), El Greco, Caravaggio ("St Catherine of Alexandria"), Bernini, Canaletto, Guardi, Anton van Dyck, Cornelis de Vos, Rubens and Gerard ter Borch.

On the **first floor** (Planta primera) are 17th century Dutch painters and 18th century English and French works. The collection of 19th century American painting includes works by the landscapists Cole, Church and Bierstadt. Romantic painting and Realism (Goya, Constable, Courbet, Caspar David Friedrich), Impressionism and Late Impressionism (Monet, Manet, Renoir, Sisley, Degas, Pissarro, Gauguin, Van Gogh, Toulouse-Lautrec, Cézanne) are also well represented, as are the Fauves and the German Expressionists, including the Brücke and Blauer Reiter groups. The ground floor (Planta baja) is devoted to 20th century painting, from Cubism by way of the avantgarde movements of the early decades of the century to Pop Art. Among the artists represented are El Lissitzky (""Proun 1 C"), Mondrian ("New York City, New York"), Picasso ("Man with Clarinet"), Braque ("Woman with Mandoline"), Juan Gris ("Seated Woman"), Rothko ("Green on Violet"), Pollock ("Brown and Silver"), Hopper, Bacon, Lichtenstein and Rauschenberg.

In the basement are a cafeteria, rooms for special exhibitions and a lecture hall.

Oratorio del Caballero de Gracia   G 9

Location
Caballero de
Gracia 5

Metro
Gran Vía

Bus
3

The Oratorio del Caballero de Gracia is one of the pleasant surprises to be encountered on the Gran Vía (see entry). In a quiet side street, close to the high-rise blocks, the cinemas, the department stores and the heavy traffic of this busy shopping street, is this little chapel with a pillared façade, built by Juan de Villanueva between 1786 and 1795 (the façade dates from 1826). In this building Villanueva (architect of the Prado, the Botanic Gardens and the Academy of History) was following the work of Italian architects, in particular Palladio, whose buildings he had seen on his travels in Italy.

★ Palacio de Liria   E 7

Location
Calle de la
Princesa 20

Metro
Ventura
Rodríguez, Plaza
de España

Buses
1, 2, 44, 74, C

The Palacio de Liria, which, with its gardens, occupies a large area adjoining the imposing Cuartel del Conde-Duque (see entry) on Calle de la Princesa, is the residence of the Dukes of Alba. It was begun in the reign of Charles III by the French architect Guilbert and completed in 1780 by Ventura Rodríguez. On the model of the Royal Palace (see Palacio Real), this massive rectangular building has severe Baroque façades articulated by pillars and columns. During the Civil War the palace was burned down to its foundations. The Alba family's works of art had been stored by the Republican government in the vaults of the Banco de España (see Plaza de la Cibeles) and escaped destruction; the palace itself was rebuilt after the war.

The Royal Palace, with its 2850 rooms, some of which are open to the public, recalls the splendours of the past

The palace contains a rich **art collection** which includes unique paintings by Andrea del Sarto, Titian, Veronese, Rubens, Ruysdael and Rembrandt. The Spanish school is represented by El Greco, Ribera, Zurbarán, Velázquez, Murillo and above all Goya (portraits of the Duchess of Alba – see Famous People, Cayetana de Alba – and the Marquesa de Lazán).

The palace is open to the public only by special permit, which must be applied for in writing, indicating the number of visitors (write to Miguel Esteban Arrogante, Calle de la Princesa 20, 28008 Madrid). Exceptionally, with luck, it may be possible to apply by telephone (915475302).

★★Palacio Real · E 9

Originally there stood on the hill between the Almudena Cathedral (see Catedral de la Almudena) and the Royal Palace an Arab fortress, the Alcázar, which was used as a residence by the Spanish kings from the 11th century and altered to serve its new purpose. When the Habsburg ruler Philip II made Madrid capital of Spain in 1561 the Alcázar was further altered, and it was subsequently much enlarged; the architects responsible were, in turn, Juan Bautista de Toledo, Juan de Herrera and Francisco de Mora. In 1734 the old Alcázar of the Habsburgs was almost completely destroyed by fire, along with much of its contents. The Bourbon king Philip V then commissioned the Italian architect Filippo Juvara (1670–1736) to build a new palace. After Juvara's sudden death he was succeeded by Giovanni Battista Sacchetti (1700–64), who simplified the design to a closed square surrounding an inner courtyard, with projecting corner blocks. The façades were modelled on Bernini's designs for the Louvre.

In 1764 Charles III and his court moved into the palace, which remained the royal residence until Alfonso XIII's flight in 1931, except for the period of French occupation. Since 1950 part of the palace has been open to the public: King Juan Carlos does not live here but in the palace of La Zarzuela (see entry). When required for state functions, however, the palace is closed to the public.

The Nuevos Museos, which include the Tapestry Museum (see below), were opened in 1962. Visitors can also see the royal weapons collection, the palace pharmacy and, in the park, the Carriage Museum (see Museo de Carruajes).

There are **conducted tours** of the palace in English, French and Spanish.

Exterior The palace is built of granite from the Sierra de Guadarrama (see entry) and white Colmenar limestone. It has massive foundations on the steep slope down to the Manzanares, on which are the gardens laid out by Francesco Sabatini (Jardines de Sabatini) and the Campo del Moro. The main (south) front looks on to the Plaza de la Armería, framed since the 19th century by two long ranges of low buildings; like the other fronts, it displays the royal coat of arms. The east front looks on to the Plaza de Oriente (see entry). The façade is articulated by central and corner projections, which are given emphasis by columns at first- and second-floor level. The receding wall is broken up by pilasters. The building is topped by a balustrade of white stone, with the dome of the palace church rising above the balustrade on the north front.

From the main entrance (Calle Bailén 2) visitors enter the **inner courtyard**, which has statues of the four Roman emperors born in Spain (Trajan, Hadrian, Theodosius and Honorius). An impressive staircase designed by Sabatini, with a fresco by Corrado Giaquinto (1700–66), "The Triumph of Religion and the Church", leads up to the principal floor of the palace.

Location
Plaza de Oriente

Metro
Ópera

Buses
3, 25, 33, 39, 50, 148, C

Open Apr.–Sept.
Mon.– Sat.
8am–6pm, Sun.
and pub. hols.
9am–3pm;
Oct.–Mar.
Mon.–Sat.
9.30am–5pm,
Sun. and pub.
hols. 9am–2pm;
closed on state
occasions

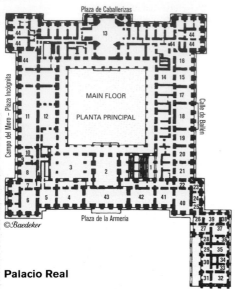

Plaza de Caballerizas

MAIN FLOOR

PLANTA PRINCIPAL

Campo del Moro - Plaza Incógnita

Calle de Bailén

©*Baedeker*

Plaza de la Armería

1 Grand Staircase	22 Vestibule
2 Hall of Halberdiers	23 King's Antechamber
3 Columned Hall	24 King's Study
4 Saleta de Gasparini	25 Nuntio's Room
5 Antecámara de Gasparini	26 Queen's Reception Room
6 Salón de Gasparini	27 Corbella
7 Antecámara de Carlos III	28 Tea Room
8 Salón de Carlos III	29 Queen's Library
9 Sala de la Porcelana	30 Music Room
10 Sala Amarilla	31 Queen's Study
11 State Dining Room	32 Royal Bedchamber
12 Music Room	33 Queen's Dressing Room
13 Chapel	34 Bathroom
14 Antesala	35 King's Bedroom
15 Antecámara	36 Bathroom
16 Cámara de María Cristina	37 Study
17 Saleta	38 Library
18 Dining Room	39 Conference Room
19 Hall of Mirrors	40 Audience Chamber
20 Hall of Tapestries	41 Salón de Grandes
21 Hall of Arms	42 Saleta
	43 Throne Room
	44 New Museums

Palacio Real

The **Sala de Alaberdos** (Hall of the Halberdiers, the palace guards) is dominated by a ceiling painting, "Apotheosis of Aeneas", by Giovanni Battista Tiepolo (1696–1770). The great Venetian was at the height of his fame when he was summoned to Madrid to paint a ceiling fresco in the Throne Room (see below). The fresco on "The Greatness of the Spanish Monarchy" is one of his finest works. The hall, now hung with tapestries, contains Empire furniture.

Then into the **Salón de Columnas** (Hall of Columns), originally a state dining room and then, in Charles III's time, as a ballroom, with a ceiling fresco by Giaquinto, "Triumph of Apollo and Bacchus".

Charles III's private apartments are one of the high points of the tour. The Saleta de Gasparini, named after the Neapolitan painter Matias Gasparini, has a ceiling painting, "Apotheosis of the Emperor Trajan", by Charles III's German court painter Anton Raphael Mengs (1728–78). The Antecámera de Gasparini also has a ceiling fresco by Mengs, "Apotheosis of Hercules". Goya's portraits of Charles IV and his wife, Maria Luisa of Parma, were painted at the end of the 18th century. There is a fine Empire clock which belonged to Charles IV.

The Salón de Gasparini, Charles III's antechamber, is a marvel of Rococo chinoiserie with its intricately patterned marble floor and beautiful silk wall hangings and covers on the furniture. Adjoining is Charles III's bedroom, in which he died in 1788. Its present décor dates from 1828, in the reign of Ferdinand VII. The ceiling fresco is by Vicente López, the portrait of Charles III by Mariano Salvador Maella (1784).

The walls and ceiling of the **Sala de la Porcelana** (Porcelain Room) are covered with Buen Retiro tiles. Beyond this are the **Sala Amarilla** (Yellow Room), its walls hung with yellow silk, and the **State Dining Room**, which has frescoes by Mengs and his pupils Francisco Bayeu and González Velázquez. On the walls are 16th century Brussels tapestries.

Staircase in the Royal Palace

Chinese porcelain and Sèvres vases, chandeliers and candelabras complete the festive décor.

The **Chapel** was built by the Italian architect Giovanni Battista Sacchetti and Ventura Rodríguez between 1749 and 1757. The painting in the dome is by Giaquinto, the sculpture by Ginés de Castro and Olivieri.

In the east wing are the **private apartments** of the Bourbon monarchs. Luxury furniture and furnishings alternate with reminders of the royal family's domestic life – photographs, a telephone, Alfonso XII's bed and Queen Maria Cristina's piano, decorated with porcelain plaques.

In the south wing of the palace are four large **state apartments**, still used today for great state occasions.
The ceiling fresco, "Apotheosis of the Emperor Hadrian" (1797), in Room 40, is by Maella. In Room 41, which has a fresco of the "Golden Fleece" by Giovanni Domenico Tiepolo, is a portrait of Charles III by Mengs. The frescoes in the two following rooms are by Giovanni Battista Tiepolo, father of Giovanni Battista. In the small Audience Chamber, which has frescoes glorifying the Spanish monarchy, are tapestries produced by the Real Fábrica de Tapices (see entry). The Throne Room (Sala de Trono) , a long, luxuriously appointed hall, is dominated by a ceiling fresco by Tiepolo, "Apotheosis of the Spanish Monarchy" (1764).

The **Nuevos Museos** (New Museums) were opened in 1962 in the former private apartments of Isabel of Bourbon in the north-west wing. Here, in Rooms 44–55, are brought together many pictures which formerly hung elsewhere in the palace. They include works by Hieronymus Bosch, Rogier van der Weyden, Caravaggio, Velázquez, El Greco and Goya – a reminder of the extraordinary richness of the royal art gallery, now mostly housed in the Prado (see Museo del Prado)

The **Tapestry Museum** occupies the former private apartments of Charles IV and his wife Maria Luisa in the east wing (Rooms 56–64). Among the older items are the series "Triumph of the Mother of God" (c. 1490), after cartoons by Quentin Metsys, and Brussels tapestries which belonged to Joan the Mad (1479–1555) and Margaret of Austria (1480–1530). In addition to the products of Flemish and French manufactories there are fine examples of the carpets and tapestries produced by the Real Fábrica del Buen Retiro.

On the ground floor is the **Royal Library**, which has 300,000 books, 4000 manuscripts, 2000 prints and drawings, 3500 maps and 3000 music scores, as well as a coin collection and a collection of Stradivarius violins.

The **Royal Pharmacy** (Real Oficina de Farmacía; entrance in Calle de Bailén) was originally established by Philip II in the Alcázar. The present pharmacy, with its old equipment, dates from the 17th–19th centuries.

The **Royal Armoury** (Real Armería; entrance from Plaza de la Armería) has occupied its present quarters since 1893. It displays on two floors more than 3000 pieces of arms and armour from the 16th century onwards.

In the **Campo del Moro** park is the Carriage Museum (see Museo de Carruajes). The Moors are believed to have set up their camp on this site in 1109: hence the name of the park.

Palacio de Santa Cruz   F 10

Address
Plaza de Provincia

Metro
Puerta del Sol

Buses
31, 50

The Palacio de Santa Cruz, now occupied by the Foreign Ministry (Ministerio de Asuntos Exteriores), was built in the 17th century as a prison. Along with the Plaza Mayor (see entry) and the Casa de la Villa it is part of the old administrative quarter of the city which grew up round the Alcázar of the Habsburgs. The design of this substantial and well-balanced two-storey building with side towers and two inner courtyards is attributed to Giovanni Battista Crescenci, an Italian architect who had also worked for Philip II on the Escorial, or Juan Gómez de Mora, architect of the Plaza Mayor. In 1786, during the reign of Charles III, the palace was converted into lawcourts by Juan de Villanueva. From 1834 to 1877 it housed the Madrid Lawcourts. Finally in 1931 it became the headquarters of the Foreign Ministry.

★El Pardo

Excursion
15 km (9½ mi.)
NW

Bus
601 from Moncloa

Open Mon.–Sat.
10.30 am–5pm,
Sun.
10am–1.30pm

The palace of El Pardo lies in a former royal hunting reserve, an area surrounded by a wall which is noted for its holm oaks and its abundance of game. To reach it, leave Madrid on N VI (the road to La Coruña) and at the Puerta de Hierro turn right into the orbital motorway M 30 North (signposted to Burgos/El Pardo); then in 3 km (2 mi.) take a road signposted to Burgos/Aeropuerto (Airport); and finally turn into M 601 to El Pardo.
    Charles V and after him Philip II built the palace on the site of a hunting lodge used by Henry IV. Work began in 1544 to the design of Luis de Vega, and after his death the palace was completed by

Gaspar de Vega. Around 1630 Philip IV had a hunting lodge, the Torre de la Parada (now in ruins), built by Juan Gómez de Mora 3.5 km (2 mi.) west of the palace. In 1747 Philip V added a church to the palace (architect François Carlier); the Puerta de Hierro (see entry) was built in the reign of Ferdinand VI; and from 1772 the palace was considerably enlarged for Charles III by his court architect Francisco Sabatini. The palace was badly damaged during the Civil War, but after the war it was renovated and became the residence of Franco until his death in 1975. The palace, a four-square building with corner towers, is now open to the public as a Museo Nacional.

The principal floor has displays of objects and works of art of historical interest, together with 200 valuable tapestries after cartoons by Goya, Bayeu and González Ruiz.

The **Casita del Príncipe** is a little summer palace built by Juan de Villanueva for Charles III's wife Maria Luisa. It is sumptuously appointed in the taste of the period, with delicate silk embroidery and pictures by Luca Giordano.

To the west of the palace are a Capucin convent and church, the most-visited place of pilgrimage in the Madrid area. The object of the pilgrimage is a polychrome recumbent figure of the dead Christ which lies in front of the high altar of the church in a glass shrine presented by Franco. The wood figure, by the Castilian sculptor Gregorio Fernández (c. 1615), is one of the finest examples of Spanish religious sculpture of the 16th–18th centuries.

Santo Cristo del Pardo

The little town just before the palace, a popular excursion from Madrid, has changed little since the 1970s. There are a number of ageing restaurants, which tend to specialise in wild boar *(jabali)* in various forms.

Parque del Oeste   B/C 5

The Parque del Oeste, one of Madrid's most beautiful parks, lies between the Montaña del Príncipe Pío (see entry) and the Moncloa district to the north-west, and as a result commuter traffic streams through the park from north-western Madrid, coming off the Carretera de Castilla. The situation was made worse in 1998, when, thanks to a transport policy favouring motor traffic, the Puente de los Franceses was extended to carry a motorway into the park. Laid out in the style of an English park around the end of the 19th century by the Madrid landscape gardener Cecilio Rodríguez, the Parque del Oeste has an area of 85 ha (210 acres)). Lying as it does near the University City (see Ciudad Universitaria), the Argüelles student quarter and the numerous student residences on the Avenida de Séneca, it is much frequented by students. During the Civil War the park was in the firing line. Between 1936 and 1939 it was the scene of bitter fighting, which left it furrowed with trenches and riddled with bomb craters and shell-holes. By 1945, however, Cecilio Rodríguez had restored it to its former appearance, with new grass, trees and monuments. One of its attractions is the rose-garden, established in 1958, which is a brilliant show of colour in spring.

Location
Paseo del Pintor Rosales

Metro
Moncloa,
Argüelles,
Príncipe Pío

Buses
21, 74

The **Paseo del Pintor Rosales**, which skirts the park from the Temple of Debod on the Montaña del Príncipe Pío (see entry) to Moncloa, is a popular promenade. Particularly in summer, its café terraces, with their views of open country and the distant Sierra de Guadarrama (see entry), attract not only the people of the surrounding district but many from farther afield. From there the Teleférico (cableway) can be taken to the Casa de Campo (see entry).

★Parque del Retiro

Location
Plaza de
Independencia/Alf
onso XII

Metro
Retiro

Buses
1, 2, 9, 15, 19, 20,
51, 52, 74

*The Fallen
Angel (figure
on a fountain)*

Amid the busy activity of the city, hemmed in by the heavy traffic of Calle de Alfonso XII, Calle de Alcalá and Calle de Menéndez Pelayo, the Retiro Park, with an area of 120 ha (296 acres), offers an oasis of calm.

The main entrance in Plaza de Independencia leads to the lake in the centre of the park. From here paths lead to the beautiful rose-garden (Rosaleda), the geometrically laid out French-style Jardín de Don Cecilio, the fountains of the Crystal Palace and to a variety of cafés where the Madrileños like to take their aperitif, in the shade or in the sun according to the time of year.

History In the time of Philip II the royal residence, the Real Sitio del Buen Retiro, adjoined the monastery of San Jerónimo founded by Henry IV. Both then lay outside the town, which was concentrated round the Alcázar. Of the palace there remain only the building now occupied by the Army Museum (see Museo del Ejército), the Casón del Buen Retiro (see entry), now an annexe of the Prado, and the Retiro Park.

In 1632 the Duke of Olivares, Philip IV's powerful minister, presented his master with the keys to the former monastery gardens, which had been laid out as a park by the Italian landscape architect Cosimo Lotti. It then became renowned as the scene of brilliant court festivities, with bullfights, naval battles on the lake, firework displays, court balls and theatrical performances.

After the rebuilding of the Palacio Real (see entry) the palace and the park fell into the background. The Ermita de San Antonio was taken over by a porcelain manufactory, an observatory was built in the park and the Museo del Prado (see entry) was built. In the 18th century some parts of the park, which had hitherto been a private royal domain, were opened to the public. Finally in 1869 the Retiro became the property of the city.

The park contains numerous **monuments**, including the monument in honour of Alfonso XII (1922) on the shores of the lake, with an equestrian statue of the king towering over a semicircular colonnade; a naturalistic group commemorating the Álvarez Quintero brothers (1934); an Art Nouveau statue of the composer Ruperto Chapí (1921); and an equestrian statue of General Martínez Campos (1907).

There are also numbers of **fountains** in the park: "Los Galápagos" ("The Turtles"; 1830), at the north-west corner of the lake; "El Angel Caído" ("The Fallen Angel"; 1878; illustration, p. 116); "La Alcachofa" ("The Artichoke"; 1776), created by Ventura Rodríguez for the Salón del Prado; and the "Fons Vitae et Mortis" ("Fountain of Life and Death") at the corner of Avenida de Fernán Núñez and Paseo de Venezuela, honouring the scientist (Nobel Prize winner in 1906) Ramón y Cajal (by Victorio Macho, 1926).

There are regular art exhibitions in the Retiro, which had three handsome **exhibition halls**: the Palacio de Velázquez, built by Ricardo Velázquez Bosco in neo-Renaissance style in 1887 for a mining exhibition, which has recently been thoroughly restored; the Palacio de Cristal, a glass and iron structure also built by Bosco in 1887 for an exhibition of exotic plants from the Philippines; and the Centro Cultural Casa de Vacas.

The steps in front of the grandiose monument to Alfonso XII are a popular meeting place; the lake appeals to boating enthusiasts

On the highest point in the park is the **Observatory**, built by Juan de Villanueva in 1790.

Parque Zoológico

West of A 9

The Zoo in the Casa de Campo was established in the 1970s, the nucleus of its stock coming from the old Casa de Fieras in the Retiro Park. It has an area of 20 ha (50 acres), with the most modern facilities for displaying and caring for its animals, both exotic and native. Like zoos the world over, it appeals particularly to children.

The Zoo is open daily 10am–9.30pm.

Location
Casa de Campo

Metro
Batán

Bus
33

Paseo de la Castellana

J 1–7

The multi-lane Paseo de la Castellana, 6 km (4 mi.) long and up to 120 m (395 ft) wide, is the northward continuation of the Paseo del Prado (see entry) and Paseo de Recoletos. It is a centre of the business and social life of the younger generation of Madrileños, ever-ready for anything new.

Its first section, between the Plaza de Colón (see entry) and the site of the old Hipódromo (now occupied by the College of Technology and the Museum of Natural Science), following the line of an old drove road, was developed in the 19th century as an aristocratic residential area – though most of the old mansions have given place to modern buildings. To the east lies the Barrio de Salamanca, an upper middle class residential district. There were plans to extend the Paseo farther north in 1929, but work did not start until 1945. The office blocks which now dominate the scene were built from the 1960s onwards.

On the north-west side of the Plaza de Colón are the **Torres de Jerez** or de Colón, twin 20-storey towers set back from one another (by

Metro
Colón, Rubén Darío, Gregorio Marañón, Nuevos Ministerios, Santiago Bernabéu, Plaza de Castilla

Buses
5, 7, 14, 27, 45, 66, 67, 125, 129, 134, 135, 147, 150

Antonio Lamela, 1976). In the early 1990s they were given an outsize green roof which increased their height to 107 m (351 ft) and earned them the name of the most tasteless buildings in Madrid.

To the north follow the IBM Building (Paseo 4; by Miguel Fisac, 1968); the Bankinter Building (Paseo 29; by José Rafael Moneo and Ramón Bescós, 1976); La Unión y Fénix Español (Paseo 37; by Luis Gutiérrez Soto, 1965), a striking double-slab building topped by a figure of a phoenix; then, after the flyover, on both sides of the Paseo, the Museo de Escultura al Aire Libre (see entry), an open-air museum of abstract sculpture; the Bankunion Building, with a wine-red façade (Paseo 47; by José Antonio Corrales Gutiérrez and Ramón Vázquez Molezún, 1975); on the Glorieta de Emilio Castelar, the Adriática de Seguros (Paseo 47; by Javier Carvajal, 1979); and on Plaza del Doctor Marañón, the Caixa Building (by J.M. Bosch Aymerich, 1978).

The **Nuevos Ministerios** (New Ministries), at the corner of Plaza San Juan de la Cruz, were built in two phases. The first section (1932–36) was in a rational style showing neo-classical influence which met the Second Republic's need for imposing government buildings. The second phase (1940–42) is in the monumental style favoured by the Franco regime.

The Paseo now comes to the **Azca quarter** (see entry), with the Picasso and Europa Towers, the BBV Building, the Palacio de Congresos (Conference Centre) and the Estadio Santiago Bernabéu.

Torres Kio

To the north of the Plaza de Castilla, an important traffic intersection, is one of Madrid's most spectacular examples of contemporary architecture, the Torres Kio: twin 115 m (377 ft) high, 27-storey towers with façades of black glass relieved by strips of light-coloured steel leaning towards each other at an angle of 14.3°. Symbolically labelled the Puerta de Europa, the Gateway to Europe, they are popularly known as the Torres Kio. (The name comes from the Kuwait Investment Office, KIO, for whose headquarters the towers were originally designed). The architects were Philip Johnson, the New York veteran of the Modern movement in architecture, and his partner John Burgee; Leslie Robertson was responsible for design and structural engineering

The Torres Kio, Madrid's "Gateway to Europe"

★Paseo del Prado

H/J 9–11

The Paseo del Prado, which links the Plaza de la Cibeles (see entry) with the Plaza del Emperador Carlos V to the south, is now a section of the busy traffic artery which runs through Madrid from north to south. It is embellished by avenues of trees and areas of grass and lined by handsome buildings and parks, among them the Botanic Gardens (see Jardín Botánico), the Prado Museum (see Museo del Prado) and the Museo Thyssen-Bornemisza (see entry) in the Palacio de Villahermosa. Originally the Paseo, which follows the course of a long dried-up stream, the Arroyo Abroñigal, was laid out for Charles III as the "Salón del Prado", a grand avenue for the Madrid of the Enlightenment. Under the direction of Jose de Hermosilla, Juan de Villanueva and Ventura Rodríguez the work was completed between 1775 and 1782. On the model of the Piazza Navona in Rome the Paseo was punctuated by three fountains – the Cibeles, Apollo and Neptune Fountains.

The Paseo begins in the Plaza de la Cibeles (see entry). To the south, at the corner of Callé de Montalbán, are the Admiralty, with the Museo Naval (Naval Museum: see Practical Information, Museums); the extension of the Admiralty, at the corner of Calle Juan de Mena, was built in 1976 by Alberto López de Asiaín. To the east, at the end of Calle Montalbán, is the Museo Nacional de Artes Decorativas (Museum of Decorative Art: see Practical Information, Museums).

Metro
Banco de España, Atocha

Buses
9, 10, 14, 27, 37, 45, 53, 150

In the green central section of the Paseo is the Apollo Fountain, with representations of the four seasons (by Alfonso Giraldo Vergaz and Manuel Álvarez, 1777). In the adjoining Plaza de la Lealtad is the Obelisk of May 2nd (by Isidro González Velázquez, 1839), which commemorates those who died in the rising of May 2nd 1808. On the northeast side of the square is the Bolsa (Stock Exchange), built in 1884 on the model of the Vienna Stock Exchange. On the south-east side of the square is the entrance to the Ritz Hotel, opened in 1910 (architect Charles Mewès).

Plaza de la Lealtad

Plaza Cánovas del Castillo, in the centre of which is the Neptune Fountain, is dominated by three buildings: on the west side the elegant Palace Hotel, opened in 1912 directly opposite the Ritz, the south corner of which also looks on to the square. Here too is the neo-classical palace of he Duke of Villahermosa (1806; see Museo Thyssen-Bornemisza), which occupies the north-east corner of the square. Farther up the Carrera de San Jerónimo is the Congreso de los Diputados (see entry), the Spanish Parliament. The Neptune Fountain (by Juan Pascual de Mena, 1780), like the nearby Fountain of Cybele, is a favourite meeting-place for Madrileños, either for a celebration or a demonstration. On one such occasion in May 1998, after Real Madrid won the Europa Cup, Neptune lost his left arm, the police then being engaged in protecting the fertility goddess Cybele, a little farther north, from the enthusiasm of half a million fans. On the southward continuation of the Paseo del Prado are the neo-classical façade of the Prado Museum (see Museo del Prado) and the railings of the Botanic Gardens (see Jardín Botánico), both on the left-hand side of the street.

Plaza Cánovas del Castillo

At the south end of the Paseo del Prado is the Plaza del Emperador Carlos V (also called the Glorieta de Carlos V). The most notable feature of this square is the Atocha Station (see entry). Immediately south of the Botanic Gardens, closing the east side of the square, is the Ministry of Agriculture, Fisheries and Food (by Ricardo Velázquez Bosco, 1897). South-west of the square, opposite the Atocha Station, is the Centro de Arte Reina Sofía (see entry), which along with the Prado and the Museo Thyssen-Bornemisza forms Madrid's "Art Triangle".

Plaza del Emperador Carlos V

★Plaza de la Cibeles   H/J 9

Metro
Banco de España

Buses
1, 2, 15, 19, 20, 51,
52, 74, 146

In the centre of the Plaza de la Cibeles, one of Madrid's most beautiful squares, is the Fountain of Cybele (Fuente de Cibeles; by Ventura Rodríguez, Francisco Gutiérrez and Robert Michel, 1782), which has become an emblem of the city. It shows Cybele, goddess of fertility and love, in a granite wagon drawn by two lions. It originally stood at the end of the Paseo de Recoletos, looking down the Paseo del Prado (see entry); then at the beginning of the 20th century it was turned through 90 degrees to face the Puerta del Sol (see entry). The Plaza de la Cibeles is now one of the most heavily trafficked squares in Madrid, with some 220,000 vehicles circling noisily round the fountain and discharging their exhaust gases. In this square the Paseo del Prado, the Paseo de Recoletos and Calle de Alcalá meet.

**Palacio de
Comunicaciones**

Four important buildings stand round the Plaza de la Cibeles. The south-east corner of the square is dominated by the monumental Palacio de Comunicaciones (Head Post Office), known to the people of Madrid as Nuestra Señora de Correos, "Our Lady of the Post", which was built by Antonio Palacios and Julián Otamendi in Historicist style in 1905–17.

Banco de España

Opposite the Post Office is the Banco de España, Spain's central bank and the successor to the Bank of San Carlos (Calle de Alcalá) founded in the reign of Charles III. It was built in 1884 by Eduard Adaro and Severiano Sainz de la Lastra in the French style favoured in the late 19th century, and was later several times enlarged. It contains paintings by such famous artists as Goya, Sorolla, Mengs and Maella.

Palacio de Linares

On the north-east side of the square is the Palacio de Linares, a 19th-century palace designed by Carlos Colubi. In the early 1980s it was threatened with demolition, but has since been renovated and now houses the

The pagan fertility goddess Cybele has become a patroness of Madrid along with the Christian Virgin of Almudena and St Isidore

This massive piece of sculpture on the Plaza de Colón commemorates the Spanish voyages of discovery

Casa de América (entrance in Calle Marqués del Duero: see Practical Information, Cultural Centres), which organises exhibitions and other events concerned with South American cultures. There is an excellent restaurant, the Paradís (see Practical Information, Restaurants).

Opposite the Palacio de Linares is the former Palacio de Buenavista, now occupied by the Ministry of Defence (Ministerio de Defensa). Standing on higher ground, the palace, built in 1777–82 (architect Juan Pedro Arnl), was designed to command the road to Alcalá. It was built for the Duchess of Alba, thought by some, erroneously, to have been Goya's lover and the model for the "Naked Maja" which is now in the Prado. When the Duchess died in 1802 the palace was bought by the city and presented to Manuel Godoy, Charles IV's powerful minister. Later it housed the collection of artillery which is now in the Army Museum (see Museo del Ejército), before being turned over to the Ministry of Defence. A well-kept park, tall railings and a military guard separate the palace from the heavy traffic of the outside world.

Palacio de Buenavista

Plaza de Colón   J 7

The Plaza de Colón, at the south end of the Paseo de la Castellana (see entry), was laid out in the 1970s, replacing the old square, originally planted with trees and surrounded by 19th century mansions, at the junction of Calle Goya and Calle Génova. The older buildings have long since been replaced by modern high-rise blocks, and the heavy traffic has transformed the square into a wide and busy thoroughfare. In 1970 the former Real Fábrica de Moneda (Royal Mint) was demolished and the square extended to the south-east round the Jardines del Descubrimiento de América (Gardens of the Discovery of America). The 3m/10ft high figure of Columbus on the 15 m (50 ft) high Columbus

Metro
Colón

Buses
5, 14, 27, 45, 150

Column (by Jerónimo Suñol, 1885) which stood in the centre of the square was moved to the south, and in 1976 four huge sculptured blocks by Joaquín Vaquero Turcios commemorating the Spanish voyages of discovery in the 15th and 16th centuries were set up in the gardens.
Underneath the gardens, sheltered from the heavy traffic in the square by a curtain of water, is the Centro Cultural de la Villa (City Cultural Centre), with a theatre and exhibition and lecture rooms. Also under the square are a car park and the terminus of the airport buses.

Just off the square, at Paseo de Recoletos 41, is the **Museo de Cera** (Waxworks Museum: see Practical Information, Museums). To the north-west are the two **Torres de Jerez** or de Colón (by Antonio Lamela, 1967). To the north-east, in Calle de Goya, is the **Edificio Carlos III**, a large office block (by Luis Gutiérrez Soto, 1945). At Paseo de Recoletos 20, at the corner of the square, is the former Biblioteca Nacional (begun 1866), now occupied by the **Museo Arqueológico Nacional** (National Archaeological Museum: see entry).

Plaza del Dos de Mayo   G 7

Metro
Bilbao, Tribunal

Buses
12, 147

The Plaza del Dos de Mayo lies in the Barrio de Maravillas *(maravillas =* miracles), now called Malasaña, between Calles Hortaleza, San Bernardo, Carranza and Sagasta. In this old craftsmen's quarter with its numerous bars and cafés are the Museo Municipal and the Museo Romántico (see entries). In the old literary cafés and more modern establishments all styles and tastes are represented. Among the best known are Café de Ruiz, in the street of that name; La Manuela, at Calle de San Vicente Ferrer 29; La Plaza, in the square; the Café Comercial, on the Glorieta de Bilbao; El Parnasillo, in Calle de San Andrés; the Art Deco café El Sol de Mayo; and the Vía Láctea, at Calle Velarde 18. In summer the terraces round the square are thronged until late at night with night owls, strollers and local people taking the air. At weekends the area is a favourite rendezvous for young people.

History In the centre of the square is the Puerta de Monteleón, a relic of the palace of the Dukes of Monteleón, built in 1690 and burned down in 1723. An artillery park was established here by Manuel Godoy, Charles IV's minister, and this area was the scene of heavy fighting on May 2nd 1808, when the people of Madrid rose against the French occupying forces. Led by two artillery officers, Daoiz and Velarde, now commemorated by a monument (by Antonio Solá) in the square, they put up a fierce resistance to Marshal Murat's troops. Among them was Manuela Malasaña, a 15-year-old local girl, who was killed in the fighting. The barracks were finally taken by the French and the defenders were shot at the foot of the Montaña del Príncipe Pío (see entry). The old doorway of the Monteleón palace and the monument in front of it serve as reminders of these dramatic events.

★Plaza de España   E 8

Metro
Plaza de España

Buses
1, 2, 4, 46, 74, 75, 148, C

The Plaza de España lies at the interface between old and modern Madrid. Here the town of the Habsburg and Bourbon monarchs – the Plaza de Oriente, the Palacio Real and the Plaza Mayor (see entries) – meets present-day Madrid, with the Gran Vía of the 1930s and the high-rise blocks of the 1950s. The Plaza de España, one of the city's most important traffic intersections and a favourite promenade of the Madrileños, lies on a platform sloping down to the Manzanares between the higher ground on which the Royal Palace is built and the Montaña del Príncipe Pío.

Cervantes, in stone, looks down on Don Quixote and Sancho Panza; in the background the Edificio españa

In the 18th and 19th centuries the square, lying near barracks and the Royal Palace, was mainly used for military purposes. Later, with the unstoppable expansion of the city to the north-west, it began to be built up. Around the turn of the 19th century the construction of the offices of the Royale Compagnie Asturienne des Mines (corner of Calle Bailén; by Manuel Martínez Angel, 1899) and the modernist building at the corner of Calle Ferraz gave it an industrial and progressive air.

In more recent times a series of new buildings have given the square its present character: the former headquarters of the Directorate of Health Services (1929) at the corner of Calle Martín de los Heros, the apartment block (1929) at the end of the Gran Vía and the high-rise buildings of the 1950s – the Edificio españa (by Joaquín and Julián Otamendi, 1948; 107 m (350 ft) high, 26 floors, rooftop café, swimming pool at a height of 96 m (315 ft), at present closed) and the Torre de Madrid (by J. and J. Otamendi, 1957; 124 m (407 ft) high). In the centre of the square

123

is a monument to Cervantes (by Rafael Martínez Zapatero, 1928; sculpture by Lorenzo Collaut Valera). Cervantes, seated in front of a massive obelisk, looks down on his two famous characters, Don Quixote and Sancho Panza. The square is a favourite haunt of children and students, tourists and office workers from the nearby Gran Vía. In the surrounding area are numerous cinemas.

★★Plaza Mayor   F 9/10

Metro
Puerta del Sol,
Ópera

Buses
3, 31, 50

The Plaza Mayor, which measures 120 by 90 m (395 by 295 ft), is one of the finest squares in Spain. It already played a central role in the life of Madrid in the time of Philip II, who commissioned his favourite architect Juan de Herrera, builder of the Escorial (see entry), in 1581 to rebuild it. Work began in 1590, and was completed in 1617–19, during the reign of Philip III, under the direction of Juan Gómez de Mora.

The Plaza Mayor was the commercial centre of Madrid and the hub of the town's life, and also the scene of formal acts of state – royal proclamations, the announcement of canonisations and executions. It was also used for entertainments and festivities – bullfights, theatrical performances and knightly tournaments. After being badly damaged by fire it was rebuilt by Juan de Villanueva in the 1790s, when the houses round the square were brought up to the same height as the Casa de la Panadería and roofed with slates. The eight streets entering the square were built over, giving the Plaza Mayor its present enclosed form.

Casa de la
Panadería

On the north side of the square, flanked by two turrets, is the Casa de la Panadería (1590). This housed the officials responsible for the distribution of the town's reserves of bread and grain, and it is believed that bread was also sold here. Above the balcony, from which the royal family watched spectacles in the square, is the royal coat of arms. The

Equestrian statue of Philip III in the Plaza Mayor; in the background the Casa de la Panadería

frescos on the façade have recently been restored. Opposite the Casa de la Panadería is the Casa de la Carnecería, also flanked by two turrets, which was responsible for the administration of the town's stock of meat. In the centre of the square is an equestrian statue of Philip III, designed by Giambologna and cast in Florence in 1613 by Pietro Tacca, which originally stood in the Case de Campo (see entry) and was moved to its present position in 1847.

The Plaza Mayor is the scene of an annual Christmas market and a weekly stamp exchange on Sunday mornings. The cafés round the square and the restaurants in the arcades are popular with tourists, visitors from the Spanish provinces and the Madrileños themselves. The square, which is closed to traffic, has two exits on each side which link it with main streets like Calle de Toledo, Calle Mayor and Calle Postas. On the side with the Casa de la Carnecería is the Arco de Cuchilleros (Cutlers' Arch), from which steps lead steeply down through the massive foundations of the square to the lower-lying Cava de San Miguel.

★Plaza de Oriente   E 9

The idea for the Plaza de Oriente came from Napoleon's brother Joseph Bonaparte, king of Spain from 1808 to 1813, who wanted the area in front of the Royal Palace to be opened up, both for aesthetic reasons and to provide better protection against possible disturbances or riots. Building work on the square, which was designed to link the eastern districts of Madrid with the palace and open up a view between the Puerta del Sol (see entry) and the palace, was interrupted after the end of the war of liberation and Ferdinand VII's return to the throne, and it was only in the reign of Ferdinand's daughter, Isabella II, that the square was completed in its present form: a circular area laid out in gardens and surrounded by buildings, the most prominent of which is the Teatro Real (see entry), also known as the Teatro de la Opera. In the centre of the square is an equestrian statue of Philip IV by the Italian sculptor Pietro Tacca (1636–40), on the basis of drawings by Velázquez and a model by the Spanish sculptor Martínez Montáñes. The statues of Visigothic kings round the square are believed to have originally been on the balustrade of the Royal Palace. There are several good cafés and restaurants round the square which are popular meeting-places in the evening and after the opera. (Illustration, p. 41)

Metro
Ópera

Buses
3, 25, 33, 39, 148

From the Plaza de Oriente Calle Lepanto runs south to the little Plaza de Ramales. A cross in the square marks the site of the church of San Juan, in which Velázquez was buried in 1660. There are plans for remodelling the square and looking for the crypt containing his tomb.

On the opposite side of the square is the Convento de la Encarnación (see entry).

Plaza de Santa Ana

See Teatro Español

★Plaza de la Villa   E/F 10

The Plaza de la Villa, which opens off the Calle Mayor, is one of the handsomest squares in the old town, with the Town Hall, the Casa de Cisneros and the Torre de los Lujanes. In the centre of the square is a monument to Admiral Álvaro de Bazán (1526–88), created by Mariano Benlliure in 1891 to commemorate the Siglo de Oro, Spain's Golden Age.

Metro
Puerta del Sol
(Calle Mayor exit)

Bus
3

Madrid's Town Hall (Casa de la Villa)

Casa de la Villa
The Town Hall (Ayuntamiento or Casa de la Villa), on the west side of the square, was begun in 1644 to the design of Juan Gómez de Mora, who also worked on the Escorial (see entry). After his death the building was completed by José de Villareal. The doorways and the upper floors of the towers were the work of José del Olma and Teodoro Ardemans, the architect of the pleasure palace of La Granja (see entry). In 1789 Juan de Villanueva added a balcony looking on to the Calle Mayor, from which the queen could watch the Corpus Christi procession, and the colonnades on the principal floor. Notable features of the interior are a fine collection of tapestries and a number of handsome rooms, including the Salón de Goya, the Council Chamber and the Patio de Cristales. Two particular treasures are a 16th century monstrance and Goya's "Allegory of Madrid". There are conducted tours Mon. 5pm.

Casa de los Lujanes
Opposite the Town Hall are the Casa and Torre de los Lujanes, which are among the few surviving buildings of 15th–16th century Madrid. They now house the libraries of the Real Sociedad Económica de Amigos del País and the Real Academia de Ciencias Morales y Políticas. The entrance doorway with the arms of the owners is one of the rare pieces of Gothic architecture surviving in Madrid.

Torre de los Lujanes
The Torre de los Lujanes became the prison of François I of France after his defeat in the battle of Pavia in 1525. Charles V's royal prisoner enjoyed a considerable measure of freedom, walking freely about the streets of Madrid and taking part in festivities organised in his honour by the Castilian nobility.

Casa de Cisneros
On the south side of the square is the Casa de Cisneros, now linked with the Town Hall by a covered bridge. It was built in 1537 by Benito Jiménez de Cisneros, a nephew of the great Cardinal Cisneros, founder of the University of Alcalá de Henares (see entry). It has preserved, in Calle del

Sacramento, a Late Gothic, Plateresque façade. The palace was purchased by the city in 1909 and is now the residence of the Mayor of Madrid. It has a fine collection of tapestries.

Plaza de la Villa de París   H/J 7

On the south side of the Plaza de la Villa de París is the former convent of Las Salesas Reales (see entry), which since the end of the 19th century has been occupied by the Palacio de Justicia (Law Courts). This imposing building, with a neo-Baroque façade (by Joaquín Rojí, 1915–26) looking on to the gardens in the square, lies in the centre of a very respectable district of Madrid which attracted the city's middle classes in the 19th century, during the reign of Isabella II. Quiet streets of substantial houses – Calles Piamonte, Conde de Xiquena, Almirante, Santa Teresa, Marqués de la Ensenada – form a peaceful oasis amid the heavy traffic of the nearby Calle de Génova, Paseo de Recoletos and Calle de Hortaleza. Bookshops and shops selling fruit, groceries and fish alternate with cafés, restaurants, modest tabernas and bars where you may meet officials from the Palacio de Justicia, students of the Instiitut Français or actors from the Teatro Nacional María Guerrero (see entry).

Metro
Colón

Buses
21, 37

Prado Museum

See Museo del Prado

★Puente de Segovia   C 10

The Puente de Segovia is Madrid's oldest bridge over the Manzanares. In 1582 Philip II commissioned Juan de Herrera, architect of the Escorial (see entry), to build the bridge to provide a better connection between the capital and the Escorial. The bridge, built of massive granite blocks, was lengthened in 1935 towards the approach roads and widened, still preserving the original arches. It now links the city centre with the outlying districts to the south-west.

Buses
25, 31, 33, 36, 39,
65

★Puente de Toledo   E 13

The Puente de Toledo is one of the finest monuments from the reign of the first Bourbon king, Philip V. It was built by Pedro de Ribera between 1718 and 1732 to replace the dilapidated old Puente Toledano.

The bridge, which spans the Río Manzanares and the four-lane orbital motorway M 30 in nine arches, is supported by solid buttresses which end in rounded balconies. Half way along the parapet, on both sides, are miniature temples containing figures of the city's patron saints Isidro and his wife María de la Cabeza (by Juan Antonio Ron,1735). A renovation of the bridge in 1997 has done little to counter its continuing destruction by exhaust gases.

From the bridge there are views of the Estadio Vicente Calderón (see entry), one of Madrid's two football stadiums, and, towards the city centre, the Puerta de Toledo (see entry).

Metro
Pirámides

Buses
23, 34, 117
Illustration, p. 130

★Puerta de Alcalá   J 8/9

The Puerta de Alcalá is one of Madrid's most familiar landmarks and emblems. This neo-classical gate of Colmenar granite was built by

Location
Plaza de la
Independencia

The Puente de Toledo; in the background the Puerta de Toledo

Metro
Retiro

Buses
1, 2, 9, 15, 19, 20,
51, 52, 74, 146

Francesco Sabatini between 1764 and 1778, replacing an earlier Baroque arch built for the reception of Philip III's wife Margaret of Austria in 1599. Situated on the road to Alcalá de Henares, it was one of the main entrances to Madrid (the others being the Atocha, Toledo, Segovia and Bilbao gates). It was part of Charles III's large-scale plans for the development of eastern Madrid, which were carried out by Sabatini, Villanueva and Ventura Rodríguez. The royal residence of Buen Retiro lay in the centre of the plan, which also included the building-up of open country in the San Jerónimo and Atocha areas, the establishment of the Botanic Gardens (see Jardín Botánico) and the building of the Museum of Natural Science (see Museo del Prado).

With its five openings, the three central ones arched and the other two rectangular, its elegant granite masonry and its Baroque limestone ornament by Francisco Gutiérrez and Robert Michel, the imposing Puerta de Alcalá became a symbol of the Enlightenment and a monument to the "king-mayor" Charles III.

Puerta de Hierro   NW of A 1

Location
On N VI road to
La Coruña

Buses
83, 133

The Puerta de Hierro (Iron Gate), a remarkable example of 18th century Spanish court architecture, stands on N VI (which runs north-west from Madrid to La Coruña), at the turn-off of the road to El Pardo. During the reign of Ferdinand VI (1746–59) the royal hunting lodge of El Pardo (see entry) and its hunting reserve were surrounded by walls, and at the same time the Puente de San Fernando – now part of the flyover carrying the orbital motorway M 30 on to N VI – and the Puerta de Hierro were built. Some years ago it was stripped of its walls, and in 1997 it was moved, stone by stone, to the Paseo del Rey, since it constituted a possible hazard to traffic. There are now plans to move it again to a more suitable spot.

The Puerta de Alcalá, the principal entrance to Madrid from the east

The bridge was designed by Francisco Nangle and Francisco Moradillo, with sculpture by Giovanni Olivieri. The building materials, as in so many Madrid buildings, were granite and white Colmenar limestone. Building work was begun in 1751 but dragged on to 1753 and cost the then considerable sum of 100,000 *reales*.

★Puerta del Sol

G 9

The Puerta del Sol took its name from the town gate which once stood here, facing the rising sun. It is the starting-point from which distances are measured on the national highways (N-numbered roads) which radiate from Madrid (illustration, p. 17) and an important traffic hub. Although over the years many typical old cafés have given place to modern cafeterias or fast food outlets, there still remain some traditional establishments such as the Yenes cafeteria on the corner of the Calle Mayor, which offers a fine view of the busy activity in the square from the first floor, and the Jabugo Sol *jamonería* on the corner of Calle Alcalá, where you can enjoy a tasty piece of Iberian ham to accompany your *caña* of beer. With its old shops and buildings, its cake-shops, its specialist shops selling fans, hats and walking-sticks, its sellers of lottery tickets and newspapers, its swarms of passers-by, its bus stops and Metro entrances, the Puerta del Sol is one of the busiest and liveliest squares in Madrid.

The original Puerta del Sol, which according to a description of 1539 was a modest brick-built gate with six defensive towers, was one of the principal town gates. It was pulled down in 1570, and many other buildings disappeared in later centuries, including the monastery of San Felipe Real (1547), the Royal Hospital (1560) and the churches of Buen Suceso (1628) and Nuestra Señora de la Victoria (1597), while the once famous fountain of La Mariblanca was replaced by a column.

Metro
Puerta del Sol

Buses
3, 5, 15, 20, 50, 51, 53, 150

Puerta del Sol

The semicircular Puerta del Sol, on the site of Madrid's old east gate, lies almost exactly in the centre of Spain

The Puerta del Sol, considered with some reason to be the geographical heart of Spain, has repeatedly played a part in modern Spanish history. The rising against the occupying French forces began here on May 2nd 1808, when the people of Madrid fought an unequal battle against Napoleon's Mamelukes and Imperial Guard. The numerous cafés were hotbeds of political discussion and plans for revolt. In 1912 the Spanish prime minister, José Canalejas, was assassinated in the square by an anarchist; and in 1931 the Second Republic was proclaimed from the balcony of the Head Post Office, which had become the Ministry of the Interior.

★Casa de Correos

The oldest building in the square, dating from the reign of Charles III, is the Casa de Correos, the former Head Post Office which, after thorough renovation, has reverted to its original name. It was designed by Ventura Rodríguez and built by Jaime Marquet. Its construction involved the demolition of two whole blocks with over twenty houses. Built of granite, white limestone and red brick on a granite base, it has a rectangular plan with two inner courtyards. The main front, with its classical lines, shows the influence of French models. Above the main entrance is a balcony topped by a pediment bearing the royal arms, lions and trophies. Under the Franco regime it was the headquarters of the notorious security police, known by Spaniards, after their uniform, as the "greys". The cellars in which troublesome opponents of the regime were imprisoned and tortured were swept away in the renovation of the building during the 1990s.

The clock-tower was added in 1866, as was the iron framework on which a golden ball announces to the crowds of Madrileños who gather here on New Year's Eve the start of the new year. The twelve strokes of midnight on the clock are followed live on television or radio by almost the whole population of Spain, who eat a grape at each stroke to ensure good fortune and the fulfilment of all their wishes in the coming year.

On the north side of the Puerta del Sol is a famous statue of a bear nibbling at a *madroño* tree (arbutus or strawberry tree), the **emblem of Madrid**. The *madroño,* formerly common in the Madrid area, was believed to have medicinal qualities, particularly for relieving swellings on the body. There are now very few left within the city: there is one specimen near the Ritz Hotel, and there are said to be over a hundred in the Retiro Park.

Puerta de Toledo   E 11/12

The Puerta de Toledo, in a spacious square two-thirds of the way along Calle de Toledo, was the last triumphal arch to be built in Madrid. Begun during the short reign of Joseph Bonaparte and designed by Antonio López Aguado, it was intended to celebrate the glories of Napoleon; but when it was completed in 1817 it became instead a symbol of Frederick VII's return to the throne and the overthrow of French rule.

Metro
Puerta de Toledo

Buses
16, 23, 35, 60

El Rastro   F 11

The Madrid flea market El Rastro, in the city's Barrios Bajos ("low districts") which slope down to the river Manzanares, is held every Sunday morning. The triangle of narrow streets and lanes between Calle de Toledo, the Ronda de Toledo and Calle de Embajadores has its centre in the Plaza de Cascorro. Here, under the monument to Eloy Gonzalo, a hero of the Cuban War of 1898, the Rastro begins.

The name of the wide Ribera de Curtidores (Tanners) is a reminder of the slaughterhouses and tanneries which once occupied this quarter. These have now given place to junk dealers and antique shops, of which the Galería Piquer and the Nuevas Galerías, on either side of the Ribera de Curtidores at Calle del Carnero, in particular may appeal to antique-hunters. On Sunday mornings a colourful mass of people crowd round the stalls, which offer anything and everything, old or new, for sale – mattresses, suitcases, boots, uniforms, baskets, ironware, crockery, wooden articles and much else besides. This little world of its own has been immortalised in the work of the painter José Gutiérrez Solana (see Famous People) and the writer Gómez de la Serna (see Madrid in Quotations).

Location
Around Plaza de
Cascorro

Metro
La Latina, Puerta
de Toledo

Buses
17, 18, 23, 35, 41,
60

At Calle de Embajadores 15, amid houses of both modest and rather grander pretensions, stands the church of San Cayetano. It was built by Pedro de Ribera and José Churriguera, the two masters of Madrid Baroque; but, after a fire in 1936, only the façade survives.

Iglesia de San
Cayetano

Close by is the Real Fábrica de Tabacos (1809), one of the earliest evidences of the industrialisation of Madrid. Employing 600 workers, it was in its day a central element in the life of the Rastro quarter. The *cigarreras* played an important part in the workers' movement in Madrid.

Real Fábrica de
Tabacos

In the 18th and 19th centuries tenement blocks known as *corralas* were built to house the population of the town's working-class districts. These buildings, which might have anything between two and seven stories, were laid out round a central courtyard *(corral),* and the individual dwellings, which usually had an area of no more than 20 sq. m (215 sq. ft), were entered from long external galleries. With such cramped accommodation indoors, the life of the community usually took place on the galleries or in the courtyard. As a result the corralas became the setting of the *zarzuelas,* the popular operettas which are a speciality of Madrid. In the Rastro quarter and in the rest of Lavapiés, a district still in need of renovation and redevelopment, a number of corralas have been restored and some are open to the public, for example as antique- and junk-dealers' shops. There is a charming example in Calle Tribulete, with its galleries on the side facing Calle Mesón de Paredes. Other examples are the Corralas de Miguel Servet at Calle Espino 6, at Calle Mesón de Paredes 79 and in Plaza de Cascorro.

Real Academia de la Historia   G/H 10

Address
Calle León 21

Metro
Sevilla, Antón Martín

Buses
6, 26, 32, 57

The elegant premises of the Real Academia de la Historia (Royal Academy of History), in granite and red brick, were built by Juan de Villanueva in 1788. The library of the Academy, which was founded in 1738, has over 200,000 books and manuscripts.

In the same building is the Museo de Antigüedades (Museum of Antiquities), whose numerous treasures include five pictures by Goya. Open by appointment only.

Real Academia Española de la Lengua   J 10

Address
Calle Felipe IV 4

Metro
Banco de España, Retiro, Atocha

Buses
9, 10, 14, 27, 34, 37, 45

In the high-class district between the Prado Museum and the Retiro Park, which also includes such imposing buildings as the Army Museum (see Museo del Ejército), El Casón (see entry), the Stock Exchange and the elegant Ritz Hotel in Plaza de la Lealtad (see Paseo del Prado), are the headquarters of the Royal Spanish Academy of Language. The Academy was founded in 1713 by the first Bourbon king Philip V on the model of the Académie Française. It has 60 members, and maintains close links with Academies in South America. Its main responsibilities are the fostering of the Spanish language and the establishment of its grammar and orthography. It produced the first volume of its excellent "Diccionario de la Lengua Española" in 1726.

In 1894 the Academy moved to its present quarters near the Casón. It has a large library and a valuable collection of first editions and autograph manuscripts.

★Real Academia de Bellas Artes de San Fernando   G 9

Address
Calle de Alcalá 13

Metro
Sol, Sevilla

Buses
3, 5, 15, 20

Open Tue.–Fri. 10am–7pm, Sat.–Mon. and pub. hols. 10am–3pm

The Real Academia de Bellas Artes de San Fernando was, like the other Royal Academies, a Bourbon foundation. Charles III (1759—88) bought a Baroque palace built by José Churriguera in 1724 for a financier named Goyaneche and commissioned Diego de Villanueva to remodel it. Villanueva gave it a new neo-classical façade and removed the Baroque ornament. The Academy of San Fernando is the seat of the Madrid Academy of Art, though it has not had any teaching functions since the 1960s. One of its earlier directors was Goya (from 1795), and among its students have been Picasso and Dalí (who was expelled from the school) as well as many other famous artists. The Madrid universities have now taken over the functions of the Academy. The Academy building contains, in addition to offices, the National Chalcography Collection (engravings) and a fine art collection (works of the 16th–20th centuries). This consists of works by former members of the Academy, donations and works of art from dissolved Jesuit houses in Córdoba and Cuenca and from the collection of Manuel Godoy, Charles IV's minister, which was confiscated in 1808.

Among the most important works in the collection are drawings by Raphael, Titian and other masters, many of them once belonging to the Jesuits, who were expelled from Spain in 1767.

The **16th century paintings** include works by Giuseppe Arcimboldo ("Spring"), Juan de Juanes and Morales.

The **17th century Spanish school** is represented by Ribera ("The Magdalene"), Alonso Cano ("Christ on the Cross"), Pereda ("Life, a

Zarzuela –
Operetta, Folk Theatre or Ballet?

The *zarzuela* is a native Madrid genre. We are not talking here about the Spanish equivalent of bouillabaisse, the mixture of fish and shellfish served with a light oil sauce, but of a type of theatrical performance in which singing, either solo or in chorus, alternates with dialogue. The name comes from the small palace of La Zarzuela outside Madrid, originally a hunting lodge favoured by Philip IV. Entertainment for Philip and his guests was provided by actors from the capital, and in their performances the usual three-act plays, which were costly to produce, soon gave place to specially written two-act pieces with numerous musical interludes which became known as zarzuelas.

The zarzuelas were mostly on heroic themes, as in the Spanish courtly theatre, but they sometimes also had tragic plots. The first zarzuelas were written by Calderón, Philip's court poet, who in 1648 produced "El Jardín de Falerina". The zarzuela soon became highly popular, and the most celebrated authors wrote librettos for setting to music. Over 500 have survived, though in most cases the music is lacking, since it was not printed.

In the second half of the 18th century musical taste changed. Italian operas became popular, at first in translation and later in the original language, and the zarzuela was forgotten. There was a revival of interest in the genre in the late 1830s, when one-act zarzuelas began to be produced – known as the *género chico* as against the *zarzuela grande*. The new type soon became enormously popular, and by the late 19th century Madrid had no fewer than ten theatres exclusively devoted to the production of zarzuelas. The zarzuela now reached out beyond the frontiers of Spain, enjoying great popularity in Germany and Italy. The plays were no longer concerned with the "big" themes: instead they dealt with everyday stories of love, jealousy and women's virtue, with the old man in love, the passionate young lover, the coquettish Manolas and the gossiping neighbours.

Then at the beginning of the 20th century the *zarzuela grande* came back into favour. Nowadays, however, few new zarzuelas are being written, and accordingly there are critics who say that the zarzuela is dead. Nevertheless new productions of old pieces are still popular, and it is still worth while to go to a zarzuela show even if you do not understand Spanish, for these unpretentious pieces have preserved all their freshness and gaiety. Moreover the programme usually includes an English summary of the plot.

You can see performances of zarzuelas in the corrala in Calle de Tribulete, an open-air theatre in the style of the old corrala courtyards, and in the Teatro de la Zarzuela in Calle Jovellanos, built in 1856 with the support of a banker and a number of artists, with seating for an audience of 2500 (illustration, p. 238).

Dream"), Pereira ("St Bruno in Meditation"; marble statue), Zurbarán (five life-size figures of monks; "Vision of St Alonso"), Murillo ("An Angel Musician appearing to St Francis", "St Diego feeding the Poor"), Velázquez, Herrera the Elder, Pacheco, Caxés, Rizzi, Escalante and Carreiñ.

There are also numerous pictures by **foreign masters**, including Domenichino, Luca Giordano, Reni, Rubens, van Dyck, Vos, Fragonard, Van Loo, Giaquinto, as well as the Spanish artists Bayeu, Paret and Preciado de la Vega, representing the 18th century.

There is an impressive collection of works by **Goya**, mostly commissioned by the Academy: "Burial of the Sardine", "Flagellants",

Goya: "Portrait of Manuel Godoy"

"Madhouse", "Inquisition Tribunal", "Bullfight in a Village", "Portrait of Leandro Fernández de Moratín", "La Tirana", "Equestrian Portrait of Ferdinand VII", "Portrait of Manuel Godoy as Generalissimo" and a self-portrait of 1815.

★Real Fábrica de Tapices   K 12

Address
Calle Fuenterrabía
3

Metro
Menéndez Pelayo

Buses
24, 37, 54, 57, 141

Open Mon.–Fri.
9.30am–12.30pm;
closed Aug.

*Tapestry
restorer at
work*

Just to the east of the Atocha Station (see entry) is the Royal Tapestry Manufactory, successor to the Real Fábrica de Tapices founded by Philip V in 1721, which was installed in its present premises in 1889. The manufactory became independent of the Crown in 1744, and is still run by a ninth-generation descendant of the original owner, Jakob van der Goten. Even though most of the works of art produced here now hang in the Royal Palace and the Escorial and the cartoons for the tapestries can be seen in the Prado, the manufactory is well worth a visit. A number of carpets and tapestries are displayed in the exhibition room, but the real interest of a visit lies in seeing the workshops, in which carpets and tapestries are still produced on looms which were in use in the time of Goya. (See Baedeker Special, p. 76). The restoration of old tapestries, most of them from the royal collections, museums or private collections, is a major source of income for the manufactory.

Riofrío

The palace of Riofrío, built as a dower-house for Isabella Farnese, Philip V's widow, stands on rising ground amid forests of holm oak, with views of the Sierra de Guadarrama (see entry). The original plan was for a palace, convent, theatre and subsidiary buildings, but only the palace was actually built. Building began in 1754 to the design of the Italian architect Virgilio Rabaglio and was completed by Fraschina and Gamones in the reign of Charles III. (Illustration, p. 45.)

The palace is a square building of four wings surrounding a central courtyard. The main entrance, over which are the arms of the Bourbons and the Farneses, leads into a granite-paved inner courtyard from which a wide double staircase leads up to the principal floor. The rooms are in 18th century taste, with Rococo furniture, silk hangings and displays of porcelain. There are a number of notable pictures by a French painter, Houasse. Part of the building houses a Hunting Museum.

The attraction of Riofrío lies in its wide views of the surrounding country, to which the Italian architecture of the palace forms a charming contrast. The snow-covered slopes of the sierra in winter and the cool mountain air in summer, the beautiful oak forests and the tame deer, who come right up to the palace, are well worth a side trip during a visit to La Granja or Segovia, which is only 10 km (6 mi.) north.

Excursion
90 km (56 mi.)
NW

Open May–Sep.
Tue.–Sat.
10am–6pm, Sun.
and pub. hols.
10am–2pm;
Oct.–Apr.
Tue.–Sat.
10.30am–1.30pm,
3–5pm, Sun. and
pub. hols.
10am–2pm

Royal Palace

See Palacio Real

Las Salesas Reales   H 11

The former convent of the Salesas Reales is a very typical example of Spanish Baroque architecture of the Bourbon period. It was founded by Barbara of Braganza, Ferdinand VI's Portuguese wife, and built by the French architect François Carlier along with Francisco Moradillo, who was responsible for some alterations to the original plans, such as the low towers on the façade and the dome of the church. In the church is the sumptuous tomb of the founders, created by Francisco Gutiérrez (sculptor of the Cybele Fountain in Plaza de la Cíbeles: see entry) to the design of Francisco Sabatini. The convent has been used since the late 19th century as a lawcourt. It was rebuilt in 1926 after being burned down in 1915 and was then given the neo-Baroque façade which looks on to the Plaza de la Villa de París. Opening times depend on the times of services in the church.

Location
Plaza de las
Salesas

Metro
Colón

Bus
37

San Andrés   E 10

The church of San Andrés, which along with the Capilla del Obispo and Capilla de San Isidro forms a unified architectural group, lies in a picturesque corner of Madrid, with views of the Plaza de los Carros and Plaza de la Paja. Its monumental west front looks on to a narrow lane, the Costanilla de San Andrés, which links the two squares. Almost the whole of the nave of the church was destroyed by fire during the Civil War but the two chapels were unscathed. The church has been in course of restoration since the 1960s and is not always open to the public.

Location
Plaza de San
Andrés

Metro
La Latina

Buses
3, 31, 50, 60, 65

There was a mediaeval church here in which San Isidro and his wife María de la Cabeza, Madrid's patron saints, were buried. After Isidro's canonisation in 1622 the church was completely rebuilt. The **Capilla de**

Las Salesas Reales

San Isidro was added on the south side of the church between 1657 and 1669. It was designed by Pedro de la Torre and built under the direction of José de Villareal, with a sumptuous Baroque interior by Manuel Pereira and other artists.

Built on to the north side of the church is the **Capilla del Obispo** (Bishop's Church; 1520–35). It can be entered only from the Plaza de la Paja (the former hay market: *paja* = 'hay'), but has been closed for restoration since 1998. It is the only surviving example of Isabelline Gothic architecture in Madrid. Notable features are the Renaissance doors (workshop of Francisco Giralte, a pupil of Berruguete) and the wooden inner doors (attributed to Francisco de Villapandó or Cristóbal de Robles). The chapel was built to house the shrine of San Isidro, which remained here from 1518 to 1657, when it was transferred to the church of San Isidro el Real (see entry). The chapel's high altar is a masterpiece of Castilian Late Gothic, in the style known as Plateresque. The architect Francisco Giralte, a native of Palencia, was buried in the chapel in 1576. To right and left of the altar are the tombs of Francisco de Vargas (d. 1524) and his wife Inés de Carvajal (d. 1518; by Giralte). The chapel also contains the tomb of Bishop Gutiérrez de Carvajal y Vargas from which it takes its name.

San Antón de los Escolapios   G 7/8

Location
Calle de Hortaleza
63

Metro
Chueca

The aisleless church of San Antón de los Escolapios was built by the great Baroque architect Pedro de Ribera, but little is now left of his work since the church's remodelling in neo-classical style by Francisco de Rivas in the reign of Charles IV. Only the layout of the interior – on a rectangular ground-plan, with semicircular side chapels and a short transept – betrays its Baroque origins. The church's most precious possession is Goya's "Last Communion of St Joseph of Calasanzio" (1819) in the second chapel on the right.

Buses
3, 7, 40, 149

At the corner of the Escuela de los Escolapios is the **Fuente de los Delfines** (Dolphin Fountain; by Ventura Rodríguez, 1770). Originally the fountain was fed by its own spring, which was credited by local people with medicinal qualities. Then it was connected to the municipal water supply system, and since 1990 it has been flowing again – but now labelled "not for drinking".

Open daily
5.30–6pm

San Antonio de la Florida

See Ermita de San Antonio de la Florida

★San Antonio de los Alemanes

G 8

On the north side of the Gran Vía, at the corner of the Corredera Baja de San Pablo and Calle de la Puebla, is the church of San Antonio de los Alemanes or de los Portugueses. Philip III founded a hospital for the Portuguese on this site in 1607, and in 1624 the church of San Antonio was built here. After the separation of Spain and Portugal Maria Anna of Austria, Philip II's fourth wife, took the hospital under her personal protection and gave it to the Germans living in Madrid. The hospital, hospice and church then became "de los Alemanes" ("of the Germans"). In 1702 Philip V gave them to the Real Hermandad del Refugio y Piedad, a confraternity which cared for the poorest people in Madrid. The name "Hospedería para Alemanes" still appears above the entrance to the hospital, and until the Civil War Germans who could show, with written confirmation from their embassy, that they lacked the money to pay for a night's lodging were given a bed here. No use seems to have been made of this right since the 1940s.

The architect of the church was a Jesuit, Pedro Sánchez, who also designed the church of San Isidro (see entry) in Calle de Toledo. This jewel of Baroque architecture is concealed behind an unremarkable grey façade: the oval ground-plan of the church was originally inscribed within an octagon, but in 1887 the octagonal exterior was filled out to fit in with the straight building line of the street. The elliptical interior with its domed roof is a classic example of overcharged Baroque ornament. The walls are covered with frescoes by Luca Giordano and the dome has a huge ceiling painting by Francesco Ricci and Juan Carreiñ. The high altar is 18th century, replacing the original retablo which was destroyed by fire. The statue of St Anthony is attributed to Manuel Pereira. On each side of the church are three side altars decorated with medallions and gilded, from which the last Habsburg rulers – Philip IV, Charles II and Maria Anna of Austria – look down on visitors.

Location
Calle de la Puebla
22

Metro
Callao

Buses
3, 40, 46, 149

★San Francisco el Grande

E 11

The Real Basílica de San Francisco el Grande occupies the site of an old Franciscan friary; begun in 1761, it was designed by a Franciscan, Francisco de las Cabezas, who is believed to have taken as his model Carlo Fontana's church of Santa Maria in Capitelli in Rome. Because of technical difficulties in the construction of the huge dome (33 m (110 ft)) across) Francisco Sabatini, Charles III's favourite architect, took over the direction of the work in 1770 and saw it to completion in 1785. He was responsible for the neo-classical façade and the rotunda. Joseph Bonaparte used the church for meetings of the Cortes. In 1878 it was declared the Panteón Nacional (National Pantheon). Among those

Location
Plaza de San
Francisco

Metro
La Latina

Buses
3, 60, 148

San Ginés

buried here are Juan de Villanueva and Ventura Rodríguez. In 1926 the church was returned to the Franciscans.

The interior, a domed rotunda with six chapels, is of impressive size and height. The paintings on the altars in the chapels date from between 1781 and 1783; among them are works by Goya ("St Bernard preaching"; first chapel on left), González Velázquez ("St Bonaventura"), Mariano Salvador Maella ("Immaculata"; first chapel on right) and Francisco Bayeu.

The church contains numerous other works of art. The choir-stalls in the ante-sacristy and chapterhouse come from the monastery of El Paular (by Bartolomeo Fernández, 16th century: see Sierra de Guadarrama). The sacristy contains a collection of pictures, including works by Francisco Pacheco, Zurbarán and Alonso Cano.

The church is at present filled with scaffolding for the renovation of the dome, which is expected to take at least until 2001. The high altar, the chapels and the collection of pictures, however, can still be seen.

San Ginés   F 9

Location
Calle del Arenal
15

Metro
Puerta del Sol

Bus
3

The origins of San Ginés, which lies close to the Teatro Real, the Plaza de Oriente, the Palacio Real and the Plaza Mayor, (see entries), go back to a Mozarabic church of the 11th/12th century which was destroyed during its rebuilding in the 17th century as an aisled church. It stands in a mediaeval part of the town which was much altered over the centuries until it reached its present form in the 19th century, in the reign of Isabella II. The church was rebuilt after a fire in 1872. Its tower dominates the surrounding streets (Calles Bordadores, Coloreros, San Martín), whose feeling of intimacy within the city recalls the novels of Benito Pérez Galdós.

After suffering heavy destruction during the Civil War the church was renovated and the 19th century neo-Plateresque ornament on the exterior was removed. The exterior masonry, with alternating courses of brick and undressed stone and without plaster cladding, reflects an old Mudéjar technique.

At the north-west corner of the church is the **Capilla del Cristo**, which is open only during services. It belonged to a lay confraternity, the Esclavitud Penitencial de Cristo, of which Philip IV was a member. His illegitimate son Juan José de Austria (d. 1679) is buried in the chapel. Among the artists involved in the decoration of the chapel were Alonso Vergaz (high altar), Pompeo Leoni (four gilded bronze angels), Alonso Cano ("Mocking of Christ"; north transept) and El Greco ("Expulsion of the Money-changers from the Temple"; in aisle to east of entrance).

Teatro Esclava

Adjoining San Ginés is the Teatro Esclava, a charming old theatre which is now occupied by a disco (Joy Esclava). Between this and the church is the Pasadizo de San Ginés, a narrow passage in which is the Chocolatería de San Ginés widely famed Chocolatería de San Ginés, where you can satisfy your hunger between 7pm and 7am in real Madrid fashion with a cup of hot chocolate and freshly fried churros.

★San Isidro   F 10

Location
Calle de Toledo 49

Metro
La Latina

In the heart of the old town, near the Plaza Mayor (see entry), the busy Plaza de Tirso de Molina and the flea market of El Rastro (see entry), is the collegiate church of San Isidro, which was Madrid's cathedral until the consecration of the Catedral de la Almudena. The church, built in 1622 in Jesuit Baroque style, occupies the site of an earlier church dedicated to St Francis Xavier which was consecrated in 1567 in the presence of Philip II. Three Jesuits – Pedro Sánchez, Juan de Haro and Francisco Bautista – were the architects of the new church, to which, soon afterwards, there was attached a school, the Colegio Imperial, in the adjoining Calle de Estudios. After the expulsion of the Jesuits in the reign of Charles III the church was remodelled by Ventura Rodríguez and dedicated to San Isidro, Madrid's patron saint, whose remains were then transferred to the church from the chapel adjoining San Ginés (see entry). Ferdinand VI (1816–23) restored the church to the Jesuits.

Instituto de San Isidro While the church was under construction Philip IV and his minister the Duke of Olivares resolved to establish a system of Estudios Reales ("royal studies") in the adjoining Colegio Imperial. This too was entrusted to the Jesuits. After their expulsion from Spain lay teachers were appointed. Among pupils at the Instituto de San Isidro, which is still well respected, have been Lope de Vega, Calderón and Quevedo (see Famous People) and in more recent times Pío Baroja, Jacinto Benavente and Vicente Aleixandre.

Buses
17, 23, 35

Open Mon.–Sat.
8am–12pm,
1–2.30pm,
5.45–8.45pm

San Marcos   E 7

In the old district of Amaniel, which lies behind the Edificio España (see Plaza de España), north-east of the Gran Vía (see entry), is the church of San Marcos, the last great monument of Madrid Baroque. It was built by Ventura Rodríguez between 1749 and 1753 to commemorate Philip V's victory over British forces at Almansa during the War of the Spanish Succession. The ground-plan of five interlocking ellipses was inspired by the work of Bernini and Borromini in Italy. The interior, with its dominant dome, is strikingly impressive. The frescoes are by Luis González, the stucco work by Robert Michel, the statue of St Mark on the high altar and the statues in the lateral recesses of the altar by Juan Pascual de Mena.

Location
Calle de San
Leonardo 10

Metro
Plaza de España

Buses
1, 2, 44, 74, C

San Martín   G 8

In Calle de la Luna, just off the busy Gran Vía, is the Baroque church of San Martín, built in 1761 by an unknown architect. The brick façade, with twin towers, could be the work of José Churriguera. The church has pictures of saints by Pedro de Mena, Gregorio Hernández, José Mora and Pedro Alonso de los Ríos and paintings by Claudio Coello, Juan Ricci and Carreño. The writer Francisco de Quevedo is said to have had an adventure with a lady in this church which compelled him to flee to Italy.

Location
Calle de la Luna

Metro
Callao

Buses
1, 2, 44, 46, 74,
147, 148

San Miguel   F 10

Near the Plaza de la Villa (see entry) and Plaza Puerta Cerrada is the Baroque church of San Miguel, built from 1739 onwards on the site of an earlier church. It was designed by the Italian architect Santiago Bonavia, who had also worked for the royal house, at Aranjuez and elsewhere, and was later succeeded in the direction of the work by Virgilio Rabaglio and after him Andrés de Rusca. Its narrow two-storey façade, flanked by low bell-towers, is built of granite and, following Italian models, convexly curved. The sculpture in the semicircular recesses is by Luis Salvador Carmona and Juan Pascual de Mena. The aisleless interior, with side chapels, a barely projecting transept and a dome, has paintings by the González Velázquez brothers and frescoes by Bartolomé Rusca.

Location
Calle de San
Justo 4

Metro
Ópera, Puerta del
Sol

Buses
31, 50, 65

San Nicolás de los Servitas   E 9

Location
Plaza de San
Nicolás

Metro
Ópera

Buses
3, 149

San Nicolás de los Servitas is Madrid's oldest church. All that survives of the original building is the brick tower, one of the few examples of Mudéjar architecture in Madrid and perhaps originally a minaret. The horseshoe arches at the entrance to the choir and the stucco decoration are also in Mudéjar style. The retablo on the high altar was the work of Juan de Herrera, architect of the Escorial (see entry). Herrera was buried in the church until his remains were transferred to his home town of Santander.

San Pedro el Viejo   E 10

Location
Calle del Nuncio

Metro
La Latina

Buses
31, 50, 65

The church of San Pedro el Viejo (Old St Peter's), also known as San Pedro el Real, is situated in the oldest part of Madrid, the area round Plaza Puerta Cerrada and Calle Segovia. It was built in the reign of

Alfonso XI (1312–40) in the old Moorish quarter, probably on the site of a mosque. Of the original church there survives its square brick west tower, one of Madrid's few remains of the mediaeval period. It is typical of the Mudéjar style, with its red brickwork, its sparse decoration and the two small horseshoe-shaped ornaments half way up the tower.

The present **church** dates from the 17th century. Like many churches in the old town of Madrid, it became impoverished in the course of time, and at various times (most recently in 1936) lost some of its furnishings by theft. The whole area round San Pedro, extending to the Plaza de la Paja (see San Andrés), is now being cleaned up and

San Piedro el Viejo

renovated, and numbers of cafés and excellent tapa bars tempt visitors to linger.

San Plácido   F 8

Location
Calle San Roque 9

Another 17th century church in the area north of the Gran Vía (see entry) is San Plácido, which belonged to the convent of San Plácido, a house of Benedictine nuns which was demolished in 1908. It shows a stylistic unity characteristic of Madrid's Late Baroque architecture with the churches of San Antonio de los Alemanes, San Martín (see entries) and La Concepción.

The convent was founded in 1623 by Doña Teresa Valle la Cerda; the architect was Fray Lorenzo de San Nicolás, a native of Madrid. The aisleless church, which has preserved its 17th century decoration and furnishings almost intact, has a short transept and a dome (with no drum) over the crossing. The high altar, with a large "Annunciation", is by Claudio Coello (1668), who was also responsible for the side altars in the transept, dedicated to St Gertrude (south) and SS Scholastica and Benito (north).

Velázquez's **"Christ on the Cross"**, now in the Museo del Prado (see entry), was painted for the convent of San Plácido.

Metro
Callao

Buses
1, 2, 44, 46, 74, 75,
147, 148

Santa María la Real de Montserrat   F 7

The church of the Benedictine convent of Montserrat, which had been founded by Philip IV in 1634, was built from 1668 onwards by Pedro de la Torre to the design of Sebastián Herrera Barnuevo and was consecrated in 1704. The church, however, remained unfinished. The original tower, attributed to Pedro de Ribera (1720), has an Oriental aspect. From 1842 to 1914 the convent was used as a women's prison, but since its renovation in 1920 it has been reoccupied by the Benedictines.

Location
Calle de San
Bernardo 79

Metro
San Bernardo,
Noviciado

Buses
21, 147

★★Segovia

The Castilian town of Segovia (pop. 57,000) lies at an altitude of 1000 m (3300 ft) on a rocky hill, almost surrounded by the little rivers Eresma and Clamores, on the northern slopes of the Sierra de Guadarrama (see

Excursion
90 km (56 mi.)
NW

A walk through the old town of Segovia is a journey through time

entry). It is the chief town of its province and the see of a bishop. With its Roman aqueduct and numerous medieval buildings Segovia is now a UNESCO World Heritage Site. For visitors to Madrid with sufficient time at their disposal a trip to Segovia is a must.

A culinary speciality of Segovia is *cochinillos asados* (roast sucking pig). Its two most famous restaurants are the Cándido, just by the Roman aqueduct, and the Duque (established 1895) at Calle Cervantes 12; but the town's other restaurants also offer the local speciality.

Access

By rail: from Atocha or Chamartín Station (RENFE). By bus: Empresa La Sepulvedana, Paseo de la Florida 11, and other companies. By car: on N VI. On a visit by car it is also worth taking in La Granja de San Ildefonso and the palace of Riofrío (see entries).

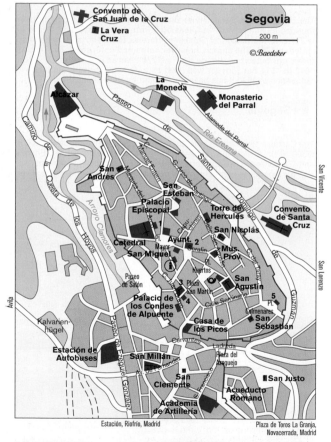

Estación, Riofrío, Madrid

Plaza de Toros La Granja,
Novacerrada, Madrid

1 Palacio del Marqués del Arco
2 La Trinidad
3 San Martín
4 Torreón de los Lozoya
5 San Juan de los Caballeros
(Museo Zuloaga)

Segovia's Roman aqueduct, one of the most impressive Roman remains in Spain

History Originally founded by the Iberians, Segovia became a centre of resistance to the Romans, who finally took it in 80 BC. Under Roman rule, situated at the intersection of two military roads, it was a place of some importance. After the Visigothic and Arab periods the town took on a new lease of life under the Counts of Castile, and it was for long a favourite residence of the Castilian kings, including Alfonso X, the Wise. In 1474 Isabella the Catholic was proclaimed queen in Segovia. The town owed its prosperity to the wool trade and the Mesta, a trading organisation comparable to the Hanseatic League in northern Europe. In 1520 the revolt of the Comuneros broke out in protest against increased taxes imposed by Charles V. Juan Bravo, one of its leaders, was born in Segovia and was in due course beheaded there. The town flourished under the Trastamara family and again, after a period of oblivion, under the Bourbons in the 18th century. It still retains something of the splendour of that period.

Sights

The finest **views** of the town are to be had from the Calvary Hill on the road to Avila (N 110) or the panoramic road in the valley, which runs alongside the two rivers and under the walls.

★★Roman aqueduct

The starting-point of a tour of the town's sights is the busy Plaza del Azoguejo, which lies below the old town and is spanned by the Roman aqueduct with its two tiers of arches. This colossal structure is believed to have been built in the reign of the Emperor Trajan in the late 1st century AD and was still in use until 1974. Part of a 17 km (10 mi.) long conduit bringing water to Segovia from the Sierra de Fuenfría, it has 118 arches ranging in height between 7 and 28.5 m (23 and 94 ft), built of granite blocks laid without mortar or cramps, and a total length of 818 m (2685 ft). It bridges the deep valley now occupied by the suburbs of Segovia, reaches the upper town and ends at the Alcázar, where the water channel runs underground. The aqueduct of Segovia is, after the walls of Tarragona, the largest surviving Roman monument in Spain and one of the finest aqueducts in the Roman world – although air pollution has left its mark on the structure.

Calle Cervantes, to the left of the aqueduct, leads up to the **old town**. At the point where it runs into Calle Juan Bravo, on the right, is the 15th century Casa de los Picos (the *picos*, "sharp points", are the facetted blocks of which it is built). Farther along, on the left, is the Casa del Conde de Alpuente, whose façade has beautiful sgraffito decoration (15th century).

Calle Juan Bravo, lined with shops, bars and restaurants, leads to the **Plazuela de San Martín**, in the centre of the former aristocratic quarter. In the little square are a monument to Juan Bravo and the house in which he was born, the Casa del Siglo XV or Casa de Juan Bravo, identifiable by the four-arched gallery running along under the roof. The massive Torreón de los Lozoya dates from the 14th century. Adjoining it are the Casa de los Bornos and the Casa de Solier (also known as the Casa de Correos).

★San Martín

The Romanesque church of San Martín (12th century) is surrounded on three sides by a colonnade with richly carved capitals. In the interior is the Gothic Capilla de Herrera, with the tombs of the Herrera family. In the Capilla Mayor is a recumbent figure of Christ by Gregorio Hernández. Adjoining the church is the old prison (Carcel Real; 17th century).

Museo de Arte Contemporáneo Esteban Vicente

Close by, in Plazuela de las Bellas Artes, is a museum devoted to the work of the painter Esteban Vicente, an Abstract Expressionist, who was born in Turégano, near Segovia. It is housed in a palace built for Henry IV in 1455. The museum also puts on periodic special exhibitions of work by contemporary painters of Segovia province. Open Tue.–Sat. 11am–2pm, 4–7pm, Sun. 11am–2pm.

San Miguel

The **Plaza Mayor**, with its street cafés and its bandstand, is the central feature of the old town. On the north side of the square is the unpretentious Ayuntamiento (Town Hall; 17th century), on the east side the Theatre and on the south-east side the Gothic church of San Miguel (by Gil de Hontañón, 1558). The church has a fine high altar by José Vallejo Vivanco (1572) and contains some interesting tombs. Isabella the Catholic was proclaimed queen in this church.

Close by, on the highest point in the old town, is the Gothic-style Cathedral, built of yellow stone between 1525 and 1593 (architects Juan and Rodrigo Gil de Hontañón). It replaced an earlier church destroyed during the revolt of the Comuneros. Notable features of the interior are the grilles, a polychrome wood "Lamentation" by Juan de Juni (1571) and an "Entombment" (to right of entrance). On the marble high altar is an ivory figure of the Virgen de la Paz (14th century). The 15th century choir-stalls came from the previous Cloister church. The cloister, also from the earlier church, was rebuilt between 1524 and 1530 from the original stones. There is an interesting **Cathedral Museum** with pictures by various artists, including Ribera. Its chief treasures, however, are its very beautiful Brussels tapestries of the 16th and 17th centuries, including a series of scenes on Queen Zenobia of Palmyra.

★Cathedral

Open daily
9.30am–6pm

The Alcázar, a magnificent example of an old Castilian stronghold, stands on a rocky promontory above the confluence of the rivers Eresma and Clamores. Dating from the 11th century, it was rebuilt by Alfonso the Wise in the 13th century and was enlarged and embellished in the 15th and 16th centuries. Here Philip II married Anne of Austria. The Torre de Juan II with its ten semicircular turrets, through which the Alcázar is entered, and the round Torre del Homenaje, with a pointed roof, at the opposite end of the complex, both date from the 14th century. The arduous climb up the Torre de Juan II is rewarded by the superb views it affords of the town, the surrounding plain and the Sierra de Guadarrama.

★Alcázar

Open daily
10am–6pm
(summer 7pm)

A walk round the Alcázar offers an introduction to the life-style of the high nobility in the 15th and 16th centuries. The tour, bearing right from the entrance, takes in the Sala del Trono (Throne Room), with its ceiling of gilded stars; the Sala de la Galera, whose arched windows offer fine views of the river valley; several rooms containing period furniture, tapestries, arms and armour; and the Chapel. Then, opening off the little

The Alcázar of Segovia

145

courtyard below the Torre del Homenaje, are three further rooms housing a small museum of military history.

★San Esteban

A little way north of the Plaza Mayor can be seen the five-storey tower of the church of San Esteban. Like most of Segovia's Romanesque churches, San Esteban has a columned loggia in which meetings of the town's guilds were held. Notable carved features are the beautifully carved capitals of the colonnades on the west and south sides of the church and a Christ on the Cross in painted wood (13th century) in the interior.

San Juan de los Caballeros

From the Plaza del Azoguejo a street runs up, passing the little Romanesque church of **San Sebastián**, to the old town. After crossing the **Plaza del Conde de Cheste**, which is surrounded by aristocratic palaces, including those of the Marqueses de Moya, the Marqués de Lozoya (14th century), the Condes de Cheste and the Marqués de Quintanar, our route ends in **Plaza Colmenares**. In this square is the former church of San Juan de los Caballeros (11th century), once the burial-place of the best families of Segovia. It now houses the **Museo Zuloaga**, which displays the works of the painter Ignacio Zuloaga and the ceramicist Daniel Zuloaga. Open Tue.–Sat. 10am–2pm, 5–7pm, Sun. 10am–2pm.

San Clemente

From the Plaza del Azoguejo the Avenida de Fernández Ladreda runs south-west to the Romanesque church of San Clemente (13th century), which has an interesting apse. Within the church, to the right of the Capilla Mayor, are 13th century wall-paintings.

San Millán

A short distance away is another Romanesque church, San Millán, built between 1111 and 1124 and thus one of the oldest churches in the town. The predominantly Baroque interior is decorated with frescoes, and in the chancel there are remains of Romanesque frescoes.

From San Millán the route continues on a narrow street running round the hill, which is surrounded almost continuously by the old **town walls**. The walls have Iberian foundations, but were developed and strengthened by the Romans and restored in the 11th/12th century. The street turns round the north-eastern tip of the town and crosses the Río Eresma, where it turns right again. From this point the Alcázar can be seen in all its majesty.

Soon after the bridge, on the left, can be seen the rather ponderous 17th century pilgrimage church of the Virgen de la Fuencisla and the **Convento de San Juan de la Cruz**, a house of Discalced (Barefoot) Carmelites founded by Juan de la Cruz in 1576 (now an old people's home). On the opposite side of the street, standing by itself, is the round church of the **Vera Cruz**, a former Templar church of 1202–17 with 13th century wall paintings. A few hundred yards farther on a side street runs over the Eresma to the **Monasterio El Parral**, a Hieronymite house founded by Henry IV in 1447 on the hillside to the left. It has a massive retablo by Juan Rodríguez (16th century) and contains the alabaster tombs of the Marqués de Villena and his wife (1528). The road continues under the town walls to return to the Plaza del Azuguejo. To the left can be seen the **Convento de Santa Cruz** (founded 1217), With an Isabelline doorway. At the convent a road goes off to the church of **San Lorenzo** in the suburb of that name. The tower and the tripartite apse are outstanding examples of the Mudéjar style.

Surroundings

Sierra de Guadarrama

Beyond San Ildefonso the N 601 climbs into the wooded hills of the Sierra de Guadarrama (see entry). On the pass, the **Puerto de Navacerrada** (alt. 1860 m (6103 ft)), is a winter sports station which attracts skiers from all over the Madrid region. The capital is now only 60 km (37 mi.) away and easily reached on N 601 or N IV (now of motorway standard).

Leave N 601, which continues north, and turn north-east into C 603, which comes in 34 km (21 mi.) to Turégano (alt. 936 m (3071 ft)), a small cathedral town with an arcaded Plaza Mayor lying at the foot of a partly ruined castle and keep of the 13th/15th centuries. Within the battlemented walls is the Romanesque church of San Miguel, with a striking bellcote.

Turégano

15 km (9 mi.) farther north C 603 comes to the little town of Cantalejo, 24 km (15 mi.) north of which is Fuentidueña, with the remains of two Romanesque churches and a massive castle.

Fuentidueña

15 km (9 mi.) north-east of Cantalejo on a minor road is the picturesque little town of Sepúlveda (alt. 1032 m (3386 ft)), high above a loop in the river Duratón. It was the Roman town of Septem Portae ("Seven Gates") and has well-preserved Roman walls, as well as several Romanesque churches. Among them is the commandingly situated church of El Salvador (11th century), with arcading and a free-standing bell-tower from which there are breathtaking views in all directions. The Castillo was founded by Fernán González.

Sepúlveda

From Sepúlveda take SG 233, signposted to Pedraza, and at the Quattro Carreteras road junction take the road to the left to reach the castle of Castilnovo (12th–15th centuries), which was originally a Moorish stronghold.

Castilnovo

Pedraza is said to have been the birthplace of the Emperor Trajan. Its powerful castle stands on a massive crag. Round the attractive Plaza Mayor, very typical of Castile, are the Romanesque Torre San Juan and the Casa de la Inquisición, now an *hostería* (inn).

Pedraza

10 km (6 mi.) beyond Pedraza the road runs into N 110, which returns to Segovia by way of **Collado Hermosa**.

For longer excursions into the country round Segovia there are many small hotels to provide accommodation (see Practical Information, Hotels).

Sierra de Guadarrama

The Sierra de Guadarrama forms part of a 100 km (62 mi.) long mountain massif which separates Old and New Castile. In Mt Peñalara it reaches a height of 2430 m (7973 ft), in the Cabezas de Hierro 2383 m (7819 ft). It is a popular weekend leisure destination for the people of Madrid both in summer and in winter. In this section some possible excursions from Madrid are described.

Excursion
60 km (37 mi.) N

Leave Madrid on N I, heading north, and just beyond Fuencarral (9 km (5½ mi.)) turn left into C 607. This leads to Colmenar Viejo (alt. 885 m (2904 ft)), near the quarries of the white Colmenar limestone used in the Royal Palace and many other buildings in Madrid. The most notable feature of an otherwise unremarkable town is the parish church of La Asunción, which has a fine Plateresque high altar of 1579, with sculpture by Francisco Giralte, a pupil of Berruguete, and an "Annunciation" by Sánchez Coello (1574).

Colmenar Viejo

C 607 continues to the little town of Cerceda, where a minor road goes off on the right to Manzanares el Real (alt. 908 m (2979 ft)). In the wide

★**Manzanares el Real**

147

valley of the Río Manzanares, here dammed to form the Embalse (reservoir) de Santillana, is the magnificent castle of the Mendoza family, in Mudéjar style, built in the 15th century and faithfully restored in the late 1970s. There are conducted tours of the castle (open Tue.–Sun. 10am–1.30pm, 3–6pm; closed pub. hols.).

★La Pedriza Nature Park

A few hundred metres west a side road goes off to La Pedriza Nature Park. Since there are restrictions on the number of visitors it is advisable to arrive early in the day. The park offers wide panoramic views. The Río Manzanares originates here as a mountain stream.

Miraflores de la Sierra

From Manzanares el Real a road runs along the Embalse de Santillana, passes through Soto el Real and comes to Miraflores de la Sierra (alt. 1150 m (3773 ft)), an old town in a beautiful setting on the southern slopes of the sierra which is a popular resort of the people of Madrid in summer.

★Monasterio El Paular

The route continues over the Puerto de la Morcuera (pass; 1796 m (5893 ft)) and runs down the beautiful valley of the Río Lozoya to the monastery of El Paular (alt. 1153 m (3783 ft)), 2 km (1½ mi.) west of Rascafría. Founded in 1390 as a Carthusian house, it is now occupied by Benedictines. The monastery was designed by a Moorish architect from Segovia, Abd ar-Rahman, and built under the direction of Juan Guas. Part of the monastery round the cloister is now a hotel. The church, which was rebuilt in Baroque style after an earthquake in 1755, has a richly furnished Capilla del Tabernáculo of 1724 and a sumptuous 15th century Dutch marble high altar.

The return route is by way of Rascafría and along the Río Lozoya, passing through the villages of Oteruelo, Alameda and Pinilla, to Lozoya. Then on C 604 to join N I, which leads back to Madrid. The slopes of the

The castle of the Mendoza family in Manzanares el Real

wide valley between the two ranges of the Sierra de Guadarrama are covered with oak forests. In Villavieja de Lozoya and Sierra Pobre are hotels which make good bases for mountain walks and other excursions.

From the monastery of El Paular C 603 runs up through dense pine forests, with magnificent views, to the Puerto de los Cotos (1830 m (6004 ft)), then down to Castilla León, and climbs again to the Puerto de Navacerrada (1860 m (6103 ft)). On both passes are ski resorts with lifts. N 601 then runs down to the beautiful little town of Navacerrada, a popular resort of the people of Madrid at weekends. The town has an art gallery, numerous restaurants and an excellent hotel (see Practical Information, Hotels). There is an antiques and junk market every Sunday morning.

★**Puerto de Navacerrada**

N 614 continues to Guadarrama, from which a side trip can be made to the palace/monastery of El Escorial (see entry).

From the Chamartín district in the northern suburbs of Madrid N I runs north by way of San Sebastián de los Reyes and San Agustín de Guadalix and past the Jamara car-racing circuit, the best known racing circuit in Spain after the one at Jerez de la Frontera.

Circuito de Jarama

In the spa of El Molar (alt. 817 m (2681 ft)) a minor road (15 km (9 mi.)) goes off to the ancient little walled town of Torrelaguna (alt. 774 m (2539 ft)), on the southern slopes of the Sierra de Guadarrama. The main features of interest are the Gothic parish church (13th–15th centuries), which has a beautiful Baroque altar, and the house in which Cardinal Jiménez was born.

Torrelaguna

Now return through the remote and picturesque Sierra Pobre to N I, which goes over a low pass (1140 m (3740 ft)) and runs past the rugged peaks of La Cabrera to Buitrago del Lozoya (alt. 977 m (3206 ft)). This ancient little town (pop. 1400) on the west side of the Embalse de Lozoya has preserved its Arab walls and towers, a castle of the 14th/15th century and a Gothic church. There is a small museum containing works by Picasso which he presented to his hairdresser, Eugenio Arias Herranz (open Mon.–Fri. 11am–1.30pm, 5–7pm (4–6pm winter), Sat. and pub. hols. 11.30am–2pm, 5–8pm (4–7pm winter), Sun. 10am–2pm).

Buitrago del Lozoya

Beyond the village of Somosierra (23 km (14 mi.) north) the road climbs to the Puerto de Somosierra (1404 m (4607 ft)), where Napoleon's forces fought their way through the Sierra de Somosierra (part of the Sierra de Guadarrama) in 1808. There are fine views of the Sierra de Ayllón to the right and over the plateau of New Castile to the south. The destruction wrought by a forest fire in 1995 will take a long time to repair.

Puerto de Somosierra

The return to Madrid is by the direct route on N I.

Teatro Español

G 10

The Teatro Español stands in the Plaza de Santa Ana, in the old Barrio de los Literarios in which Cervantes, Quevedo and Lope de Vega (see Famous People) lived. It is one of Madrid's oldest theatres, opening on September 21st 1583 as the Corral del Príncipe with two comic plays by Lope de Rueda. Innumerable comedies by the great dramatists of the Golden Age were performed in the Corral del Príncipe. The theatre was roofed over in 1745. The Romantic movement enjoyed a series of triumphs with the first performances of such plays as "Don Alvaro" (1835) by the Duke of Rivas, "El Trovador" (1836) by García Gutiérrez and "Los Amantes de Teruel" (1837) by Hartzenbusch. The theatre's café was the

Location
Plaza de Santa Ana

Metro
Sol, Antón Martín

Buses
6, 26, 32, 57

The Teatro Español in the Plaza de Santa Ana

regular meeting-place of the Romantics, the "Parnasillo" group, the intellectuals and artists of the capital. The Teatro Español was given its present name in 1849, and thereafter was for many years a national theatre. It is now one of Madrid's municipal theatres and one of the best of all its theatres.

Plaza de Santa Ana

The Plaza de Santa Ana owes its name to a Carmelite convent founded here in 1586. The square was given its present aspect in 1610, during the reign of Joseph Bonaparte, when the convent and seven other buildings were demolished, trees were planted and the square was embellished with a fountain. The monument to Calderón (see Famous People) on one side of the square dates from this period. The Hotel Victoria on the west side of the square, with a very individual façade, was built in 1918 to the design of Jesús Carrasco (see Practical Information, Hotels).

Teatro Nacional María Guerrero   J 8

Location
Calle Tamayo y
Baus

Metro
Colón

Bus
37

The Teatro Nacional María Guerrero, known for short as the María Guerrero, is situated on the so-called "left bank" of the Paseo de Recoletos, in the area round the Palacio de Justicia and the former Palacio de Buonavista (now housing the Ministry of Defence) which is noted for its concentration of literary cafés, restaurants and boutiques.

The theatre, which takes its present name from the great actress María Guerrero (see Famous People), opened in 1885 as the Teatro de la Princesa and was for many years the home of the company headed by María Guerrero and her husband Fernando Díaz de Mendoza. It is now the principal house of the National Dramatic Centre (see Practical Information, Theatres).

Teatro Real

E 9

The building of the Theatre Royal, which stands in the Plaza de Oriente opposite the Palacio Real (see entries), began in 1818 after the demolition of the old Caños del Peral theatre; the architect was Antonio López Aguado, a pupil of Juan de Villanueva. After various interruptions the Teatro Real (also known as the Teatro de la Ópera) was finally inaugurated by Queen Isabella II on November 19th 1850 with a performance of Donizetti's opera "La Favorita". Among the theatre's greatest successes have been productions of Verdi and Wagner operas, works by Stravinsky and performances by the Russian ballet. In 1925 extensive alterations to the building were carried out by Antonio Flórez, including the building of new façades. Between 1960 and 1966 it was converted into a concert hall. The construction of the Auditorio Nacional de Música (see entry) prepared the way for another change of function, and after thorough restoration the theatre was reopened in 1997 as an opera house and performances of the characteristically Spanish type of opera, the zarzuela, returned to the Teatro de la Zarzuela (see Baedeker Special, p. 134, and Practical Information, Music). Illustration, p. 19.

Location
Plaza de Oriente

Metro
Ópera

Buses
25, 33, 39

Tours Sat., Sun. and pub. hols. at 10.30am

Templo de Debod

See Montaña del Príncipe Pío

★★Toledo

Toledo (alt. 529 m (1736 ft); pop. 66,000), capital of the autonomous region of Castilla–La Mancha and of Toledo province and the seat of the Archbishop Primate of Spain, is picturesquely situated on a granite crag in a loop on the Río Tajo (Tagus), which at this point has carved out a deep channel. Once the capital of Castile, Toledo was for centuries the scene of encounters between Jews, Muslims and Christians and on that account has sometimes, rather over-enthusiastically, been called the "Jerusalem of the West". Its magnificent buildings and treasures of art make it one of the great tourist cities of Spain. It is famous for its steel swords ("Toledo blades") and its inlay work in gold and silver, a craft tradition brought in by the Moors.

Excursion
70 km (43 mi.) S

By rail: from Atocha Station. By bus: from the Estación Sur, Calle Canarias (Metro: Palos de la Frontera). By car: N IV (signposted to Talavera), then N 401; stops recommended in Illescas (see below), Aranjuez (see entry) and Chinchón (see Aranjuez, Surroundings).

Access

History Toledo, one of the oldest towns in Spain, was once the capital of an Iberian tribe, the Carpetani. It was also a place of importance under the Romans, who captured the town in 192 BC, calling it Toletum, and valued it for its excellent strategic situation. Under the Visigoths the town was again a capital (534–712) and the meeting-place of many church councils. At the Council of Toledo in 589 the Visigothic king Reccared adopted the Catholic faith. In 712 Arab troops took the town, which had both Christians and a small Jewish community among its inhabitants, calling it Tolaitola. Until 1085 Toledo was the seat of an emir owing allegiance to the Caliph of Córdoba. The town now acquired a third religion, Islam. The Arabs built mosques and Koranic schools, but allowed members of the other two faiths freedom of worship. The different population groups lived in their own quarters of the town. The official language was Arabic (the use of which was not prohibited until 1580). In later centuries Toledo flourished thanks to its weapon manu-

General view of Toledo

facture and its silk and wool industries, and began to attract scholars as well as merchants. In 1087 it became the residence of the king of Castile and the religious centre of the whole of Spain. As the "town of three religions" Toledo developed into a centre of European intellectual life and learning. Archbishop Rodrigo Jiménez founded the famous school of translators without which the history of European philosophy would have taken a different course: Jewish, Muslim and Christian scholars translated works on medicine, astronomy, history and the natural sciences, sacred writings, even poetry into the language of Christendom. The archbishop himself wrote the first comprehensive history of Spain. King Alfonso X, the Wise, continued this work. And while there was still bitter fighting between Christian and Muslim armies in the south of the Iberian peninsula, rabbis, high church dignitaries and learned Muslims worked side by side in Toledo until the late 13th century.

When Granada, the last Moorish kingdom in Spain, fell to the Catholic Monarchs in 1492 and the Muslims were expelled from Spain, a period of nearly seven centuries of mainly peaceful cohabitation, with mutual tolerance and respect, came to an end. The Inquisition established its tribunal in Toledo Cathedral. Some 12,000 Jews were compelled to leave the town, while their property was confiscated. Of their ten synagogues and five Talmudic schools only two survived the storm. The great days of the town (and of the whole country) were finally at an end, and Toledo lost its political importance when Philip II transferred his residence to Madrid.

During the Spanish Civil War the Alcázar was besieged by Republican forces and completely destroyed.

Sights

With its ring of Gothic and Moorish walls, its towering Alcázar and its Cathedral, Toledo is a magnificently impressive sight. The layout of the **old town** with its narrow and irregular streets and blind alleys, the

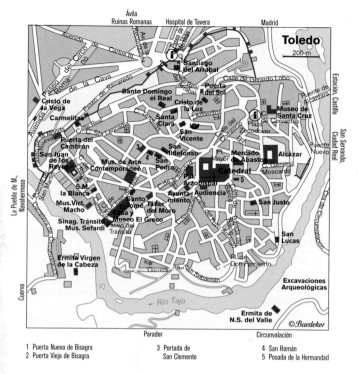

Ávila
Ruinas Romanas   Hospital de Tavera   Madrid

Toledo
200 m

©Baedeker

1 Puerta Nueva de Bisagra
2 Puerta Vieja de Bisagra

3 Portada de
   San Clemente

4 San Román
5 Posada de la Hermandad

houses with their few windows, their grille-covered balconies and open
inner courtyards show Muslim influence, while Christian times have left
their mark in the numerous churches, religious houses and hospices.
The whole town is an open-air museum of Spanish history, earning
Toledo its place as a UNESCO World Heritage Site.

The finest **views** of the town are to be had from the south bank of the
Tagus, for example from the Ermita de Nuestra Señora de la Cabeza or
the Ermita de la Virgen del Valle. There is also a good view from the
Parador Nacional Conde de Orgaz (see Practical Information, Hotels).

On the east side of the Plaza del Ayuntamiento is the Cathedral, the land-
mark and emblem of the town and the "Catedral Primada" of Spain. It
was built between 1227 and 1493 on the site of the town's principal
mosque, which itself had replaced a Visigothic church. It is Spain's finest
Gothic cathedral after that of Burgos. The building of the cathedral was
initiated by Archbishop Rodrigo Jiménez de la Rada. The first architect
was a Frenchman named Martin, who was followed by Petrus Petri. In
the 90 m (295 ft) high north tower (1380–1440), from which there are fine
views, is the famous bell known as the Campana Gorda, cast in 1753,
which weighs 17 tonnes. The south tower, which has a Baroque dome,
remained unfinished. Illustration, p. 156.
    On the west front are three handsome Gothic doorways (1418–50)
with rich sculpture and relief decoration. On the central doorway, the
Puerta del Perdón, is a figure of the Virgin (by Juan Alemán) sitting on

★Cathedral

Open daily
10.30am–1pm,
3.30–6pm
(summer 7pm)

Catedral de Toledo

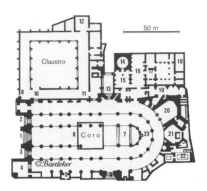

1 Puerta del Perdón
2 Puerta de la Torre
3 Puerto de los Escribanos
4 Capilla Mozárabe
5 Puerta Llana
6 Puerta de los Leones
7 Capilla Mayor
8 Trascoro
9 Puerta del Mollete
10 Puerta de la Presentación
11 Puerta de Santa Catalina
12 Capilla de San Blas
13 Puerta de la Chapineria
   (Puerta del Reloj)
14 Ochavo
15 Capilla del Virgen del Sagrario
16 Sacristía
17 Vestuario (Vestry)
18 Ropería (Wardrobe)
19 Capilla de Reyes Nuevos
20 Capilla de Santiago
21 Capilla de San Ildefonso
22 Sala Capitular
23 Transparente

the bishop's throne on Assumption Day and presenting San Ildefonso with a priest's vestments. Of the beautiful side doorways the finest is the Puerta de los Leones (Lion Doorway), in richly ornamented Gothic style (1458–66), at the end of the south transept. On the north side of the cathedral, between the cloister and the sacristy, is the oldest of the doorways, the Puerta de la Chapinería or Puerta del Reloj (Clock Doorway; 13th century). From the cloister the Puerta Catalina leads into the interior of the cathedral.

Interior The cathedral is entered through the left-hand doorway on the west front, the Puerta de la Mollete (the Muffin Doorway), at which the poor were given food. The nave, 110 m (361 ft) long (not counting the Capilla de San Ildefonso), with double aisles and 88 piers formed of clustered shafts, is truly impressive. The choir's magnificent stained glass dates from between 1418 and 1561. Also in the choir (Coro), which is enclosed by a Plateresque *reja* of 1548, are choir stalls *(sillería)* of walnut-wood, a masterpiece of Renaissance carving. In the lower section, the Sillería Baja, the stalls are backed by 54 historical reliefs by Rodrigo Alemán depicting scenes from the conquest of Granada. In the upper section, the richly carved Sillería Alta (completed in 1543), the left-hand side has carvings of Biblical scenes by Alonso Berruguete, including an alabaster "Transfiguration", while the right-hand side has carvings by Felipe Vigarny. On the free-standing altar in the choir is a Romanesque figure of the Virgen Blanca (*c.* 1300).

The richly gilded **Capilla Mayor** has a magnificently decorated Plateresque *reja* of 1548. The huge altar (1504) of gilded and painted larchwood has four tiers of life-size figures depicting New Testament scenes; in the centre is a fine pyramidal monstrance. On either side of the high altar are the tombs *(sepulcros reales)* of Sancho II and his son (right) and Alfonso VII (left). On the left of the Capilla Major is the tomb of Cardinal González de Mendoza. On the rear side of the Capilla Mayor, the walls of which are decorated with numerous figures of saints and reliefs, are the tomb of Cardinal Diego de Astorga and the Transparente, a massive marble altar in Churrigueresque style dedicated to the Virgin with a painted openwork dome (1722).

The chapels in the **ambulatory** (Girola) all contain finely carved tombs. In the central chapel, the Capilla de San Ildefonso, is the tomb of Cardinal Albornoz (14th century; in the centre); adjoining it on the left is the Capilla de Santiago, in rich Gothic style, with the magnificent Gothic marble tombs of Condestable Álvaro de Luna and his wife (1488).

Immediately adjoining this chapel is a passage leading to the **Capilla de Reyes Nuevos**, sumptuously decorated in Plateresque style, which contains the tomb of Enrique II de Trastamara.

From the ambulatory a splendidly decorated doorway leads into the **chapter house** (Sala Capitular) of 1512, which has a superb artesonado ceiling. The 13 wall paintings depicting archbishops of Toledo are mostly by Juan de Borgoña; two are by Goya (1804 and 1823).

To the left of the ambulatory is the entrance to the **sacristy** (1592–1616), which now contains a small **picture gallery**. On the altar is the "Unclothing of Christ" ("El Expolio"; 1579) by El Greco; to the right of the altar is Goya's "Arrest of Christ" (1788); and on the walls is a series of 16 figures of apostles by El Greco. There are also paintings by Morales, van Dyck, Raphael, Titian and Mengs and a sculptured figure of St Francis by Pedro de Mena. The display of pictures extends into the adjoining Vestuario and the Salas Nuevas (New Rooms) of the Cathedral Museum.

On the west side of the sacristy is the **Ochavo**, an octagonal chamber with a tall dome, painted by Ricci and Carreño in 1670. It contains around 400 relics. The adjoining Capilla de la Virgen del Sagrario has a richly clad and much revered figure of the Virgin enthroned (c. 1200).

The **cathedral's treasury** (Tesoro Mayor) is housed in the Capilla de San Juan under the north tower. Its greatest treasure is a famous monstrance by Enrique de Arfe (1524), almost 3 m (10 ft) high and weighing 172 kg, with 260 silver gilt statuettes.

Immediately to the right of the main entrance is the **Capilla Mozárabe** (1504), in which at 9.30am on weekdays and 9.45am on Sundays mass is said according to the Mozarabic rite, which goes back to Visigothic times.
   In the right-hand aisle is the inner side of the Puerta de los Leones, with fine 16th century wood reliefs. Above it is the Imperial Organ of 1594, with a stone sounding-board.

On the north side of the cathedral is the **cloister** (Claustro), which was begun in 1389. On the walls of the lower cloister (Claustro Bajo) are frescoes by Francisco Bayeu and Maella (1776). At the north-east corner is the Capilla de San Blas (closed), with Florentine ceiling paintings of the early 15th century. Adjoining the upper cloister (Claustro Alto) is a room (entered from Calle Hombre de Palo) in which the *gigantones,* the 6 m (20 ft) high figures clad in 18th century garb which feature in traditional processions, are kept.

Outside the west front of the cathedral is the Plaza del Ayuntamiento. On the north side of the square is the 18th century **Palacio Arzobispal** (Archbishop's Palace), on the north-west and south-west sides the **Ayuntamiento** (Town Hall; 1618), with two handsome corner towers and a beautiful tile frieze of 1595 in the chapter room, designed by Jorge Manuel Theotocopuli, El Greco's son.

Plaza del Ayuntamiento

North-west of the cathedral are a number of notable churches. Calle del Nuncio Viejo leads to Calle Alfonso X, and in a square opening off this street on the left is the imposing Baroque façade of the twin-towered church of San Ildefonso, which contains two works by El Greco.

San Ildefonso

A little way to the west can be seen the Moorish tower of the former church of San Román (13th century), which now houses the **Museo de**

San Román

los Concilios y de Cultura Visigoda. The church has 13th century frescoes and a fine 18th century retablo. The museum displays Visigothic antiquities, including crowns, sculpture and jewellery.

Farther north-west is the monastery of **Santo Domingo el Antiguo**. In the church is El Greco's tomb.

𝔁

Alcázar

On the highest point in Toledo, above the eastern slope of the hill, is the Alcázar, which can be reached on a street running up from the Plaza de Zocodover. Built on the site of a Roman fort, the Alcázar has a square ground-plan with corner towers and a façade designed by Covarrubias and Herrera (16th century). It was burned down by the French in 1810, and after rebuilding was occupied by a military academy from 1882 onwards. At the beginning of the Civil War it withstood a 68-day siege and bombardment by Republican forces. Rebuilt after the war, it now houses a museum of the Civil War and a collection of weapons and uniforms. Consideration is being given to the possible transfer of the Army Museum in Madrid (see Museo del Ejército) to the Alcázar. (The museum is at present closed for renovation.)

Open Tue.–Sat.
9.30am– 1.30pm,
4–5.30pm, Sun.
10am–1pm,
4–5.30pm

The busy Plaza de Zocodover, triangular in plan, was already the hub of the town's life and its market square in Moorish times (its name comes from the Arabic Suq ed-Dawab, "cattle market"). It was probably also the scene of executions and the burning of heretics at the stake – activities reflected in the name of the nearby Moorish town gate, the **Arco de la Sangre** (Arch of Blood).

Plaza de
Zocodover

The Arco de la Sangre leads to the former Hospital de Santa Cruz, built in the 15th/16th century for Cardinal Mendoza, Isabella the Catholic's confessor, by Enrique de Egas, in Renaissance style with an early Plateresque doorway. On the doorway the cardinal is shown kneeling before the Cross between SS. Peter, Paul and Helen. The hospital is now occupied by the Museo de Santa Cruz, which comprises a number of different collections.

In the archaeological section, displayed in rooms round the patio, are prehistoric, Roman and Visigothic antiquities.

The art collection begins in three rooms on the ground floor. The most notable items on display are a number of Flemish tapestries of the 15th and 16th centuries and a carpet with signs of the zodiac made for the cathedral. There are also a number of works by old masters, including a Flemish portrait of Philibert II of Savoy and a "Christ in Chains" by Morales, as well as Don John of Austria's standard from his flagship in the battle of Lepanto in 1571. The finest paintings and works of sculpture are displayed on the upper floor. They include a retablo dedicated to the Virgin with figures by Alonso Berruguete, works by Luis Tristán, a pupil of El Greco, Ribera and the Master of Sigena, a "Crucifixion" by Goya and an outstanding collection of El Grecos, including his "Assumption", a late work. Also on the upper floor is the museum's collection of applied and decorative art.

★★Museo de
Santa Cruz

Open Tue.–Sat.
10am–6.30pm,
Sun. 10am–2pm,
Mon. 10am–2pm,
4–6.30pm

Below the Museo de Santa Cruz, to the east, the Puente de Alcántara (closed to motor traffic) crosses the gorge of the Tagus. The bridge was originally Roman but was completely rebuilt by the Moors in 866 and was given its present form mainly in the 13th and 14th centuries. At the west end of the bridge is the Puerta de Alcántara, a gate-tower built in 1484, and at the east end a Baroque gate of 1721. From the bridge there is a magnificent view of the town, rising steeply up the hill to the Alcázar.

★Puente de
Alcántara

Downstream can be seen the Puente Nuevo (1933) and some remains of

Castillo de San
Servando

◀ *The elegant tower of Toledo Cathedral dominates, along with the Alcázar, the townscape of Toledo*

the Roman aqueduct. High above the left bank of the river rears the 11th century Castillo de San Servando.

★Puerta del Sol

North-west of the Plaza de Zocodover is the Puerta del Sol, a massive twin-towered gate in Mudéjar style (14th century) which formed part of the town's inner (older) ring of walls.

Cristo de la Luz

Through the Puerta del Sol and beyond a small park is Toledo's only surviving mosque, which was built around 1000 on the remains of a Visigothic church. In 1182 it was extended by the addition of an apse and consecrated as the church of Cristo de la Luz. The church, built of brick, thus consists of two parts. The older part has nine domes and six narrow intersecting aisles, with four sturdy columns supporting twelve arches and the domes. The other part has two domes, one round and the other semicircular. The choir has remains of Romanesque wall paintings. On the façade of the church is a Kufic inscription, "Allah is great".

Santiago del Arrabal

From the Puerta del Sol Calle Real del Arrabal leads to the Puerta de Valmardón, part of the inner, Arab circuit of walls, and continues north to the outer district (arrabal) of Santiago, with the Mudéjar-style church of Santiago (13th century).

★Puerta Vieja de Bisagra

Near the church, in the town walls, is another Moorish gate, the Puerta Vieja de Bisagra (early 9th century). Alfonso VI is said to have entered the town through this gate in 1085.

Puerta Nueva de Bisagra

Along the town walls to the right is a double gateway, the Puerta Nueva de Bisagra (rebuilt 1550), a magnificent example of military architecture. On the town side is an inner gate topped by two towers leading into a forecourt containing a statue of Charles V; on the outside is a large imperial coat of arms.

★Hospital de Tavera

From the Puerta Nueva the park-like Paseo de Merchán leads to the outer district of Las Covachuelas, in which is the large complex of the Hospital de Tavera (1541–99). The church (1561) has a marble façade by Alonso Berruguete. In the interior, under the dome, is the handsome tomb (also by Berruguete – his last work) of Cardinal Tavera, founder of the Hospital. The retable was designed by El Greco.

Some of the **residential apartments**, which were decorated and furnished in 17th century style for the Duchess of Lerma, are open to the public. They are of interest mainly for the fine paintings they contain, including works by Titian, Claudio Coello ("Portrait of the Infanta Clara Eugenia"), El Greco (including his last work, the "Baptism of Christ"), Tintoretto ("Birth of the Messiah") and Zurbarán. Regrettably, the faithfully reconstructed 16th century pharmacy is not open to the public, but the library and archives (with El Greco's "Holy Family") can be seen.
The apartments are usually open daily 10am–1.30pm, 3.30–6pm.

★★Santo Tomé

To the west of the Cathedral, in Plaza Santo Tomé, which lies on the edge of the old Jewish quarter, the Judería, is the church of Santo Tomé. Originally a mosque, it was remodelled in Gothic style by the Count of Orgaz in the 14th century, with the addition of a handsome Mudéjar-style tower. In an adjoining building is displayed one of El Greco's principal works, **"The Burial of the Count of Orgaz"** (1586), which depicts the legend that St Stephen and St Augustine conduct the dead to heaven (open daily 10am–1.45pm, 3.30–6.45pm, winter till 5.45pm).

Museo de Arte Contemporáneo

To the north of Santo Tomé, in Calle de las Bulas, is the Museo de Arte Contemporáneo, which is devoted to the art of the 20th century.

To the south of the church is the Taller del Moro (Moor's Workshop), actually a 15th century palace, which now houses a small Museo de Arte Mudéjar, with examples of Mudéjar stone-carving.

Taller del Moro

In the same square is the Palacio de Fuensalida, in which Isabella the Catholic died in 1539.

Palacio de Fuensalida

Calle de los Alamillos leads to Calle Samuel Levi, in which is the Casa El Greco. The house originally belonged to Samuel Ha-Levi, a Jewish banker's son who became Pedro I's treasurer and was tortured to death on the king's orders after the bankrupt royal treasury was restored to order with his help. It is not certain that El Greco actually lived in this house or died in it in 1614, but it is a fine example of a 15th century Toledan mansion. It was renovated in 1906 and furnished with period furniture and works by El Greco. Open Tue.–Sat. 10am–1.45pm, 4–5.45pm, Sun. 10am–1.45pm.

★Casa y Museo El Greco

In the adjoining building is the Museo el Greco, which was established in 1910. It shows in three rooms on the first floor more than 20 paintings by El Greco, including the famous "View of Toledo" , "Christ with the Apostles", "The Crowning with the Crown of Thorns" and "St Bernardino in the Chapel". In other rooms are paintings by other famous Spanish masters, including Zurbarán and Miranda.

A few yards away from the El Greco House is the Sinagoga del Tránsito, founded by Samuel Ha Levi. After the expulsion of the Jews in 1492 it was handed over to the knightly Order of Calatrava. With an unpretentious exterior, the interior has sumptuous Mudéjar decoration at the east end of the choir and on the upper part of the walls, and a beautiful cedarwood artesonado ceiling. The gallery on the right-hand side was for women only. On the upper part of the side walls is a frieze with the arms of Castile and León and above this a frieze in Hebrew script in praise of Jahweh, Samuel Ha-Levi and Pedro I, as well as a gallery with 54 arches, decorated with delicate stone tracery.

★★Sinagoga del Tránsito

In the adjoining rooms is the Museo Sefardí, which is devoted to the history and culture of the Jews in Spain (the Sephardim). Among the exhibits is the Tarragona Sarcophagus, with a trilingual inscription in Hebrew. Latin and Greek. Open Tue.–Sat. 10am–1.45pm, 4–5.45pm, Sun. 10am–1.45pm.

Museo Sefardí

The church of Santa María la Blanca is a former synagogue, the second of Toledo's surviving synagogues. Built in the 12th/13th century in Mudéjar style, it was handed over to the Order of Calatrava and since 1405 has been a Christian church. The interior has a fine artesonado ceiling and pine-cone capitals on its 28 horseshoe-shaped arches. Open daily 10am–1.45pm, 3.30–7pm, winter 5.45pm.

★Santa María la Blanca

North-west of the Judería is the Franciscan friary of San Juan de los Reyes, built in 1476 after the victory over the Portuguese at Toro as the burial-place of the Catholic Monarchs and their descendants but completed only in the 17th century. On the outer walls of the church (begun in 1553), which has an Isabelline main doorway by Covarrubias, are the chains of Christians freed from Moorish captivity.

★Monasterio de San Juan de los Reyes

Open daily 10am– 1.45pm, 3.30– 7pm, winter 6pm

In the interior, finely decorated by Juan Gris, the most notable features are a frieze of the arms of the Catholic Monarchs borne by eagles in the transept, the vaulting of the gallery in the choir and the altar by Felipe Vigarny and Francisco de Comontes. To the south-east is the cloister (1504), one of the finest achievements of the Late Gothic style in Spain; the upper gallery has an elaborate artesonado ceiling.

Puerta del Cambrón	North-west of the church a road runs down to the Puerta del Cambrón (Gate of the Thorn-Bush), an imposing double gateway originally built by the Visigoths, rebuilt in the 11th century by the Moors and again rebuilt in the 16th century.
Ermita del Cristo de la Vega	From the Puerta del Cambrón a road leads under the bypass to the Ermita del Cristo de la Vega, outside the town walls. There was a small church here in the 4th century which was rebuilt after 660 after St Leocadius appeared here to St Ildefonso, archbishop of Toledo. The apse of this church still survives.
Puente de San Martín	South-west of the church of San Juan and the Puerta del Cambrón is the Puente de San Martín (1212, rebuilt 1390), from which there is a magnificent view of the Tagus gorge 30 m (100 ft) below.

Surroundings

Illescas	On the way from Madrid to Toledo it is worth stopping in Illescas, which lies 2 km (1½ mi.) west of N 401. In this beautiful little town (alt. 588 m (1929 ft)) Charles V met his prisoner, François I of France, after the battle of Pavia in 1525. The church of the Hospital de la Caridad had five pictures by El Greco, now in the Museo de Santa Cruz in Toledo: an "Annunciation", a "Nativity", a "Coronation of the Virgin", "Compassion" and "San Ildefonso". The parish church has a very beautiful bell-tower.
Aranjuez	54 km (34 mi.) north-east: see entry
Chinchón	See Aranjuez

Torre de España   O 8

Location Avenida de Guadalajara	The Torre de España television tower, popularly known as El Pirulí, was completed in time for the World Cup football matches of 1982.
Metro O'Donnell	The 220 m (720 ft) high tower to the south of the Parque de la Fuente del Berro, near the M 30 motorway, is a new landmark in Madrid. It is not open to the public. Madrid's only high viewpoint is the Faro de Moncloa near the Ciudad Universitaria (see entry).

Town Hall

See Plaza de la Villa

Las Ventas   O 6

Location Alcalá 221	For aficionados of bullfighting Madrid's bullring of Las Ventas, known as La Monumental, is the most important in the world. Until the 18th century bullfights *(corridas)* took place in the Plaza Mayor (see entry); then in 1754 Madrid's first bullring, designed by Ventura Rodríguez, was inaugurated in Calle de Alcalá. Built of stone, with wooden benches, it could seat 12,000 spectators. When the town grew towards the north-east the bullring was moved from its site in Calle de Alcalá – now occupied by the Palace of Sport – to the outer district of Las Ventas. The new bullring, in neo-Mudéjar style, has seating for 23,000 spectators. It was inaugurated in 1934 by the toreros Juan Belmonte, Marcial Lalanda and Cagancho. After the Civil War it was the scene of triumphs by such
Metro Ventas	
Buses 12, 21, 38, 53	

Madrid's Las Ventas bullring, known as La Monumental

celebrated matadors as Manolete, Arruza, Dominguín, Litri, Bienvenida and Ordóñez.

The leading Spanish bullfighting school, the Escuela Nacional de Tauromaquía, is on the outskirts of Madrid. The bullfighting season begins in May and ends in October. The high point of the season is the Feria de San Isidro between May and June, when there are bullfights every day. See the Baedeker Special, p. 162.

The Museo Taurino (Bullfighting Museum) at Las Ventas displays posters, costumes, bullfighting weapons and mementos of leading matadors (open Tue.–Fri. 9.30am–1pm, Sun. 10am–1pm).

Museo Taurino

Viaducto

E 10

Sacchetti, architect of the Royal Palace (see Palacio Real), had a long cherished plan for providing a direct link between the Palace and the church of San Francisco el Grande (see entry) by building a bridge over Calle de Segovia, but his revolutionary town-planning project became reality only in 1874. Work on the construction of the Viaduct began in the brief reign of King Amadeo d'Aosta, and it was completed in 1874, under the short-lived First Republic. The first Viaduct, an iron structure on stone foundations, was 130 m (426 ft) long by 13 m (43 ft) wide and spanned Calle de Segovia at a height of 23 m (75 ft). This first bridge soon began to show its age, and was completely rebuilt fifty years after its construction. The rebuilding began under the Second Republic but was not completed until 1942. Further restoration work has been carried out in recent years

The area round the Viaduct, which has been the scene of many suicides and attempted suicides, offers fine views of the Casa de Campo (see entry) and the sea of roofs of the old town.

Location
Calle de Bailén

Metro
Ópera/La Latina

Buses
3, 148

The "Alternative"

For aficionados of bullfighting Madrid's Plaza de Toros at Las Ventas is, along with Pamplona and ahead of Seville, Ronda and Bilbao, the most important bullring in the world. The most glorious moments in the life of a torero are when he is carried in triumph on the shoulders of his *cuadrilla* through the *puerta grande*, the main entrance of a bullring; and the Puerta Grande of Las Ventas is *the* gate of gates in the world of *tauromaquía*. On July 8th 1995, after a tremendous *novillada* (a fight with wild young bulls), this gate opened for the first time for a woman, Cristina Sánchez. But there was more to come. In May 1998 this 25-year-old girl passed her test as a master bullfighter. She had thus conquered what had been since time immemorial a male domain, achieving what other women had tried from time to time to do over the past 200 years. This ceremony, which can take place in other bullrings but brings the highest fame in Madrid, is called *tomar la alternativa*, "taking the alternative". It is called *dar la alternativa* when an experienced bullfighter gives a young torero in his *cuadra* (team) the opportunity of fighting his own bull in the same corrida as himself. When a matador retires from the ring and cuts off his pigtail this is called *cortar la coleta*.

It cost the world of *tauromaquía* an effort to accept a *mujer torero* – the term which has been provisionally adopted for a female bullfighter – who would not show, under the close-fitting *taleguilla* (bullfighter's breeches), always on the left, that which a man and torero must have to fight a bull. But the very critical Madrid public, who are roused to their cries of *"olé"* only by a first-class performance in the ring and tolerate the playing of pasodobles by the band only between fights, confirmed by their enthusiastic response to Cristina Sánchez's success that she possessed the two most important virtues of a bullfighter, *cojones y arte,* courage and skill – though there were still occasional cries on the lines of "Go and wash the dishes, that's your job".

What for many northern Europeans, and now for some Spaniards, is merely a bloody spectacle is for aficionados a high art. They speak of the *arte de lidiar,* the art of gaining control of the bull, winning the contest with him and mastering him not merely in the physical sense. For them the bullfight is one of the last surviving approximations to the age-old contest between man and animals. The advocates of bullfighting argue that Spanish fighting bulls, the *toros bravos,* are honoured and feted as scarcely any other animals in the world are. They have names and pedigrees and are spoiled for four years on the best grazing land in Andalusia, Extremadura, Castile and Navarre, and then die a stylish death in accordance with ancient rituals in less than a quarter of an hour. They enjoy more respect and better treatment than cattle in other countries, whose inglorious career is confined to the stock farm, the cattle-transporter and the slaughterhouse.

Historical traces of the fight between man and bull reach far back into prehistoric times in many different cultures. Until the present rules for the corrida evolved in the 18th century there were very varying forms of bullfight. During and after the Reconquista it was usually only members of the highest classes of society who fought bulls on horseback at court festivities or exercises in the use of weapons. In the course of the 18th century, when

the Bourbon rulers increasingly discouraged such sports at court, it was the servants of nobles who fought bulls on foot before an audience. The present-day art of bullfighting was originated by Francisco Romero, born about 1700 in the Andalusian town of Ronda. The systematic breeding of fighting bulls also began in the 18th century, and the pedigrees of the most celebrated bulls still date back to that period. Goya's series of etchings, "Tauromaquía", illustrated the historical moment at the end of the 18th century when the mounted bullfighter gave place to the *torero a pie,* who fought the bulls on foot.

Every year, between Easter and the end of autumn, there are around 1800 bullfights in Spain, in which some 11,000 fighting bulls are killed. The most important are the Corridas de San Isidro, when there are some 45 corridas in Madrid alone. Then, in the late afternoon, the aficionados gather in their thousands in the *plaza de toros.* Those who can afford it escape from the almost intolerable heat of the sunny side *(sol)* of the arena by buying the much more expensive tickets for the shady side *(sombra).* All of them sit on small leather cushions. After a good fight the spectators wave white handkerchiefs to award the matador the bull's ear as a trophy.

The ceremony begins with the *paseíllo,* the colourful entry of all the participants in the bullfight to the music of a pasodoble. The heavily embroidered costumes – those of the matadors, embroidered in gold, being known as the *traje de luces,* the "suit of lights" – are a survival from the aristocratic days of bullfighting and have changed very little since the 19th century. As a rule there are six fights during the afternoon, divided into three *tercios.* Before the bull can be killed by the matador in the third and final sequence of the ritual he must be first teased and weakened by the *cuadrilla.*

In the first *tercio de capa* the matador "greets" the bull with a brightly coloured cloak, and teases him so that the spectators can judge his qualities and the torero can assess the bull's strong points and weaknesses. During this *tercio* the picadors enter the ring. The bull attacks their well padded horses, again revealing his strength and his character, while its rider weakens the bull's neck muscles with his lance.

Each of the torero's dance-like movements has a name in the language of bullfighting. Only when the bull's will to fight has been broken and the torero can venture to turn his back on him, to the plaudits of the crowd, can the *coup de grâce* be give, The bull must lower his head to that the sword

Tercio de capa: the matador greets the bull

In the second *tercio* the banderilleros enter the ring. With short, rapid, dancelike footsteps they make straight for the bull and at the last moment step aside and plant two *banderillas* (darts ornamented with banderoles) in the bull's neck and shoulders. This is done three times, with a pair of banderillas being planted in the bull's neck each time.

The trumpets then blow for the third *tercio*, the *faena*. The matador enters the ring, and the main and final stage of the fight begins. The intelligence and skill of the man must now triumph over the half-ton weight of the bull. The torero must now gain control of the bull with a piece of scarlet cloth, the *muleta,* and steer him past his body. There is a proverb that says "A bull can only be deceived once: the second time he goes for the body."

(estoque) can be plunged in at a particular point in the back of his neck so as to hit the right artery and bring about the bull's death within seconds. If the matador delays the final stroke too long or fails to hit the vital spot the bull is despatched with a sword or dagger.

Ernest Hemingway, an aficionado, has described better than anyone else the anguish and respect of the torero in his contest with the bull, the drama and elegance but also the sadness of this ritual act of death in the arena. Courage, defiance of death and physical strength, but also an aesthetic sense and in certain movements a sense of eroticism are all concentrated on a hot afternoon in the bullring in a single figure, the torero. He is the incarnation of the proverbial Spanish machismo, now belonging to the past.

At the near end of the Viaduct, at the corner of the Calle Mayor, is the Palacio Uceda, built in the 16th century by a pupil of the Herreras, which now houses the Capitanía General and the Council of State. Beside the palace are steps leading down to Calle de Segovia and the winding lanes of the old Moorish quarter, the Morería.

Palacio Uceda

At the west end of the bridge the Cuesta de los Ciegos runs down to Plaza Gabriel Miró and the Jardines de las Vistillas. From the gardens, a popular place of resort, particularly on summer evenings, there are fine views over the roofs of Madrid.

Jardines de las Vistillas

La Zarzuela

The predecessor of the royal palace of La Zarzuela was an estate of that name between Madrid and El Pardo which was bought in 1625 by Don Fernando, Philip IV's brother. On this property, which passed into the king's hands a few years later, a hunting lodge in the Italian style was built by Juan Gómez de la Mora. Alterations were carried out in the reign of Charles IV. During the Civil War it was completely destroyed. The present palace of La Zarzuela, a modern and functional building which is now the home of the royal family, was built in the 1950s and has little resemblance to the hunting lodge of the Habsburg kings. The palace is not open to the public.

Excursion
15 km (9 mi.) NW

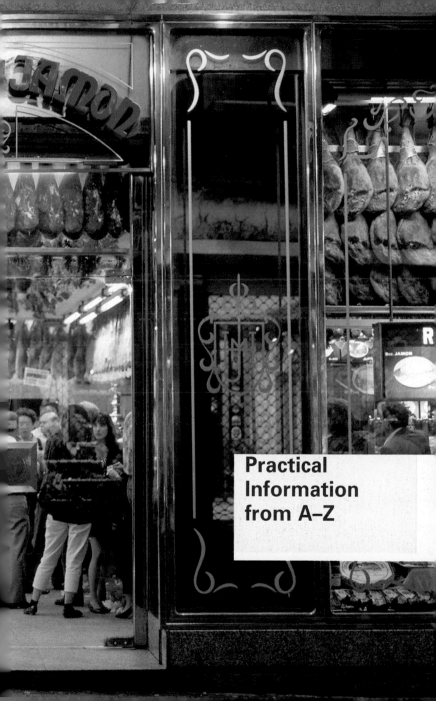

**Practical
Information
from A–Z**

Air Travel

Madrid's Barajas Airport lies 16 km (10 mi.) east of the city in the direction of Barcelona. Within the terminal building are a branch of the Spanish National Tourist Office, facilities for changing money, baggage lockers and shops.

Information

General information and flight information: tel. 913058334, 35 and 36
Left luggage: 7am–noon (maximum 7 days)
AENA (the Airport Company): tel. 913936000

Airport buses

Airport buses ply between the airport and the underground town terminal in Plaza de Colón (tel. 914316192: see Sights from A to Z , Plaza de

Taxis

Colón) every 15 minutes between 7am and 10pm. The journey takes

Metro

25 minutes. There are also plenty of taxis (see Taxis). An extension of the Metro: (Line 8) to the airport is due to come into operation at the end of 1999.

Airlines

In Madrid

Iberia
Velázquez 130 and Santa Cruz de Marcenado 2; tel. 915877592
Barajas Airport; tel. 915873664

British Airways
Barajas Airport; tel. 913058343

American Airlines
Pedro Teixeira 8 (5th floor); tel. 915972068 or 901100001

Iberia offices
abroad

United Kingdom:
Venture House
27–29 Glasshouse Street
London W1R 6JU
Tel. (020) 78300011

USA and Canada:
6100 Blue Lagoon Drive, Suite 200
Miami, FL 33126
Tel. (1800) 7724642

Banks

Opening hours

Banks *(bancos)* and savings banks *(cajas de ahorro)* are usually open Mon.–Fri. 9am–2pm. These times also apply to branches of some savings banks in shopping centres and at rail stations and airports. At airports there are banks and exchange offices open round the clock.

Breakdown Assistance (auxilio en carretera)

Motorways

On motorways there are almost always emergency telephones at convenient intervals. Help in the event of an accident or breakdown can also be obtained through the Guardia Civil or the traffic police *(policía de tráfico),* who patrol the motorways.

◀ *Museo del Jamón: an establishment with many branches in Madrid*

General emergency: 012
City police: 092
National police: 091
Traffic police: 914577700

Emergency
telephone
numbers

Breakdown and tow-away assistance can be obtained within Madrid through the city police (tel. 092), within the Madrid region through the traffic police (tel. 914577700).

Breakdown
service

Information on road conditions can be obtained by telephoning the Dirección General de Tráfico at 900123505 (toll free).

Road conditions
report

Breakdown assistance, as well as motoring information is also provided by the Spanish motoring organisation RACE.

Motoring
organisations

Real Automóvil Club de España
Calle José Abascal 10 E-28003; tel. 915947400
Breakdown assistance for AA members; tel. 915933333

Real Motoclub de España
Calle Orfila 10; tel. 913085813 or 913085661 (6–10pm)

Motorcycling club

In cases of emergency the Radio Nacional corporation will broadcast emergency messages for visitors travelling in Spain.

Emergency
messages

Business Hours

Banks are normally open Mon.–Fri. 9am–2pm and in winter Sat. 9.30am–1pm. Some branches of savings banks *(cajas de ahorro)* open on Saturday afternoons.
See also Banks and Currency

Banks

Chemists are closed on Saturday afternoon. Proposals for the liberalisation of opening hours are under consideration. For information on out-of-hours rota services by chemists tel. 098.

Chemists

Churches are almost always closed. They are open only for morning and evening services, at weekends and for church festivals.

Churches

The opening times of museums are given in the Sights from A to Z section of this guide. See also the list of museums in the entry (below) on museums.

Museums

District offices are open 8.30am–2pm. The head post office is open 9am–midnight (see Sights from A to Z, Plaza de la Cibeles).

Post offices

See also Postal and Telecommunications Services, Telephone.

Department stores in the Corte Inglese chain (Spain's only department store chain) are open 10am–9pm.

Shops

Ordinary shops are generally open Mon.–Sat. 9am–2pm and 5–8pm, but there are many exceptions. On several occasions during the year, particularly in the pre-Christmas period, the municipal authorities allow shops to open on Sundays. Some markets on the outskirts of Madrid are normally open on Sundays.

Shops in the VIPS chain, which offer a wide range of goods as well as cafés and restaurants, are open until 3am. There are VIPS shops at Gran Vía 43, Julián Romea 4, O'Donnell 17, Orense 16 and 79, Paseo de la Castellana 85, Paseo de la Habana 17, Princesa 5 and Velázquez 84 and 136.

Tourist offices   Tourist offices in Madrid (for addresses see Information) are open Mon.–Fri. 9am–7pm, Sat. 9am–1pm.

Camping

There are a range of camping sites in the Madrid area. Information about camping sites in Spain can be obtained from the Directorate-General of Tourism.

Madrid   Camping Osuna; tel. 917410510
Avenida de Logroño, at km 8 on N II (Madrid–Barcelona)
Camping Madrid; tel. 913022835
at km 7 on N I (Madrid–Burgos)

Arganda   Camping Arganda; tel. 918712663

Aranjuez   Soto del Castillio; tel. 918911395
at km 46.8 on the Madrid–Cádiz road

El Escorial   Camping-Caravaning El Escorial; tel. 918902412

Car Rental (coches de alquilar)

It is worth hiring a car for excursions from Madrid rather than for sight-seeing in the city. The hire charge for a lower-category car from one of the international rental firms, with unlimited mileage, is likely to range between 8000 and 12,000 ptas a day depending on the length of hire. Prices may, however, vary according to how busy the firm is. Local rental firms are often considerably cheaper.

Car rental firms in Madrid   Avis, Gran Vía 60; reservations, tel. 915484204/5
Europcar, Avenida de Partenon; reservations, tel. 917211222
Hertz, Gran Vía 88; reservations, tel. 915425805
Autos América, Cartagena 23; tel. 913567919
Viajes American Express, Plaza de las Cortes 2; tel. 913225500
Budget/Interrent, Alcántara 59; tel. 9 14 02 14 80 (weekend 913293337)
Unión Rent; reservations, tel. 902201040

Driving licence   When hiring a car you must produce your driving licence; most national licences are accepted.

Chemists

Chemists' shops are identified by a green cross on a white ground.

Opening hours   Chemists are open Mon.–Fri. 9.30am–2pm, 5–8pm, Sat. 10am–2pm.
Changes in the regulations on chemists' opening times are in contemplation, and it is expected that they will be permitted to open longer both during the day and in the evening. In the meantime there is a rota system under which certain chemists are open outside the normal hours. The address of the chemist on duty in a particular district is given in a notice ("Farmacia de Guardía") in all chemists' windows and in the newspapers. The chemist on duty can supply both prescribed and non-prescription drugs and other articles, but there is usually an additional "out of hours" charge.
For information about chemists on duty, tel. 098.

Cinemas

Madrid is a film-mad city. Along the Gran Vía (see Sights from A to Z, Gran Vía) are numbers of cinemas, usually showing the usual international films. The products of the rising Spanish film industry, which in the last twenty years has produced so many box-office hits and candidates for Oscars, with such directors as Carlos Saura and Pedro Almodóvar, can be seen in the arts and repertory cinemas. Film fans will find what they want in Calle Martín de los Heros with its two first-run cinemas, the Alphaville and Cines Renoir, which specialise in foreign and classic films.

Most cinemas have three shows a day, around 4, 7 and 10pm, as well as night showings on Saturday and Sunday.

Out of the profusion of cinemas in Madrid only a few representative houses can be mentioned here, all showing films with the original sound-track:
Alphaville, Martín de los Heros 14 (4 houses)
Bellas Artes, Marqués de Casa Riera 2 (one house)
Bogart, Cedaceros 7 (one house)
Cine Doré, Santa Isabel 3. In this cinema is the Filmoteca Española (shows Tue.–Sun. at 4.30, 6.30, 7.30, 9.30 and 10.30pm; café and restaurant, open 1pm–12.30am; bookshop, open 4–10pm).
Cines Renoir, Martín de los Heros 12 (5 houses)
Ideal Multicines, Doctor Cortezo 6 (9 houses)
Multicines Picasso, Francisco de Rojas 10 (4 houses)
Palacio de la Música, Gran Vía 35 (3 houses)

The Week of Experimental Films takes place at the beginning of February. The Madrid Film Festival, IMAGFIC, is held annually in spring; originally devoted exclusively to science fiction, it is now a shop-window for the international film. Between July and September, during the Veranos de la Villa ("City Summers"), is the season of the open-air cinemas, particularly the one in the Parque del Oeste. In November the Filmoteca (see above, Cine Doré), in association with the Centro de Arte Reina Sofía, runs the Festival of Film Directors and the Festival of Women's Films.

Film festivals

To find out what's on in Madrid's cinemas, see the weekly "Guía del Ocio" ("Leisure Guide") or ask the city tourist office (see Information).

What's on

Cultural Centres

Madrid has a large number of cultural centres and foundations in which conferences, exhibitions and a variety of other events are held, offering visitors a wide range of cultural experiences.

Centro Cultural de la Villa de Madrid (see Sights from A to Z, Plaza de Colón), Plaza de Colón/Serrano; tel. 915756080. Buses 21, 51, 53.

City Cultural Centre

Each district of Madrid has several cultural centres, the addresses of which can be obtained from the City Cultural Centre.

District cultural centres

Ateneo (see Sights from A to Z, Ateneo Artístico, Científico y Literario), Prado 21; tel. 914296251. Lectures and other events.
Canal de Isabel II, Sala de Exposiciones, Santa Engracia 125; tel. 914451000.
Casa de América (centre for cultural exchange with Latin America), Palacio de Linares, Paseo de Recoletos 2; tel. 915954800.

Other institutes

Casa Monte (a foundation of the Caja de Madrid), San Martín 1; tel. 913792461. Exhibitions. Open daily 11am–2pm and 5–9pm, Sun. and pub. hols. 11am–2pm.

Centro Cultural Conde-Duque (see Sights from A to Z, Cuartel del Conde-Duque), Conde-Duque 1. Metro: Argüelles, Ventura-Rodríguez; buses 1, 2, 44. C. Information on exhibitions: tel. 915885824 and 915885834 (daily). Information on programme and libraries: tel. 915885735 (Mon.–Fri.).

Círculo de Bellas Artes (see entry in Sights from A to Z), Alcalá 44; tel. 913605400 and 9102422442. Lectures, film shows, etc.

Club de los Amigos de Unesco, Plaza Tirso de Molina 8; tel. 913691652.

Expo Fomento, Paseo de la Castellana 67 (Nuevos Ministerios). Architectural exhibitions.

Filmoteca Española (with library and café), Cine Doré, Santa Isabel 3; tel. 913691125. See Cinemas.

Fundación la Caixa, Serrano 60 and Paseo de la Castellana 51; tel. 914354833. Exhibitions, etc.

Hemeroteca Municipal (Municipal Newspaper Archives): for address and telephone number see above, Centro Cultural Conde-Duque.

Hemeroteca Nacional (National Newspaper Archives), in the National Library (see Sights from A to Z, Museo Arqueológico), Paseo de Recoletos 20.

Ibero-American Centre (see Sights from A to Z, Museo de América), Avenida de los Reyes Católicos 6; tel. 915492641. Lectures and cultural cooperation between Spain and South America.

Instituto Alemán (German Institute), Zurbarán 21; tel. 913913944. Lectures, discussions, exhibitions.

Instituto Francés (French Institute), Marqués de la Ensenada 12; tel. 913084950.

Instituto Italiano (Italian Institute), Mayor 86; tel. 915427680.

National Library (see Sights from A to Z, Museo Arqueológico), Paseo de Recoletos 20; tel. 915807800. Lectures, exhibitions, etc.

Planetarium, Parque Tierno Galván. Metro: Méndez Alvaro; buses 8, 102, 112, 117. See Museums, Planetario de Madrid.

Sala de Exposiciones, Palacio de Cristal, Palacio de Velázquez and Casa Vacas, Parque del Retiro (see Sights from A to Z, Parque del Retiro). Open daily 10am–6pm; closed Mon.

What's on

Information on current exhibitions and other events can be obtained from newspapers and the weekly "Guía del Ocio" ("Leisure Guide").

Currency

Since January 1st 1999 Spain, along with eleven other countries of the European Union (but not Britain), has been a member of the European Monetary Union, with the euro as their common currency. Until the euro comes into actual circulation, however, the exchange rates between the participating currencies are fixed by the European Central Bank. In spite of the introduction of the euro the Spanish national currency, the peseta, remains in circulation until June 2002. There are banknotes for 1000, 2000, 5000 and 10,000 pesetas and coins in denominations of 1, 5, 10, 25, 50, 100, 200 and 500 pesetas. There are also coins for 2000 pesetas, but these are seldom found in circulation. Older banknotes are still valid, but only recently minted coins are accepted: banks no longer exchange the older coins.

Currency regulations

There are no limits on the amount of Spanish currency that may be taken into or out of Spain, but amounts of 100,000 ptas in cash or open cheques must be declared, on pain of confiscation by the customs authorities.

Eurocheques up to 25,000 ptas can be cashed in Spain; but they are now less and less used, since the system is thought to be too complicated and too expensive. Even banks want to be rid of the system, and charge excessive commission. Foreign visitors should come equipped with travellers' cheques and/or draw money from automatic dispensers with their Eurocard.

If you lose your Eurocheque card you should report this at once to the issuing authority so that a stop can be put on it.

Eurocheques

Credit cards are widely used in Spain. and are accepted in almost all hotels, restaurants and shops, even small ones. The commonest are Master/Eurocard and Visa, followed at some distance by Diners Club and American Express (tel. 3225500)

If you lose a credit card you should at once inform the issuing authority at the telephone number given above or direct to their home number.

Credit cards

The best way to get pesetas is to draw them from an automatic dispenser with your Eurocard. The easiest way of paying for anything, with the lowest charges, is by credit card. In both cases the cost is charged to your account at the current exchange rate. This is also the case with the cashing of Eurocheques, though this involves the production of your passport and perhaps standing in a queue. There are high charges, on the other hand, for drawing money from a cash dispenser with your credit card. Even though "no commission" may be advertised, the exchange rate is likely to be poor. Even banks usually change money slightly below the official rate, as well as charging commission at about the same rate as for the use of a Eurocheque card in an automatic cash dispenser.

Banks change money during normal business hours, but many hotels, travel agencies and exchange offices will change it outside those hours.

Changing money

Automatic cash dispensers are known as *cajeros automáticos* or *tele-bancos*. The commonest are those of the 4 B, Servired and Red 6000 systems, all three of which are linked with the Eurocard network. Cash dispensers are usually found at all banks and are open 24 hours a day. After keying in your personal identity number (PIN) you can usually draw up to 25,000 or 30,000 ptas. It is advisable to use dispensers which are in the outer vestibule of a bank, with a door which can be closed as a protection against thieves.

Automatic telling machines

See entry

Banks

Customs Regulations

Since January 1st 1993 the countries of the European Union (EU), including Spain, Britain and Ireland, have belonged to a common economic area, the European internal market, within which there are in principle no restrictions on the movement of goods for personal use or consumption between the countries of the Union. There are, however, certain maximum quantities beyond which the customs authorities will require to be convinced that the goods are for personal and not for commercial or industrial use. These limits are in general: 800 cigarettes, 400 cigarillos, 200 cigars, 1 kilogram (2.2 lb) of tobacco, 10 litres of spirits, 20 litres of fortified wines, 90 litres of wine (including a maximum of 60 litres of sparkling wine) and 110 litres of beer. There are spot checks by customs officers to ensure that travellers are exporting or importing no more than they require for their own use.

Goods bought in duty-free shops (duty-free goods are due to end

Diplomatic Representation

Entry to Spain from non-EU countries — Travellers over the age of 17 coming from non-EU countries can take in the following quantities without payment of duty: 200 cigarettes or 50 cigars or 250 grams of tobacco, 2 litres of wine and 2 litres of sparkling wine or 1 litre of spirits with an alcohol content of over 22° vol. or 2 litres of spirits under 22° vol., 50 grams of perfume and a quarter of a litre of eau de cologne, 500 grams of coffee or 200 grams of instant coffee and 100 grams of tea or 40 grams of tea extract.

Diplomatic Representation

Embassies in Spain

United Kingdom — Calle Fernando el Santo16, Madrid
Tel. 913080618

USA — Calle Serrano 75, Madrid
Tel. 915872200

Canada — Calle Núñez de Balboa 35, Madrid
Tel. 914314300

Spanish embassies

United Kingdom — 39 Chesham Place, London SW1X 8SB
Tel. (0171) 2355555

USA — 2375 Pennsylvania Avenue NW, Washington DC 20037
Tel. (202) 4520100

Canada — 74 Stanley Avenue, Ottawa, Ontario K1M 1P4
Tel. (613) 7472252 and 7476181

Electricity

The standard voltage in Spain is 220 AC, though some old buildings may have 125 volts. There are occasional fluctuations in voltage and sometimes short power failures.

Electric plugs have two round pins. A suitable adaptor should be taken.

Emergencies

Emergency telephone numbers

General 112

Fire (Bomberos) 080

Police (Policía Nacional) 091

Municipal Police (Policía Municipal) 092

Guardía Civil 062

Events

Madrid has a variety of feast-days and festivals, mostly of religious origin, throughout the year. Each district *(barrio)* of the city has its patron saint, whose feast-day is celebrated by a popular festival – often including not only a pilgrimage but also various entirely secular activities such as a fair and musical and theatrical performances. We list below a few selected events.

Cabalgata de los Reyes. Spanish children used to receive their Christmas presents from the Three Kings at Epiphany, but many parents now celebrate Christmas on December 24th or 25th. On the evening before the official festival of the Three Kings, however, there is still a procession of gaily coloured floats from Calle de Alcalá by way of the Puerta del Sol and Calle Mayor to the Plaza Mayor.   *January 5th*

San Antón: festival in honour of the patron saint of the Hortaleza district.   *January 17th*

Carnavales de San Blas: carnival parades, music and the "Burial of the Sardine", which marks the beginning of Lent.
ARCO: International Art Fair (see Trade Fairs).   *February 3rd*

Semana Santa: solemn processions mark the beginning of Holy Week (Maundy Thursday). Opening of the bullfighting season at Las Ventas bullring.   *March/April*

Cumbre Flamenco: various events centred on flamenco (see Music).
Fiesta de la Primavera (Spring Festival) in the Hortaleza district.   *April*

Fiesta del Dos de Mayo, commemorating the 1808 war of liberation from the French (see Sights from A to Z, Plaza del Dos de Mayo). The main celebrations are on the Plaza del Dos de Mayo and Plaza de las Comendadoras.   *May 2nd*

San Isidro: celebrations in honour of Madrid's patron saint. Among the events are a popular festival on the San Isidro meadow, a firework display, ballet, Ópera and theatrical performances and jazz and rock concerts.
A high point in the celebrations is the Feria de San Isidro in the Las Ventas bullring (see Sights from A to Z, Las Ventas), which draws bullfighting aficionados from far and wide.
International Drama Festival in various Madrid theatres.
Antiquarian Book Fair on the Paseo de Recoletos.   *May 8th–15th*

Parque de Europa: popular festival in La Latina district.
Large Book Fair in the Retiro Park.   *May–June*

San Juan: Festivals in honour of the patron saint of the Batán, Retiro and Manoteras districts.   *June*

San Antonio de la Florida: Festival in the Argüelles district centred on the Ermita de San Antonio de la Florida (see entry in Sights from A to Z)   *June 9th–13th*

Beginning of the series of events known as the "Clásicos en Verano" ("Classics in Summer") and the "Veranos de la Villa" ("Summers of the City") organised by the municipal authorities, with films, music, theatre and ballet (see Theatres and Music).   *End of June*

Festivals in many districts (particularly Chamberí) in honour of the Virgen del Carmen, with fireworks, dancing and music.
 Tetuán de las Victorias: a variety of events commemorating the Spanish victory at Tetuán in 1860.   *July*

Excursions

August 6th–15th	Fiesta de San Cayetano, San Lorenzo and La Paloma: traditional celebrations in honour of the three patron saints in the Lavapiés and Rastro districts. The high point is the Verbena de la Paloma at the church of that name in Calle de la Paloma. Popular festival in the Entrevías district.
September	September 1st–14th: festival in the Barrio de Goya district. September 3rd–11th: Fiesta de la Melonera (festival of Arganzuela, celebrated since the 18th century). Beginning of the Autumn Festival of the Madrid Region (music, theatre, ballet: see Music and Theatres). Fiesta de Otoño: festival of St Michael, patron saint of the Chamartín district.
October 8th–12th	El Pilar: popular festivals in the Pilar and Salamanca districts. October 12th: Día de la Hispanidad, commemorating the discovery of America.
November 9th	Feast-day of the Virgen de la Almudena, the city's patroness.
December	Christmas Market on the Plaza Mayor (Christmas trees, Nativity groups, etc.): see Sights from A to Z, Plaza Mayor. New Year's Eve: ringing-in of the New Year on the Puerta del Sol (see Sights from A to Z, Puerta del Sol).
Information about events	The "Guía del Ocio" ("Leisure Guide") – published every Friday and usually available on all news-stands – lists the week's events (theatres, cinemas, exhibitions, etc.). Tourist information offices (see Information) distribute a monthly listing of events, "Qué hacer?". Information about cultural events is given in the publication "Información Cultural", available in the Ministry of Culture's bookshop at Gran Vía 51, and the periodical "Villa de Madrid", published by the municipal authorities and available in the Town Hall in Plaza de la Villa and the Ateneo at Calle del Prado 21, and in the newspapers.
See also	Music; Night Life; Theatres; Ticket Offices

Excursions

For visitors to Madrid with sufficient time at their disposal there are a great variety of places to visit in the surrounding area. Most of the excursions suggested in the Sights from A to Z section of this guide – the old university town of Alcalá de Henares, Guadalajara, Aranjuez, Toledo, Chinchón, the Escorial, the Valle de los Caídos, Riofrío, Segovia, La Granja, the Sierra de Guadarrama – are no more than 100 km (60 mi.) from the capital and can be reached on a day trip.

Among other places well worth visiting if time is available are Avila in Old Castile (110 km (68 mi.) north-west); Cuenca (165 km (103 mi.) south-east), with its famous *casas colgadas* ("hanging houses"); and the old university town of Salamanca (210 km (130 mi.) north-west). All three are UNESCO world heritage sites.

Excursions of this kind can be undertaken by public transport (bus, rail) or by hired car. There are also numerous organised trips; information about these can be obtained from tourist information offices (see Information).

You can also apply direct to the following travel agencies:
Pullmantur, Plaza de Oriente 8; tel. 915411066
Trapsatur, San Bernardo 23; tel. 915416320
Julia Tours, Gran Vía 68; tel. 915599605

The old university town of Alcalá de Henares, birthplace of Cervantes, is full of interest and within easy reach of Madrid

The Spanish railway company RENFE runs excursions to places round Madrid. There is, for example, the "Strawberry Train" (Tren de Fresa), with turn-of-the-century coaches, which plies between Madrid and Aranjuez. Information about such trips can be obtained from the Railway Museum at Paseo de las Delicias 61 (tel. 902228822). Tickets can be bought at the railway stations (for reservations tel. 913289020) or through a travel agency.

Rail trips

Excursions are also organised by the municipal tourist office, the Patronato de Turismo, Plaza Mayor 3 (tel. 915881636 or 913665477). A quarterly brochure obtainable from tourist information offices (see Information) lists the excursions on offer.

Municipal tourist office

Food and Drink

No one can say that the cuisine of Madrid lacks variety. As the melting-pot of the Spanish provinces it has assimilated the culinary specialities of all parts of Spain; and even eating habits vary (see Baedeker Special, p. 222).

Specialities

Land and sea, warm water and cold water, rich and fertile regions as well as barren and poverty-stricken ones: these contrasts in the geography of Spain are reflected in the variety of Spanish cuisine, all available in Madrid.

Popular all over Spain is the *tortilla de patata,* a potato omelette with many variations. *Huevos revueltas* (scrambled eggs) are also popular everywhere, served with a variety of vegetables or with *gambas* (prawns). Another favourite egg dish is *huevos a la flamenca* (raw eggs on tomato slices, sausage, ham, potatoes and a variety of vegetables, baked in the oven).

A typical Andalusian speciality for hot weather is *gazpacho,* a soup made from white bread, oil, garlic, tomatoes, paprika and cucumbers, served ice-cold in endless variations.

A great favourite of Madrileños is *callos* (tripe), served with olive oil, onions, paprika, *chorizo* (paprika sausage), *morcilla* (black blood sausage) and *jamón serrano* (salted ham).

Another typical Madrid dish is *cocido,* a stew of chick peas, meat, paprika sausage, bacon and vegetables. After cooking the solid elements are served separately from the stock, which is served as the first course *(sopa de cocido).* Also worth trying are *riñones al jerez* (kidneys in sherry) and braised bull's tail *(rabo de toro* or *rabo de buey).* At El Pardo you can have *jabalí* (wild boar). Two specialities of Old Castile are *cordero asado* and *cochinillo asado* (roast lamb and roast suckingpig). Other typical dishes are various stews such as *fabada asturiana* (red beans), *caldo gallego,* a vegetable hotpot from Galicia, the *olla aranesa* of Catalonia and the *judías blancas* (haricots) of La Granja. Spaniards are fond of red meat *(carne roja),* preferably ox meat *(buey).* A traditional dish for the poor is *migas* (breadcrumbs fried in oil with bacon and vegetables).

Seafood

Most kinds of seafood are best baked on a hot metal plate *(plancha)* or boiled in salt water *(cocido).* Particularly in southern Spain it is often fried *(pescaito frito)* or grilled. White fish such as sea bass *(lubina)* and sea bream *(besugo)* are best served *a la espada* (sliced through the backbone into separate pieces). *Pulpo a la gallega* (octopus boiled on paprika potatoes) is a Galician speciality. The Basques like to cook fish in the oven *(al horno);* classic Basque specialities are *merluza a la vasca* (hake) and *bacalao al pil pil* (salt cod with a delicate béchamel sauce and garlic). *Calamares en su tinta* (squid in its own ink) is also a Basque invention, though it has been taken over by the Valencians as a variant on their internationally known paella. Paella itself is usually known simply as *arroz* (rice) and served in innumerable variants.

Ham

Air-dried ham is a particular Spanish speciality. It is generally referred to as *jamón serrano,* but *jamón ibérico* is a very special kind. Only ham from a *cerdo ibérico* (an "Iberian pig", mostly free-range) is so designated; and to qualify for the even higher qualification of *de bellota* the pig must have spent its whole life grazing on acorns from holm-oak and cork-oak pasturage. This is a culinary delight of which the people of Madrid are particularly fond. The production of such delicacies has a particularly long tradition at Jabugo in the Andalusian province of Huelva, at Trevélez (Granada) and in Extremadura.

Vegetables

Spanish cuisine uses a great variety of vegetables – tomatoes, paprika, cucumbers, onions, garlic, etc. Among traditional dishes are *espinacas al estilo de Jaén* (spinach), *cazuela de habas verdes* (bean stew) and *habas con jamón* (beans with ham). Also popular are green asparagus from Navarre and peppers from Padrón in Galicia. The trouble with these little green peppers is that you cannot tell in advance which are sharp and which are sweet. Both are best when just grilled on a *plancha.*

Desserts and cakes

Spaniards like very sweet cakes, either as dessert at the end of a meal or in between times. Most of them are of Moorish origin, as is indicated by their use of cinnamon and sugar, which the Arabs brought to Spain. Other popular desserts are *flan* (caramel custard) and sweet egg yolk. Alternatives are fruit and *tarta helada* (ice-cream tart). A luxurious spe-

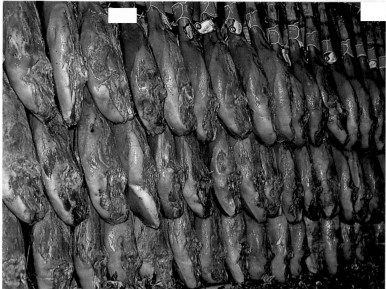

Air-dried Spanish ham (jamón): well worth taking home as a present

ciality is *churros con chocolate* (fried chou pastries dipped in hot chocolate), which are often eaten for breakfast.

See Language

Menu
(*lista de comidas*)

Drinks

After a meal or in between times Spaniards like to have a *café solo* (espresso), served in a small cup. *Café con leche* (coffee with plenty of milk) is mainly drunk for breakfast. There is also a half-way house, *café cortado* (coffee with a little milk).

Coffee

In addition to the internationally known soft drinks, freshly pressed fruit juices *(zumos)* are popular. Spaniards also drink a lot of mineral water. Madrid's tap-water is of excellent quality.

Cold drinks

Beer *(cerveza)* is now almost more popular than wine. The favourite kind is light-coloured lager type, served in small glasses *(cañas)*.

Beer

After a meal many people like a glass of brandy (usually from Jerez de la Frontera or El Puerto de Santa María) or an aniseed-flavoured schnapps. Particular delicacies are grape brandies – the *orujo blanco* of Galicia or the *marc de cava* of Catalonia.

Spirits

There are of course many excellent Spanish wines. The most famous is, naturally, sherry *(jerez),* which comes from the south of Spain. Of the more than 600 registered brands of sherry the best known internationally is probably the very dry Tio Pepe. Visitors should sample at least one real *fino,* one of the delicate sherries of distinctive character from the renowned wine-growing areas of Macharnudo, Añina, Carrascal and Balbaina near Jerez de la Frontera. First-class sherry,

Wine and sherry

known as manzanilla, also comes from the bodegas of Miraflores, near Sanlúcar de Barrameda.

Another Andalusian speciality is the very sweet dessert wine of Málaga.

Wine regions

The main wine-growing regions of Spain (for wines other than sherry) are Rioja, Ribera del Duero, Navarre and Catalonia. Quality wines from these regions are entitled to be labelled DO *(denominación de origen)*. Some wine-producers, particularly in Catalonia, use the French Cabernet Sauvignon grape, alongside the native Monastrell grape; others, particularly in the Rioja and Ribera del Duero regions, use the Spanish Tempranillo grape to produce a variety of quality and top-quality cask-matured wines. A distinction is made in Spain between table wines (with no indication of vintage), wines with the year of vintage and Crianza wines, which are aged for 6 to 12 months in wooden casks and put on the market in their third year. Even higher categories are Reserva, in which the wine must have been aged in casks for at least a year and comes on to the market in its fourth year, and Gran Reserva, in which the Crianza lasts for two years, followed by three years fermenting in bottle, reaching the market only in its sixth year.

Montilla is a sherry-like aperitif produced from Pedro Jiménez grapes grown on the warm limestone soils of Montilla and Moriles, some 180 km (110 mi.) inland from Córdoba. Among the best Spanish red wines are the full-bodied Torres wines of Catalonia. On the coast of Catalonia is the world's largest winery for the production of sparkling wines. This Paradés wine is well matured and very dry.

Tarragona is known for its sweet, slightly sparkling wines, Priorato for strong dry red wines. In the La Mancha plain south-east of Madrid the strong red wines of Valdepeñas are made from a mixture of red and white grapes and are drunk young. The Valencia and Utiel-Requeña areas produce red wines which are heavier and above all sweeter than those produced in the interior of the country.

Other important wine-growing areas are in Galicia (Albariño and Ribeiro), Aragon (the heavy Cariñena wines) and Navarre, which is famed for the first-class red wines of Señorío de Sarría.

Sangría, Sol y Sombra

Sangría is a mixture of wine, sugar, mineral water, fruit juice and brandy. Sol y Sombra is a cocktail based on Spanish brandy (e.g. Fundador, Osborne, Terry).

Drinks menu *(lista de bebidas)*

See Language

Galleries

Madrid has more than 140 art galleries. They are to be found mainly in Calle Claudio Coello and side streets opening off it in the Retiro and Salamanca quarter, in the city centre and in the Chamberí and Almagro districts. A regular publication, a leaflet called the "Guía de Arte", with listings of current exhibitions, can be obtained in tourist information offices (see Information) and in the galleries themselves. This information can also be obtained from the newspapers and from the weekly "Guía del Ocio" ("Leisure Guide": see Events).

Art Fair

The Feria Internacional de Arte Contemporáneo ARCO (see Trade Fairs), held annually in February, gives a good general view of the contemporary art scene.

Getting to Madrid

By car

There are various ways of getting from Britain to Madrid by car. One route is down through France by way of Bordeaux to the Spanish frontier at Hendaye, then on the motorway (toll) via San Sebastián to Burgos, and from there on N I (E 5), of motorway standard, to Madrid. The distance from San Sebastián to Madrid is 470 km (290 mi.). An alternative route is to follow a more easterly course through France to Perpignan and the Spanish frontier at La Junquera and continue via Barcelona to Zaragoza and from there on N II (E 90), of motorway standard, to Madrid. The distance from Barcelona to Madrid is 630 km (390 mi.).

Eurolines run a twice-weekly service from London to Madrid, leaving at 10pm on Mondays and Fridays and arriving at midnight on the following day. Information: Eurolines, 52 Grosvenor Gardens, London SW1; tel. (020) 77308235.

By bus

By Eurostar from London to Paris and then by overnight train from Paris Austerlitz to Madrid, the journey takes about 20 hours. Information: Rail Europe; tel. (0990) 848848.

By rail

There are daily flights by British Airways and the Spanish national airline Iberia from London Heathrow and Gatwick. Air UK has a daily flight from Stansted, and Viva Air (a subsidiary of Iberia) a daily flight from Gatwick. There are also charter flights from Gatwick, Manchester and Edinburgh.

By air

Information: British Airways, 156 Regent Street, London W1R 6LB; tel. (020) 74344700 and (0345) 222111; Iberia, Venture House, 27–29 Glasshouse Street, London W1R 6JU; tel. (020) 78300011.

Help for the Disabled

Federación Española de Deportes de Minusválidos
(Spanish Federation of Sports for the Handicapped)
Calle Ferraz 16; tel. 915414880 and 915419912

Information

Asociación de Parapléjicos y Grandes Minusválidos de la Comunidad de Madrid
(Association of Paraplegics and Severely Handicapped of Madrid Region)
Avenida Rafael Alberti 37; tel. 913031214
Asociación Española de Parapléjicos y Grandes Minusválidos (ASAPYM)

(Spanish Association of Paraplegics and Severely Handicapped)
Hospital Nacional de Parapléjicos, Finca de la Peralera
Apartado de correo (PO Box) 497, 45080 Toledo; tel. 925255379

Hotels

In addition to hotels *(hoteles)* with their own restaurant the following types of accommodation are distinguished in Spain: apartment hotels *(hoteles-apartamentos),* which have cooking facilities in the rooms but no restaurant or café; *hostales,* modest hotels which may not have a restaurant; guesthouses *(pensiones),* usually small, offering accommodation and full board; *paradores de turismo,* hotels belonging to the state-run chain of paradors; and *casas rurales,* which are often similar to guesthouses or apartment hotels and are usually let only for a period of several days. Designations such as Albergue, Fonda, Cortijo, Finca, Hospedería, Palacio or Posada in the name of a hotel refer to the particular architectural or historical qualities of the establishment.

Hotels

All hotels and *hostales* are required to keep "complaint books" *(libros or hojas de reclamación)*.

Categories

Hotels in Spain are classed in categories and awarded stars according to the facilities and amenities they offer. A one-star hotel must have at least a wash-hand basin in the rooms; a two-star hotel will have rooms with a private bath and will provide breakfast; a three-star hotel will also have telephones and television in the rooms and will have its own restaurant; four stars imply comfort and luxury; and five stars mark a luxury hotel. The highest category is *gran lujo* (top-class luxury) with five stars and the letters GL.

Prices

The official classification is not, however, an entirely reliable indication of price levels. In the following listings, therefore, an additional classification according to price category is used. A star (★) indicates a hotel with a particularly high standard of amenity. Attentive service can now be taken for granted in Madrid hotels. For a selection of particularly inviting hotels for excursions into the surroundings of Madrid see Baedeker Special, p. 188.

Hotel prices in Madrid are fairly uniform over the year, even during festivals like San Isidro and major trade fairs. But since most hotels depend on business travellers for much of their trade it may be possible at slack periods such as weekends and the month of August to negotiate a reduction when booking.

Hotel tariffs must be posted up in rooms. They do not normally include either breakfast (400–2000 ptas) or the value-added tax IVA. In many hotels the tax is added only in the final bill.

The following guide prices in the various price categories are for a double room without breakfast. The second figure is the high season rate. The tariff for a single room is 20–30 per cent lower than that of a double room.

L	over 30,000 ptas
A	20,000–29,900 ptas
B	10,000–19,900 ptas
C	up to 9,900 ptas

Hotel Guide

In addition to the hotels recommended here Madrid has many smaller *hostales*, sometimes lacking in amenity, with room prices around 3000 ptas. For a complete listing, consult the "Guía Oficial de Hoteles", which can be bought in tourist information offices, most bookshops and the larger news-stands.

Hotel booking agencies

Madrid has no central booking agency, but information about beds available can be obtained from the Brujula Viajes travel agency at the following addresses:
Chamartín Station, at Platform 7; tel. 913157894
Atocha Station, at Cercanías; tel. 915391173
Plaza de Colón, platform for airport buses; tel. 915759680

Madrid hotels (selection)

Five-star GL hotels

★NH Santo Mauro (L–A), Zurbano 36; tel. 913196900, fax 913085477, 36 rooms; dogs permitted. A relatively small hotel with a high standard of luxury; idyllic garden; swimming pool in former family vault of Duques de Santo Mauro; modern but cosy in Barcelona-style design.

★Ritz (L), Plaza de la Lealtad 5; tel. 915212857, fax 915328776; 158 rooms; dogs permitted. Prestige and style in their purest form. Since 1910 the hotel favoured by newly appointed ambassadors.

Villa Magna (L), Plaza de la Castellana 22; tel. 915871234, fax 914312286;

194 rooms; dogs permitted. A grandiose attempt to re-create the Ritz in a modern high-rise block.

Husa Princesa (A–B), Princesa 40; tel. 915423500, fax 915423501; 275 rooms. Centrally situated between Argüelles and Plaza de España; modern.

Five-star luxury hotels

Mindanao (B), Paseo San Francisco de Sales 15; tel. 915495500, fax 915445596; 281 rooms.

Occidental Miguel Ángel (L), Miguel Ángel 29; tel. 914428199, fax 914425320; 227 rooms. High-tech hotel on Paseo de la Castellana with classic décor.

★Palace (L), Plaza de las Cortes 7; tel. 913608000, fax 913608100; 440 rooms; dogs permitted. Since 1913 a high-class hotel patronised by bohemians like Hemingway and tourists following in their wake. Recently included in the ITT Luxury Collection.

Tryp Monte Real (A), Arroyofresno 17; tel. 913162140, fax 913163934; 77 rooms. Quiet situation in the residential district of Puerta de Hierro, near the Monte del Pardo woods.

★Wellington (L), Velázquez 8; tel. 915754400, fax 915764164; 273 rooms. Its attractive features are its situation in the select Salamanca district, near the Retiro Park, and its solid elegance.

Agumar (B–A), Paseo Reina Cristina 7; tel. 915526900, fax 914336095; 245 rooms. Recently renovated. Situated near Atocha Station, within easy reach of the great museums on the "Paseo del Arte".

Four-star hotels

Alameda (B), Avenida Logroño 100; tel. 917474800, fax 917478928; 145 rooms. Shuttle service to exhibition centre and airport.

Arosa (B), Salud 21; tel. 915321600, fax 915313127; 139 rooms; dogs permitted. Directly on Gran Vía. Recently renovated.

Barajas (B), Avenida Logroño 305; tel. 917477700, fax 917478717; 230 rooms. Convenient for exhibition centre and airport. Dogs permitted.

★La Casa Grande (A), Torrejón de Ardoz, Calle Madrid 2; tel. 916753900, fax 916750691; 8 rooms. Situated near the airport and Alcalá de Henares, this small hotel occupies a 16th century property which once belonged to the Jesuits. It contains a collection of icons, the result of the Habsburg rulers' relationships with the Tsars. In a suite now equipped with a sauna is a Baroque bed in which Catherine the Great once slept.

Carlton (B–A), Paseo de las Delicias 26; tel. 915397100, fax 915278510; 112 rooms. Near the Centro de Arte Reina Sofía.

Castellana Intercontinental (L), Paseo de la Castellana 49; tel. 913100200, fax 913195853; 306 rooms.

Castilla Plaza Silken (A), Paseo de la Castellana 220; tel. 913231186, fax 9131554406; 139 rooms. Weekend rates.

Chamartín (B), Augustín de Foxá; tel. 913344900, fax 917330214; 378 rooms.

Husa Conde de Orgaz (A–C), Avenida Moscatelar; tel. 913884099, fax 913880009; 91 rooms. Near airport and exhibition centre; good connection with city. Weekend rates.

★Emperador (A), Gran Vía 53; tel. 915472800, fax 915472817; 232 rooms. Centrally situated. Terrace with swimming pool and magnificent views.

★Emperatriz (A), López de Hoyos 4; tel. 915638088, fax 915639804; 158 rooms. Pleasant, comfortable but unfussy décor. Fine views from terraces of suites.

★Gran Hotel Conde Duque (A–B), Plaza Conde Valle Suchil 5; tel. 914477000, fax 914483569; 143 rooms. Quiet central situation in Argüelles district.

★Gran Versalles (A), Covarrubias 4 and 6; tel. 914475700, fax 914463987; 145 rooms. Central but quiet situation near Plaza Alonso Martínez.

★Holiday Inn Crowne Plaza (A), Edificio España, Plaza de España; tel. 915471200, fax 915482389; 306 rooms. Situated in the monumental Edificio España and well suited for sightseeing in central Madrid.

Liabeny (B), Salud 3; tel. 915319000, fax 915327421; 222 rooms. Central and comfortable.

Melia Madrid (L), Princesa 27; tel. 915418200, fax 915411988; 266 rooms. The most centrally situated hotel in this excellent Spanish chain, between Argüelles and Plaza de España.

Mayorazgo (B), Flor Baja 3; tel. 915472600, fax 915412485; 200 rooms. Centrally situated near the Northern Station; recently modernised.

NH Nacional (B), Paseo del Prado 45; tel. 914296629, fax 913691564; 369 rooms. The newest, and after the Santo Mauro (see above) the leading hotel of the progressive and well-run Catalan hotel chain in Madrid, between the Prado and the Centro de Arte Reina Sofía.

★NH Prisma (A), Santa Engracia 120; tel. 914419377, fax 914425851; 110 rooms. All rooms are suites with office/sitting-room and kitchen.

Serrano (B), Marqués de Villamejor 8; tel. 914355200, fax 914354849; 34 rooms. A small, quiet hotel in the Husa chain, in the Salamanca district.

Sofitel Madrid (L), Tutor 1; tel. 915419880, fax 915425736; 97 rooms. Central, with pleasant comfortable rooms, renovated in 1997. Dogs permitted.

★Santo Domingo (A–B), Plaza Santo Domingo 13; tel. 915479800, fax 915475995; 120 rooms. Opened 1995. An attractive and centrally situated hotel in the Style chain near Plaza de Callao. From rooms 502–507 on the top floor there are wide views over the roofs of the city; from room 508 there is a view of the Royal Palace. Dogs permitted.

★Tryp Reina Victoria (A), Plaza de Santa Ana 14; tel. 915314500, fax 915220307; 201 rooms. Now under statutory protection as a national monument, the hotel has been since time immemorial the haunt of bull-breeders and bullfighters. Restored to four-star status since its renovation in 1989. It lies in one of the liveliest quarters in Madrid.

Tryp Fenix (L), Hermosilla 2; tel. 914316700, fax 915760661; 226 rooms. Fine views of Castellana and Plaza de Colón. At present in course of renovation.

Villa Real (L), Plaza de las Cortes 10; tel. 914203767, fax 914202547; 115 rooms. Centrally situated facing the Cortes; more than comfortable.

Abeda (B), Alcántara 63; tel. 914011650, fax 914027591; 90 rooms.

Aramo (B), Paseo Santa María Cabeza 73; tel. 914739111, fax 914739214; 105 rooms

Aristos (B), Avenida de Pío XII 34; tel. 913450450, fax 913451023; 25 rooms. The accent here is on personal service. Guests can always be reached by mobile telephone.

Avión (B), Carretera de Barcelona, km 14.2; tel. 917476222, fax 9174727 36; 64 rooms. Near airport.

Carlos V (B), Maestro Victoria 5; tel. 915314100, fax 915313761; 67 rooms. A popular hotel, centrally situated near the Puerta del Sol.

Los Condes (B), Libreros 7; tel. 915215455, fax 915217882; 68 rooms. A family hotel on the Gran Vía.

Green Prado (B), Prado 11; tel. 913690234, fax 914292829; 45 rooms. Recently renovated, the hotel lies in the night-owls' quarter of Las Huertas, near the great museums. Consequently it is rather expensive.

Inglés (B), Echegaray 10; tel. 914296551, fax 914202423; 58 rooms. Cheap in its category, but over-valued with three stars.

Italia (C), Gonzalo Jiménez de Quesada 2; tel. 915224790, fax 915212891; 58 rooms. A comfortable *hostal* at the corner of the Gran Vía.

★Lorenzo (C), Infantas 26; tel. 915213057, fax 915327978; 16 rooms. A well-kept and comfortable *hostal* just off the Gran Vía. It stands on Plaza V. de Mella, on which building work is expected to continue until 2000.

Mercator (B–C), Atocha 123; tel. 914290500, fax 913691252; 89 rooms. Conveniently situated near the great museums.

Moderno (B), Arenal 2; tel. 915310900, fax 915313550; 97 rooms. Classic-style hotel near the Opera.

★NH Balboa (B), Núñez de Balboa 112; tel. 95630324, fax 915626980; 122 rooms. Situated in the shopping district of Salamanca. One of the most reliable and pleasantest hotels in its price category.

★NH Embajada (A), Santa Engracia 5; tel. 915940213, fax 914473312; 100 rooms. Well situated near Plaza Alonso Martínez; a very pleasant hotel, but also very dear.

Príncipe Pío (B), Cuesta de San Vicente 14; tel. 915470800, fax 915411117; 157 rooms. Near the centre; reasonably priced in its category.

Puerto de Toledo (B), Glorieta Puerta de Toledo 4; tel. 914747100, fax 914740747; 152 rooms. A functional and reasonably priced hotel near the Rastro quarter.

Regina (B), Alcalá 19; tel. 915214725, fax 915214725; 137 rooms.

★La Residencia de El Viso (B), Nervión 8; tel. 915640370, fax 915641965; 12 rooms. This hotel, in a turn-of-the-century villa, sets itself out to cater for business travellers, giving them the feeling, rarely enjoyed in other hotels, of being at home in Madrid. Excellent cuisine and beautiful garden.

Hotels

Reyes Católicos (B), Ángel 18; tel. 913658600, fax 915659867; 38 rooms.

Señorial (B), Leganitos 41; tel. 915427870; 60 rooms.

Sol in Alondras (B), José Abascal 8; tel. 914474000, fax 915938800; 72 rooms. Light and spacious rooms near the city centre in Chamberí.

Tirol (B), Marqués de Urquijo 4; tel. 915481900, fax 915413958; 95 rooms. A reasonably priced hotel in Argüelles.

Trafalgar (B–C), Trafalgar 35; tel. 914456200, fax 914466456; 48 rooms. Quiet and central.

Tryp Capitol (B), Gran Vía 41; tel. 915218391, fax 915217729; 147 rooms. Weekend rates.

Tryp Centro Norte (B), Mauricio Ravel 10; tel. 917333400, fax 913146047; 200 rooms. Near Chamartín. Weekend rates.

Tryp Gran Vía (B), Gran Vía 25; tel. 915221121, fax 915212424; 174 rooms.

Tryp Rex (B), Gran Vía 43; tel. 915474800, fax 915471238; 147 rooms.

Tryp Washington (B), Gran Vía 72; tel. 915417227, fax 915475199; 120 rooms.

Two-star hotels	Alexandra (C), San Bernardo 29–31; tel. 915420400, fax 915592825; 78 rooms.

Cliper (C), Chinchilla 6; tel. 915311700, fax 915311707; 54 rooms.

Francisco I (B), Arenal 15; tel. 915480204, fax 915422899; 58 rooms.

Isis (C), Antonio López 169; tel. 914763211, fax 914756924; 45 rooms.

Londres (C–B), Galdo 2; tel. 915314105; 57 rooms.

Mediodía (C), Plaza del Emperador Carlos V 8; tel. 915273060, fax 915307006; 165 rooms. Situated near Atocha Station. In need of renovation.

México (C), Gobernador 24; tel. 914292500, fax 914291001.

★Mora (C), Paseo del Prado 32; tel. 914201569, fax 914200564; 62 rooms. Renovated 1994. Sound-proof windows and air-conditioning. View of Botanic Gardens.

París (B), Alcalá 2; tel. 915216496, fax 915310188; 121 rooms.

Ramón de la Cruz (B), D. Ramón de la Cruz 14; tel. 914017200, fax 914022126.

One-star hotels	Europa (C), Carmen 4; tel. 915212900, fax 915214696.

★Monaco (C–B), Barbieri 5; tel. 915224630, fax 915211601; 28 rooms. King Alfonso XIII is said to have stayed here incognito at the beginning of the 20th century. The décor is still in the style of that period, though there is talk of renovation.

Terán (C), Aduana 19; tel. 915226424; 62 rooms.

Excursion hotels	See Baedeker Special, p. 198.

Information

Outside Spain

Spanish National Tourist Office
22–23 Manchester Square
London W1M 5AP
Tel. (020) 74868077

United Kingdom

Spanish National Tourist Office
666 Fifth Avenue
New York NY 10103
Tel. (212) 2658822

USA

Spanish National Tourist Office
Water Tower Place, Suite 915 East
845 North Michigan Avenue
Chicago IL 60611
Tel. (323) 6421992

Spanish National Tourist Office
8383 Wilshire Boulevard, Suite 956
Beverly Hills CA 90211
Tel. (323) 6587188

Spanish National Tourist Office
1221 Brickell Avenue
Miami FL 33131
Tel. (305) 3581992

Spanish National Tourist Office
2 Bloor Street West (34th floor)
Toronto
Ontario M4W 3E2
Tel. (416) 9613131

Canada

Internet

www.tourspain.es
www.munimadrid.es
www.paginas-amarillas.es

In Madrid

Oficina Municipal
Plaza Mayor 3
Tel. 913664874 and 913665477

Calle Duque de Medinaceli 2 (adjoining Palace Hotel)
Tel. 914294951 (closed at lunchtime, Sat. afternoon and Sun.)

Mercado Puerta de Toledo
Tel. 913641876

Barajas Airport
Terminal T 1
Tel. 913058656

Chamartín Station
Tel. 913159976

Sleep like a Marquis, a Monk or a Miller. . .

"Where have all the Madrileños gone?", a visitor might wonder as he strolls across the almost traffic-free Plaza de la Cibeles on a Sunday morning. The answer is that they are picnicking or cycling in the Sierra de Guadarrama, eating suckingpig in Segovia or have withdrawn to Guadalupe in the Montes de Toledo. Visitors can now explore at their leisure an almost empty city, or, like the Madrileños, they can seek refuge in the cool sierras or relax in one of the following excursion hotels.

The beautifully situated Parador de Cuenca

Belmonte (Cuenca)

The **Palacio de Buenavista Hospedería (C) occupies a 16th century palace. From the same period dates the Castillo, which can be explored at leisure and offers magnificent views over the La Mancha plain. 153 km (95 mi.) from Madrid; 22 rooms; Calle José Antonio González 2; tel. 969187580, fax 969187588.

Chinchón

On a trip to Aranjuez you can spend the night in the ****Parador de Chinchón (B–A) in this picturesque little town on the northern edge of La Mancha. The hotel occupies a former Augustinian monastery. 50 km (30 mi.) from Madrid; 38 rooms; Avenida Generalíssimo 1; tel. 918940836, fax 918940908.

Cuenca

The **Posada de San José (C) is the secret heart of this beautiful town. Simple but stylish, it occupies one of Cuenca's famous 17th century "hanging houses" (casas colgadas). 167 km (104 mi.) from Madrid; 30 rooms; Calle Julián Romero 4; tel. 969211300, fax 969230365.

If you want something more luxurious there is the ****Parador de Cuenca (B), housed in the 16th century Convento de San Pablo, with a swimming pool, tennis, a sauna – and the magical view of the casas colgadas. 62 rooms; Hoz del Huécar; tel. 969232320, fax 969232534.

La Granja de San Ildefonso

A short distance from the Royal Glass Factory and near the palace of the Bourbon kings with its beautiful fountains is the **Hotel las Fuentes (B), housed in the 19th century Isabelline palace of the Counts of Guijasalva. 87 km (55 mi.) from Madrid; 9 rooms; Calle Padre Claret 6; tel. 921471024, fax 921471741.

Guadalupe

In spite of its modest amenities a stay in the **Hospedería del Real Monasterio de Guadalupe (C) is a delight. The rooms open off the Gothic arcades of the monastery, which has a restaurant serving specialities of the region. 206 km (128 mi.) from Madrid; 47 rooms; Plaza Juan Carlos 1; tel. 927367000, fax 927367177.

An equally stylish alternative, in the luxury category, is the ****Parador de Guadalupe (B), in the former Hospital San Juan Bautista, which dates from the 16th century. 40 rooms; Calle

Marqués de la Romana 12; tel. 927367075, fax 927367076.

Navacerrada (Sierra de Guadarrama):
For a quiet night in the sierra there is the **Hotel Nava Real (C), occupying a 19th century mansion in the little town of Navacerrada. 52 km (32 mi.) from Madrid; 12 rooms; Calle de las Huertas; tel. 918531000, fax 918531240.

Patones de Arriba (Sierra de Guadarrama)
The ***El Tiempo Perdido (A) aims to offer every amenity to stressed city-dwellers in quest of their temps perdu – not merely by providing sports facilities and a swimming pool but by creating a very particular ambience, with first-class cuisine and peace and quiet – absolute peace and quiet in this remote village in the Sierra Pobre, 80 km (50 mi.) north of Madrid. Children and dogs are welcome. Travesía del Ayuntamiento 7; tel. 918432152, fax 918432148.

Rascafría (Sierra de Guadarrama)
The ****Santa María de El Paular (B), in a former Benedictine monastery in the valley of the Lozoya, offers complete relaxation in the beautiful scenery of the sierra, with tennis courts and a swimming pool among the attractions. Dogs are permitted. 46 km (29 mi.) from Madrid; at km 28.5 on M 604; tel. 918691011, fax 918691011.

Sotosalbos (Segovia)
The ***Hostal del Buen Amor (C), 14 km (9 mi.) from Segovia, is a good base from which to explore the surrounding area with its numerous castles and Romanesque churches. 12 rooms; Calle Eras 7; tel. 921403020, fax 921403022.

Sigüenza (Guadalajara)
The modest but attractive ***Hostal Molino de Alcuneza (B–C), near the historic town of Sigüenza, occupies an old water-mill which has been lovingly restored by its owners. 107 km (66 mi.) from Madrid; at km 0.5 on Carretera de Alboreca; tel. 949391501, fax 949391508.

Solosancho (Ávila)
Near the northern Castilian town of Ávila, under the north side of the Sierra de Gredos, is the **Hotel Sancho Estrada (B–C), in an old castle which was restored for the purpose. All the rooms except numbers 302 and 303 have small windows, while suite 110, in a tower, has no windows at all but is nevertheless particularly attractive. 137 km (85 mi.) from Madrid; Castillo de Villaviciosa; tel. and fax 920291082.

Toboso (La Mancha)
It might have been devised by Cervantes himself: the country hotel **Casa de la Torre (C) is modelled on "Don Quixote", from the furnishings to the menu. Its lies on the tourist Ruta de Don Quijote, in the town of his imaginary mistress Dulcinea del Toboso. 142 km (88 mi.) from Madrid; 7 rooms; Antonio Machado 16; tel. and fax 925568006.

Toledo
The ideal place to stay on a visit to Toledo is the ***Hostal del Cardenal (B–C), which occupies a palace built as a summer residence for Cardinal Lorenzana in the 18th century. It lies just beside one of the town gates, the Puerta de Bisagra, and has a beautiful garden. Dogs welcomed. 71 km (44 mi.) from Madrid; Paseo Recaredo 24; tel. 925224900, fax 925222991.

The finest view of Toledo is from the ****Parador Conde de Orgaz (B), opposite the town. 74 rooms; Cerro del Emperador; tel. 925221850, fax 925225166.

Villeveja de Lozoya (Sierra de Guadarrama)
In the northern part of the Sierra de Guadarrama, in the wide valley of the Río Lozoya, just off N I (the road to Burgos), is the Hospedería El Arco, in which are the foundations of a Moorish palace and a horseshoe arch. Dogs permitted. 64 km (40 mi.) from Madrid; 9 rooms; Calle Arco 6; tel. 918680911, fax 918681320.

Information by telephone: tel. 010 or 915404040
Punto de Información del Ministerio de Cultura
Plaza del Rey 1
Tel. 917017000
Internet: www.mcu.es

Patronato Municipal de Turismo
Plaza Mayor 3
Tel. 913664874

Young people

Oficina Nacional de Turismo e Intercambio de Jóvenes
Fernando el Católico 88
Tel. 915437412

Ofiicina de Información Juvenil "Sol"
Vestíbulo Principal (Metro: Puerta del Sol)
Tel. 915219511

Outside Madrid

Alcalá de Henares

Oficina de Turismo, Callejón de Santa María 1
E-28800 Alcalá de Henares; tel. 918892694

Aranjuez

Oficina de Turismo, Puente de Barcas
E-28300 Aranjuez; tel. 918910427

San Lorenzo de El Escorial

Oficina de Turismo, Floridablanca 10
E-28200 San Lorenzo de El Escorial; tel. 918901554

Guadalajara

Oficina de Turismo, Plaza de los Caídos 6
E-19071 Guadalajara; tel. 949211626

Segovia

Oficina de Turismo, Plaza Mayor 10
E-40001 Segovia; tel. 921460334

Toledo

Oficina de Turismo, Puerta de Bisagra
E-45003 Toledo; tel. 925220843

Language

As the mother tongue of over 220 million people Spanish is the most widely spoken of the Romance languages and, after English, the world's most important commercial language.

English is spoken by many older Spaniards and almost all young ones. But it adds greatly to the pleasure of a visit to Madrid, and may avoid some problems, to have at least some acquaintance with the language. In the larger hotels and shops English is widely understood, but visitors travelling on their own will find it a great help to have some idea of the pronunciation of Spanish, the basic rules of grammar and a few everyday expressions.

Pronunciation

Vowels are pronounced in the "continental" fashion, without the diphthongisation normal in English. The consonants *f, k, l, m, n, p, t* and *x* are normally pronounced much as in English; *b* has a softer pronunciation than in English, often approximating to *v* when it occurs between vowels; *c* before *e* or *i* is pronounced like *th* in "thin", otherwise like *k*;

ch as in English; *d* at the end of a word or between vowels is softened into the sound of *th* in "that"; *g* before *e* or *i* is like the Scottish *ch* in "loch" otherwise hard as in "go"; *h* is silent; *j* is the Scottish *ch*; *ll* is pronounced like */* followed by consonantal *y*, i.e. like *lli* in "million" (in many areas like *y* without the *l*); *ñ* like *n* followed by consonantal *y*, i.e. like *ni* in "onion".

The general rule is that words ending in a vowel or in n or s have the **stress** on the second-last syllable; words ending in any other consonant have the stress on the last syllable. Any departure from this rule is indicated by an acute accent on the stressed vowel. Thus Granada and Esteban, with the stress on the second-last syllable, and Santander and Jerez, with the stress on the last syllable, are spelt without the acute accent: contrast Málaga, Alcalá, Sebastián, Alcázar, Cádiz, etc. For this purpose the vowel combinations *ae, ao, eo, oa* and *oe* are regarded as constituting two syllables, all other combinations as monosyllabic: thus *paseo* has the stress on *e, patio* on *a,* without the need of an acute accent to indicate this. The accent is, however, required when the first vowel in the combinations *ia, ie, io, iu, ua, ue, ui, uo* and *uy* is to be stressed (e.g. *sillería, río),* and when the second vowel in the combinations *ai, au, ay, ei, eu, ey, oi, ou* and *oy* is to be stressed (e.g. *paraíso, baúl).*

There are two definite articles in Spanish, the masculine *el* (plural *los)* and the feminine *la* (plural *las).* There is a neuter form *lo* which is used only in certain combinations such as *lo bueno,* the good. The indefinite articles are *un* and *una.*

Declension: the genitive form is expressed by the preposition *de,* the dative by *a,* which in the masculine singular are combined with the definite article to form *del* and *al.*

In the case of personal nouns the accusative case is preceded by the preposition *a:* e.g. *Veo a Juan,* "I see Juan".

Yes/No	Sí/No	
Perhaps	Quizás/Tal vez	
Certainly!/Right!	¡De acuerdo!/ ¡Está bien!	
Please/Thank you	Por favor/Gracias	
Thank you very much	Muchas gracias	
Not at all	No hay de qué/De nada	
Excuse me	¡Perdón!	
Sorry?/What did you say?	¿Cómo dice/dices?	
I do not understand you	No le/la/te entiendo	
I speak only a little ...	Hablo sólo un poco de ...	
Can you help me, please?	¿Puede usted ayutarme, por favor?	
I should like ...	Quiero/Quisiera/Me gustaría ...	
I (do not) like ...	(No) me gusta ...	
Have you ...?	¿Tiene usted ...?	
What does it cost?	¿Cuánto cuesta?	
What time is it?	¿Qué hora es?	

Good morning!	¡Buenos días!	
Good day!	¡Buenos días!/¡Buenas tardes!	
Good evening!	¡Buenas tardes!/ ¡Buenas noches!	
Hallo!	¡Hola!/ ¿Qué tal?	
My name is ...	Me llamo ...	
What is your name?	¿Cómo se llama usted, por favor?	
How are you?	¿Qué tal (está usted)?	
Well, thank you.	Bien, gracias. ¿Y usted/tú?	
And how are you?		
Goodbye!	¡Adiós!/ ¡Hasta la vista!/ ¡Hasta luego!	

Language

	See you soon!	¡Hasta pronto!
	See you tomorrow!	¡Hasta mañana!
Travelling	Left/Right	A la izquierda/A la derecha
	Straight ahead	Todo seguido/Derecho
	Near/Far	Cerca/Lejos
	How far is it?	¿A qué distancia está?
	I should like to hire ...	Quisiera alquilar ...
	a car	un coche
	a boat	una barca/un bote/un barco
	Please, where is ...	Por favor, ¿dónde está ...
	the (rail) station?	la estación (de trenes)?
	the bus station?	la estación de autobuses?
	the Metro	el Metro?
	the airport?	el aeropuerto?
	To the hotel, please	Al hotel, por favor
Breakdown	I have broken down	Tengo una avería
	Would you please send	¿Pueden ustedes enviarme
	a recovery vehicle?	un cochegrúa, por favor?
	Is there a repair garage	¿Hay algun taller
	near here?	por aquí cerca?
Filling station	Where is the nearest filling station, please?	¿Dónde está la estación de servicio/la gasolinera más cercana, por favor?
	I should like ... litres of	Quisiera ... litros de
	standard grade petrol	gasolina normal
	super grade/diesel	súper/diesel
	lead-free/leaded	sin plomo/con plomo
	... octane	de ... octanos
	Fill up, please	Lleno, por favor
Accident	Help!	¡Ayuda!/¡Socorro!
	Watch out!	¡Atención!
	Caution!	¡Cuidado!
	Please call	Llame enseguida
	an ambulance	una ambulancia
	the police	a la policía
	the fire brigade	a los bomberos
	Have you a first aid kit?	¿Tiene usted un botiquín de urgencia?
	It was my fault	Ha sido por mi culpa
	It was your fault	Ha sido por su culpa
	Can I have your name	¿Puede usted darme
	and address, please?	su nombre y dirección?
Dining	Is there near here	¿Hay por aquí cerca
	a good restaurant?	un buen restaurante?
	a reasonably priced restaurant?	un restaurante no demasiado caro?
	Is there a restaurant here? acogedora?	¿Hay por aquí una taberna
	I should like to book a table for 4 people for this evening	¿Puede reservarnos para esta noche una mesa para cuatro personas?
	Your health!	¡Salud!
	Bill, please	¡La cuenta, por favor!
	Did you like the meal?	¿Le/Les ha gustado la comida?
	It was an excellent meal	La comida estaba excelente
Shopping	Where can I find	Por favor, ¿dónde hay
	a market?	un mercado?

a chemist's?	una farmacia?	
a baker's	una panadería?	
a photographic shop?	una tienda de artículos fotográficos?	
a shopping centre?	un centro comercial?	
a foodshop?	una tienda de comestibles?	

Could you recommend	Perdón, señor/señora/señorita, ¿podría usted recomendarme	Hotel
a hotel?	a hotel?	
a guesthouse?	una pensión?	
I have booked a room	He reservado una habitación	
Have you	¿Tienen ustedes	
a single room?	una habitación individual?	
a double room?	una habitación doble?	
with shower/bath?	con ducha/baño?	
for one night?	para una noche?	
for a week?	para una semana?	
with sea view?	con vista(s) al mar?	
What is the price of the room with	¿Cuánto cuesta la habitación con	
breakfast?	desayuno?	
half-board?	media pensión?	

Can you recommend	¿Puede usted indicarme	Doctor
a good doctor?	un buen médico?	
I have	Tengo	
diarrhoea	diarrea	
a temperature	fiebre	
a headache	dolor de cabeza	
toothache	dolor de muelas	

Where is there near here	Por favor, ¿dónde hay por aquí	Bank
a bank?	un banco?	
an exchange office?	una oficina/casa de cambio?	
I should like to change	Quisiera cambiar	
... pounds/dollars	... libras/dólares	
into pesetas	en pesetas	

What is the cost of	¿Cuánto cuesta	Post office
a letter	una carta	
a postcard	una postal	
to Britain/ the USA?	para Gran Bretaña/los Estados Unidos?	

0 cero	13 trece	50 cincuenta	Numbers
1 un, uno, una	14 catorce	60 sesanta	
2 dos	15 quince	70 setenta	
3 tres	16 dieciséis	80 ochenta	
4 cuatro	17 diecisiete	90 noventa	
5 cinco	18 dieciocho	100 cien, ciento	
6 seis	19 diecinueve	200 doscientos, -as	
7 siete	20 veinte	1000 mil	
8 ocho	21 veintiuno, -a,	2000 dos mil	
9 nueve	veintiún	10,000 diez mil	
10 diez	22 veintidós		
11 once	23 veintitres	1/2 medio	
12 doce	24 veinticuatro	1/4 un cuarto	

Menu *(Menú)*

desayuno	breakfast	General
almuerzo, comida	lunch	

Language

cena	dinner
camarero	waiter
cubierto	place setting
cuchara	spoon
cucharita	teaspoon
cuchillo	knife
tenedor	fork
taza	cup
plato	plate
vaso	glass
sacacorchos	corkscrew

Breakfast

café solo	espresso
café con leche	coffee with milk
cortado	espresso with a dash of milk
café descafeinado	decaffeinated coffee
té con leche/limón	tea with milk/lemon
infusión (de herbas)/tisana	herb tea
chocolate	chocolate
zumo de fruta	fruit juice
huevo pasado por agua	soft-boiled egg
huevos revueltos	scrambled eggs
pan/panecillo/tostada	bread/roll/toast
croissant	croissant
churros	fritters
mantequilla	butter
queso	cheese
embutido/fiambres	sausage/cold meat
jamón	ham
miel	honey
mermelada	jam

Entremeses/sopas (hors-d'oeuvres, soups)

aceitunas	olives
alcachofas	artichokes
almejas	shellfish
anchoas/boquerones	anchovies
caracoles	snails
chorizo	paprika sausage
ensaladilla rusa	Russian salad
gambas al ajillo	prawns in garlic sauce
jamón serrano	air-dried ham
mejillones	mussels
morcilla	blood sausage
panecillo	roll
pinchos	appetisers
pulpo	octopus
salchichón	salami-type sausage
salpicón de marisco	seafood salad
tortilla (a la) española	omelette with potatoes (and onions)
tortilla a la francesa	plain omelette
caldo	broth, bouillon
gazpacho	cold vegetable soup
sopa de ajo	garlic soup
sopa de pescado	fish soup
sopa de verduras	vegetable soup (sopa juliana, sopa jardinera)

Platos de huevos (egg dishes)

huevo	egg
huevo duro	hard-boiled egg
huevo pasado per agua	soft-boiled egg
huevos a la flamenca	eggs with beans
huevos fritos	fried eggs

huevos revueltos	scrambled eggs	
tortilla	omelette	
frito	fried	Pescados y
asado	roast	moriscos
ahumado	smoked	(seafood)
a la plancha	grilled on a hot iron plate	
cocido	stew	
almeja	river mussel	
anguila	eel	
atún	tunny	
bacalao	salt cod	
besugo	sea bream	
bogavante	lobster	
calamares a la romana	breaded rings of squid	
calamares en su tinta	squid in its own sauce	
camarón	shrimp	
cangrejo	crab	
dorada	dorada	
gambas	prawns	
langostinos	giant prawns	
lenguado	sole	
lubina	sea bass	
merluza	hake	
ostras	oysters	
paella	a rice dish with seafood and/or meat	
parrillada de pescado	dish of grilled fish	
perca	perch	
pez espada	swordfish	
pulpo	octopus	
rape	monkfish	
rodaballo	turbot	
salmón	salmon	
trucha	trout	
asado	roast	Carne y aves
buey	ox, bullock	(meat and
cabrito	kid	poultry)
callos	tripe	
carnero	mutton	
cerdo	pork	
chuleta	cutlet	
cocido	stew	
cochinillo	sucking-pig	
conejo	rabbit	
cordero	mutton, lamb	
escalope	escalope	
filete ruso	rissole	
guisado	stew	
higado	liver	
lomo	loin	
parrillada de carne	dish of grilled meat	
pato	duck	
pollo	chicken	
riñones	kidneys	
solomillo	sirloin	
ternera	veal	
vaca	beef	
aguacate	avocado	Ensalada y
berenjenas	aubergines	verduras (salads
calabacín	zucchini	and vegetables)

cebollas	onions
col de Bruselas	Brussels sprouts
coliflor	cauliflower
escarola	endive
espárragos	asparagus
garbanzos	chick peas
guisantes	peas
hongos/setas	mushrooms
judías	kidney beans
lechuga	lettuce
lentejas	lentils
patatas	potatoes
patatas fritas	chips
pepino	cucumber
pimiento	pepper (red or green)
tomate	tomato
zanahorias	carrots

Postres, queso y fruta (desserts, cheese and fruit)	albaricoques	apricots
	arroz con leche	rice pudding
	cerezas	cherries
	ciruelas	plums
	flan	caramel custard
	fresas	strawberries
	higos	figs
	macedonia de frutas	macédoine of fruit
	melocotón	peach
	melón	melon
	naranja	orange
	natillas	custard
	pera	pear
	piña	pineapple
	plátano	banana
	queso	cheese
	queso de cabra	goat's-milk cheese
	queso de oveja	ewe's-milk cheese
	sandía	water-melon
	tarta	cake, tart
	toronja	grapefruit
	uvas	grapes
	bombón	sweet, candy
	café helado	iced coffee
	chocolate	chocolate
	churros	fritters
	copa de helado	sundae
	dulces	sweets
	galletas	biscuits
	helado variado	mixed ice
	nata	cream
	tarta de frutas	fruit tart

Bebidas (drinks)	bebidas alcohólicas	alcoholic drinks
	aguardiente	brandy
	amontillado	a dry, slighty nutty sherry
	botella	bottle
	caña	a small glass of beer
	cava	a sparkling wine produced by the *méthode champenoise*
	cerveza	beer
	copa	(small) glass
	fino	a dry sherry
	jarra	carafe, jug

litro	litre
oloroso	a strong dark sherry
(semi-) secco	(semi-) dry
vaso	glass
vino blanco	white wine
(vino de) Jerez	sherry
vino rosado	rosé wine
vino tinto	red wine
bebidas no alcohólicas	soft drinks
agua mineral	mineral water
batido	milk shake
gaseosa	aerated water
horchata	orgeat
jugo de tomate	tomato juice
leche	milk
aranja	orange juice

Language courses

A brochure on language courses and cultural opportunities for foreigners, "Cursos de Lengua y Cultura para Extranjeros en España", can be obtained from the State Secretariat for Culture (Plaza del Rey 1; tel. 917017156) or from the Ministry of Culture at Calle de Alcalá 36.
The Madrid universities also offer language courses:
Universidad Complutense, Secretaría de los Cursos para Extranjeros, in the Facultad de Filosofía y Letras, Avenida de la Complutense, E-28040 Madrid; tel. 913945336
Universidad Autónoma, Servicio Idiomas, Carretera de Colmenar Viejo, at km 15.5; tel. 913974633
Language courses in connection with exchange visits are run by Tandem Escuela Internacional, Calle Marqués de Cubas 8; tel. 915322715

Libraries

Archivo Histórico Nacional, Serrano 115; tel. 915618005
Biblioteca Municipal Central, Centro Cultural Conde-Duque, Conde-Duque 7; tel. 91588. (The Central Municipal Library – the central unit of Madrid's 25 municipal libraries – includes a music library, a historical library and the Hemeroteca, a newspaper and periodical archive).
Biblioteca Nacional: see Sights from A to Z, Museo Arqueológico
Central de Bibliotecas Públicas de Madrid, Felipe el Hermoso 4; tel. 914459845 (for information on district lending libraries)
Consejo Superior de Investigaciones Científicas, Serrano 117; tel. 915854753 (a specialist library on the humanities, open to the public)

Lost Property (Objetos perdidos)

Oficina de Objetos Perdidos
Plaza de Legazpi 7; tel. 915884346

Information

Head Post Office, Plaza de la Cibeles
Counter 20: Información de cartería y entrega de documentos depositados en buzones; tel. 902197197
When a wallet or handbag is stolen, the thief is likely to be interested only in cash and may get rid of documents, etc., by putting them into a post-box. Any such items are kept in the Head Post Office.

Objects left in a taxi are handed in at Plaza Chamberí 4 and after three weeks or so are sent to the municipal lost property office (see above).

Taxis

Markets (Mercados)

Food markets	Mercado de San Miguel: see entry in Sights from A to Z
	There are other food markets in all Madrid's districts. Among the best are the Mercado de la Paz, Calle de la Ayala/Lagasca (Metro: Serrano or Velázquez); Mercado Antón Martín, Calle de Santa Isabel 5 (Metro: Antón Martín); Mercado Argüelles, Calle Altamirano 7 (Metro: Argüelles); Mercado Ballesta, Calle Ballesta 9 (Metro: Gran Vía); Mercado La Cebada, Plaza de la Cebada (Metro: La Latina); and Mercado Maravillas, Calle Bravo Murillo 122 (Metro: Cuatro Caminos).
Stamps and coins	Every Sunday morning there is a busy stamp and coin market in the Plaza Mayor (see Sights from A to Z, Plaza Mayor).
Craft market	Every Saturday afternoon (and daily 6–10pm Dec. to Jan. 5th) around 60 craft workers set up their stalls in Plaza de las Comendadoras (Metro: San Bernardo or Noviciado).
Christmas markets	There are Christmas markets in the Plaza de las Comendadoras (see above, Craft market) and the Plaza Mayor (pre-Christmas period to Epiphany).
Flea market	See Sights from A to Z, El Rastro
Artists' market	On Sundays and public holidays from 9am artists display their work for sale in Plaza del Conde de Barajas.
Arts and crafts, antiques	See Shopping, Souvenirs

In the Mercado de San Miguel

Sunday morning in the Plaza Mayor

Medical Aid

British visitors to Spain can get emergency medical treatment in Spain under the reciprocal arrangements between the countries of the European Union. For this purpose they must produce the E 111 form, which they should obtain before leaving home (it is contained in the "Health Advice for Travellers" leaflet obtainable from post offices or social security offices). But this gives only limited cover – though the scope of the reciprocal arrangements was widened by a decision of the European Court in Luxembourg in 1998 – and you will be well advised to take out short-term insurance cover as well. Visitors from non-EU countries should certainly do so.

In case of acute illness you should apply to the accident and emergency department *(Urgencias)* of a hospital or summon help by dialling the emergency number 012 (see Emergencies).

The Instituto Nacional de Salud (National Health Institute), or Insalud for short, at Calle Sagasta 6 (tel. 913387770), runs the 200 health centres *(centros de salud)* at which treatment is provided. It will give you the address of the health centre to apply to in a particular district and will send a doctor in an emergency. .

To ask for an emergency doctor, dial 091 or 012.

The following are the main hospitals in and around Madrid:

Clínica Nuestra Señora de la Concepción, Fundación Jiménez Díaz
Avenida Reyes Católicos 2; tel. 915441600

Ciudad Sanitaria La Paz
Paseo de la Castellana 261; tel. 913582600
(particularly to be recommended as a children's hospital and for problems during pregnancy)

Hospital 12 de Octubre
Carretera de Andalucía, km 4.5
Tel. 913908000 and 913908090

Hospital Ramón y Cajal
Carretera de Colmenar, km 9.1 (at M 30)
Tel. 913368900

Hospital de la Cruz Roja
Avenida Reina Victoria 24; tel. 915534300

The Spanish Red Cross runs a system providing medical aid for foreigners:
Cruz Roja Española, Ayuda al Extranjero
Juan Montalvo 3; tel. 915333105
Open Mon.–Fri. 9am–1pm

Motoring

Road system

Spanish motorways *(autopistas)* are subject to tolls *(peaje)*. They have rest areas at regular distances of not more than 30 km (18 mi.). There are also *autovías,* which are of motorway standard but are toll-free. They are well provided with filling stations and restaurants, which are usually reached on a signposted *vía de servicio*.

National highways

The *carreteras nacionales* (national highways), which are identified by the letter N and a number, are mostly well engineered and well maintained. Some of them, with at least four lanes, rank as *autovías* (see above). They are usually well provided with filling stations and services. Spain's most important main roads are the six trunk roads which radiate from Madrid, labelled on kilometre stones in red and white in Roman numbers:

N I	to Burgos, San Sebastián and France
N II	to Barajas and Barcelona
N III	to Valencia
N IV	to Cádiz and Andalusia
N V	to Badajoz, Extremadura and Portugal
N VI	to La Coruña and Galicia

Provincial roads

Regional or provincial roads *(carreteras comarcales)* are identified by the letter C (or in the Madrid Region by M) and a number. Important main roads are usually well engineered and in good condition. Un-numbered minor roads, however, may hold surprises for the driver.

Driving in Spain

When driving in Spain you must be prepared to cope with a variety of infractions of the highway code by other drivers. Many drivers on motorways overtake on the right, contrary to the rules, so when returning to the right-hand lane you must look out for drivers coming up on the right. Red lights are frequently ignored, endangering pedestrians as well as other motorists. At zebra crossings motorists generally pay little heed to pedestrians trying to cross. At a roundabout vehicles on the roundabout have priority over those entering it or leaving it; but drivers frequently turn sharply out of the inner lane to exit from the roundabout without regard for other drivers continuing round on the outer lane.

Right of way

In Spain, as in the rest of continental Europe, traffic goes on the right, with overtaking on the left. In general vehicles coming from the right (even coming out of a side street in town, unless otherwise indicated) have priority. Vehicles on a roundabout have priority over vehicles entering it or leaving it.

Turning left

On main roads outside built-up areas a sharp left turn is sometimes not permitted: instead drivers must turn off on the right into a slip road which then turns left and crosses the main road at right angles. This is called a *raqueta*.

Overtaking

When overtaking you must turn on your left-hand indicator, keep it on while overtaking and then turn on the right-hand indicator to return to your lane.

On mountain roads cars with trailer caravans are not permitted to overtake.

Lights

On well lit roads (except expressways or motorways) you must only use your sidelights.

Speed limits

Speed limits in Spain are:
in built-up areas: 50 k.p.h (31 m.p.h)
outside built-up areas: 90 k.p.h (55 m.p.h)
on roads with at least two lanes in each direction: 100 k.p.h (62 m.p.h)
on motorways: 120 k.p.h (74 m.p.h)

cars with trailers: 70 k.p.h (43 m.p.h); on motorways 80 k.p.h (49 m.p.h)

Seat-belts must be worn in both front and back seats. Children under 10 must sit in the back of the car.

Seat-belts

Towing of another car by a private car is prohibited.

Towing

Lead-free petrol, leaded premium petrol and diesel fuel are available at all filling stations.

Fuel

The central area of Madrid is well provided with multi-storey and underground car parks *(aparcamientos)*.

Parking

If you intend to drive your own car or a hired car in Madrid you should bear in mind the restrictions on parking in the city centre — the rules known for short as ORA. For on-street parking there is a charge for each half-hour, with a maximum stay of 90 minutes. Parking tickets can be obtained in all tobacconists' *(estancos)*.

ORA

Wrongly parked cars can be towed away to a pound by the dreaded *grúa municipal* (literally, "crane"). To discover where to reclaim your car, tel. 913450050.

Removals

The consequences of an accident while driving abroad can be serious. If you are involved in an accident, even if you are not yourself at fault, you may find your car impounded and perhaps released only after the completion of an necessary legal proceedings, and in bad accidents the driver may be arrested. In the event of an accident you should at once inform the insurance company named on your green card so that arrangements can be made for a bail bond if required.

Accidents

See entry

Breakdown
assistance

Museums

All Madrid's major museums are described in the Sights from A to Z section of this guide. In addition there are many smaller or specialised museums that can be seen only by appointment.

Armería
Arms and armour: see Sights from A to Z, Palacio Real

Calcografía Nacional (National Chalcography Collection)
Open daily 10am–2pm, Sat. 10am–1.30pm
See Sights from A to Z, Real Academia de Bellas Artes de San Fernando

Casa de Lope de Vega: see Sights from A to Z, Casa de Lope de Vega

Casón del Buen Retiro: see Sights from A to Z, Casón del Buen Retiro

Centro de Arte Reina Sofía: see Sights from A to Z, Centro de Arte Reina Sofía

Colección Banco de España
Collection of pictures
Open Mon., Tue., Thu. by appointment only (tel. 91338/5365 or 6037 or 51759); closed Jul.–Sep.
See Sights from A to Z, Plaza de la Cibeles

Colección Benedito
Pictures and sketches by the painter Manuel Benedito (1875–1963), displayed in his studio, Calle Juan Bravo 4; tel. 915754687.
Seen only by appointment; closed Jul.–Oct. Metro: Núñez de Balboa; buses 9, 19, 51

Colección de la Biblioteca Musical
Music library with instruments, autograph manuscripts, scores, etc. (lending library)
Calle Conde-Duque 11; Metro: Ventura Rodríguez, buses 1, 2, 44, 74, C
Open Mon.–Fri. 9am–9pm

Colección Municipal · Ayuntamiento y Casa de Cisneros
Tapestries, furniture and pictures belonging to the city of Madrid
Conducted tour Mon. 5pm
See Sights from A to Z, Plaza de la Villa

Colección del Observatorio Nacional
Collection of the Spanish National Observatory, Calle Alfonso XII 3
Conducted tours by appointment only (tel. 915270107 or 915271935).
Buses: 10, 14, 19, 26, 32, C

Convento de San Plácido
Convent museum
Open Sun.–Fri. 10am–noon, 4–6pm
See Sights from A to Z, San Plácido

Fundación Casa de Alba
Collection of art from five centuries, furniture and tapestries belonging to the Dukes of Alba, Palacio de Liria, Calle de la Princesa 20
Seen by appointment on written application (in exceptional cases tel. 915475302)
See Sights from A to Z, Palacio de Liria

Gabinete de Antigüedades de la Real Academia de la Historia
See Sights from A to Z, Real Academia de la Historia

Hemeroteca Municipal
Municipal Newspaper Archives
See Sights from A to Z, Cuartel del Conde-Duque

Instituto Valencia de Don Juan
See Sights from A to Z, Instituto Valencia de Don Juan

Jardín Botánico (Botanic Gardens)
See Sights from A to Z, Jardín Botánico

Monasterio de las Descalzas Reales
See Sights from A to Z, Monasterio de las Descalzas Reales

Monasterio de la Encarnación
See Sights from A to Z, Convento de la Encarnación

Museo Africano (African Museum)
The collection of the Centro de Animación Missionaria de los Combonianos, Calle Arturo Soría 101; tel. 914152412
Open for groups Mon.–Fri., for other visitors Thu. 6.30pm, Sun. 11.30am; closed Jul.–Sep. Metro: Arturo Soría; buses 11, 70

Museo de Aeronáutica y Astronáutica (Museum of Flying and Space Travel)

Carretera de Extremadura at km 10.5; tel. 915443567
Historic aircraft, numerous aircraft models, engines, instruments, etc.
Open Tue.–Sun. 10am–2pm. Bus H 1 (Madrid–Alcorcón); Cercanías C 5
(Cuatro Vientos)

Museo de América
See Sights from A to Z, Museo de América

Museo Arqueológico Nacional
See Sights from A to Z, Museo Arqueológico Nacional

Museo de Artes y Tradiciones Populares (Museum of Folk Art and
Traditions)
Facultad de Filosofía y Letras, Universidad Autónoma de Canto Blanco,
Carretera de Colmenar Viejo, km 15; tel. 913974270
Open 11am–2pm, Tue. and Thu. 5–8pm; closed Sat., Sun. and pub. hols.
Metro: Ferrocarril, Atocha and Chamartín; bus from Plaza Castilla

Museo Cajal
The legacy of Santiago Ramón y Cajal (Nobel Prize for Medicine, 1906)
has not yet found a permanent home. It is expected to be housed in a
new museum in the Instituto Cajal, Calle Doctor Arce 37; tel. 915854743

Museo de la Casa de la Moneda (Museum of the Mint)
Calle Doctor Esquerdo 36; tel. 915741054 and 914096343
This museum, housed in 30 rooms in the former Mint, offers a fascinat-
ing introduction to the world of money, with 30,000 coins and notes,
prints, drawings, dies and punches of the 16th–18th centuries and much
else besides.
Open Tue.–Fri. 10am–2.30pm, 5–7.30pm, Sat., Sun. and pub. hols.
10am–2pm.; in Aug. only in morning. Metro: Goya; buses 2, 28, 30,
56, C

Museo de Cera Colón (Wax Museum)
Paseo de Recoletos 41
More than 400 wax figures illustrating the history of Madrid from the
beginnings to the present day
Open daily 10am–2pm. Metro: Colón; buses 5, 14, 27, 45, 53
See Sights from A to Z, Plaza de Colón

Museo de Carruajes (Carriage Museum)
See Sights from A to Z, Museo de Carruajes

Museo Cerralbo
See Sights from A to Z, Museo Cerralbo

Museo de la Ciudad (City Museum)
See Sights from A to Z, Museo de la Ciudad

Museo del Ejército (Army Museum)
See Sights from A to Z, Museo del Ejército

Museo de Escultura al Aire Libre (Museum of Open-Air Sculpture)
See Sights from A to Z, Museo de Escultura al Aire Libre

Museo Español de Arte Contemporáneo (Museum of Contemporary
Art)
See Sights from A to Z, Centro de Arte Reina Sofía

Museo de la Farmacia Hispana (Museum of Pharmacy)
Facultad de Farmacia, Ciudad Universitaria; tel. 913941793
History of Spanish pharmacy

Seen only by appointment. Metro: Ciudad Universitaria; buses 62, 82, G, D

Museo Geominero
Calle Ríos Rosas 23; tel. 913495759
Collection of fossils, minerals and rocks
Open Mon.–Sat. 9am–2pm. Metro: Ríos Rosas; buses 3, 12, 37, 45, 74

Museo Lázaro Galdiano: see Sights from A to Z, Museo Lázaro Galdiano

Museo del Jamón: see Shopping, Souvenirs

Museo Municipal: see Sights from A to Z, Museo Municipal

Museo Nacional de Arte de Artes Decorativas (National Museum of Decorative Art)
Calle Montalbán 12; tel. 915326845
With its reproductions of living rooms, bedrooms and fully equipped kitchens as well as numerous individual items, the Museum of Decorative Art gives an excellent picture of how people lived in Spain in the 15th and 16th centuries. Altogether it has some 15,000 exhibits displayed in 58 rooms on five floors.
Open Tue.–Fri. 9.30am–3pm, Sat. and Sun. 10am–2pm Metro: Banco de España; buses 1, 2, 9, 10, 15, 20, 51, 52, 74

Museo Nacional de Ciencias Naturales (Museum of Natural Science)
Calle José Gutiérrez Abascal 2; tel. 914111328, 915618600 or 915618607
The pride of this museum, founded in the reign of Charles III, is its dinosaurs; it is also particularly strong in zoology, mineralogy, palaeontology and geology.
Open Tue.–Fri. 10am–6pm, Sat. 10am–8pm, Sun. and pub. hols. 10am–2.30pm. Metro: Gregorio Marañón; buses 7, 12, 14, 27, 40, 45

Museo Nacional de Antropología (National Museum of Anthropology)
Calle Alfonso XII 68; tel. 915395995
Open Tue.–Sat. 10am–7.30pm, Sun. 10am–2pm. Metro: Atocha-RENFE; buses 10, 14, 19, 26, 32, 37, 57, 140, C

Museo Nacional Ferroviario (National Railway Museum)
Paseo Delicias 61; tel. 902228822
Open Tue.–Sun. 10am–3pm; closed Aug. Metro: Delicias; buses 6, 8, 18, 19, 45, 55, 58, 85, 86

Museo Nacional del Prado: see Sights from A to Z, Museo Nacional del Prado

Museo Naval (Naval Museum)
Calle Montalbán 2/Paseo del Prado 5
Housed in the Ministry of the Navy, the Naval Museum illustrates the history of Spanish seafaring. Among the exhibits is the first map of the New World (1492).
Open Tue.–Sun. 10.30am–1.30pm; closed pub. hols. Metro: Banco de España; buses 1, 2, 9, 10, 15, 20, 51, 52

Museo Postal y de Comunicaciones (Postal and Telecommunications Museum)
Calle Montalbán (in Head Post Office
Open Mon.–Fri. 10am–1.30pm, 5–7pm, Sat. 10am–1.30pm; closed Aug. Metro: Banco de España; buses 1, 2, 9, 10, 15, 20, 51, 52, 74

Museo de la Real Academia de Bellas Artes de San Fernando
See Sights from A to Z, Real Academia de Bellas Artes de San Fernando

Museo de Reproducciones Artísticas y Gliptoteca
Avenida de los Reyes Católicos 6
Reproductions of sculpture, mainly Greek and Roman, and Renaissance casts.
Open Tue.–Sat. 10am–6pm, Sun. 10am–2pm. Metro: Moncloa

Museo Romántico (Romantic Museum): see Sights from A to Z, Museo Romántico

Museo Sorolla: see Sights from A to Z, Museo Sorolla

Museo Taurino (Bullfighting Museum): see Sights from A to Z, Las Ventas

Museo Thyssen-Bornemisza: see Sights from A to Z, Museo Thyssen-Bornemisza

Palacio Real (Royal Palace): see Sights from A to Z, Palacio Real

Panteón de Goya: see Sights from A to Z, Ermita de San Antonio de la Florida

Panteon de Hombres Políticos Ilustres (Pantheon of Famous Statesmen)
Calle Julián Gayarre 3
Open Mon.–Fri. 9.30am–1.30pm; closed pub. hols. Metro: Menéndez Pelayo, Atocha-RENFE; buses 10, 14, 26, 32, C

Planetario de Madrid (Madrid Planetarium; by Salvador Pérez Arroyo, 1986)
Parque Enrique Tierno Galván, Calle Pedro Bosch
Presentations Mon.–Fri. at 5.30 and 6.45pm, Sat., Sun. and pub. hols. at 11.30am and 12.45, 5.30, 6.45 and 8pm. Metro: Méndez Álvaro; buses 6, 8, 102, 112, 117

Real Basílica de San Francisco el Grande: see Sights from A to Z, San Francisco el Grande

Real Fábrica de Tapices (Royal Tapestry Manufactory): see Sights from A to Z, Real Fábrica de Tapices, and Baedeker Special, p. 74

Real Sitios de El Pardo: see Sights from A to Z, El Pardo

Temple de Debod: see Sights from A to Z, Montaña del Príncipe Pío

See Sights from A to Z, Alcalá de Henares (Casa Natal de Cervantes; Museo Arqueológico de Alcalá, Paseo del Juncal)   Outside Madrid

See Sights from A to Z, Aranjuez (Reales Sitios de Aranjuez)

See Sights from A to Z, El Escorial (Monasterio)

See Sights from A to Z, La Granja

See Sights from A to Z, Segovia

See Sights from A to Z, Sierra de Guadarrama (Buitrago de Lozoya; Picasso Museum)

See Sights from A to Z, Toledo

Music

The centre of Madrid's musical life is the Auditorio Nacional de Música (see entry in Sights from A to Z). The following is a list of other concert halls and musical institutions.

Auditorio de la Fiera de la Casa de Campo, Avenida Portugal (in the Casa de Campo exhibition centre: see Sights from A to Z, Casa de Campo); tel. 935889393). Metro: Lago

Centro Cultural de la Villa de Madrid, Plaza de Colón; tel. 915756080 See Sights from A to Z, Plaza de Colón. Metro: Colón

Real Conservatorio Superior de Música, Calle Santa Isabel 53; tel. 915392901. Metro: Atocha

Theatre in Círculo de Bellas Artes, Marqués de Casa Riera 2; tel. 915318503 or 7700 See Sights from A to Z, Círculo de Bellas Artes. Metro: Banco de España

Theatre in Cuartel del Conde-Duque, Conde-Duque 9–11; tel. 9158858 21 See Sights from A to Z, Cuartel del Conde-Duque. Metro: Ventura Rodríguez

Concert hall in Casa de Campo; tel. 914632900 An open-air stage, mostly used for rock concerts by popular groups. Metro: Batán

Teatro Monumental, Alcalá 65; tel. 914291281. Home of the National Radio Orchestra. Metro: Antón Martín

Auditorio de la Escuela Superior de Canto (concert hall of the Academy of Singing; no concerts July–Sep.), San Bernardo 44; tel. 915328533. Metro: Noviciado

Salón de Actos del Ateneo (see entry in Sights from A to Z), Prado 21; tel. 914296251. Metro: Sevilla, Antón Martín

Salón de Actos de la Fundación Juan March, Castello 77; tel. 914354240. Metro: Núñez de Balboa

Salón de Actos del Instituto Alemán, Zurbarán 21; tel. 913193235. Metro: Alonso Martínez

Hall of Real Academia de Bellas Artes de San Fernando (see entry in Sights from A to Z). Metro: Moncloa, Ciudad Universitaria

Teatro Albéniz, Paz 11; tel. 915318311 A municipal theatre, used for dance and musical productions (e.g. during the Festival de Otoño). Metro: Sol

Theatre and concert hall in Campo de las Naciones exhibition centre (see Trade Fairs).

Teatro Real (Teatro de la Ópera: see Sights from A to Z, Teatro Real), Plaza de Oriente; tel. 915160660 and 915160606 (tickets). Metro: Ópera

Teatro de la Zarzuela (see Baedeker Special, p. 134), Jovellanos 4; tel. 915245400. Metro: Sevilla, Banco de España

Seasons for zarzuela, ballet and concerts
The zarzuela and ballet season is from October to July.
The season for concerts by Spanish and foreign ensembles and orchestras is from October to June, and there may be some special concerts in July as well.

Madrid's cultural life continues even during the summer break. From July to September the city runs the Veranos de la Villa ("City Summers"), mainly in the Centro Cultural de la Villa and the Cuartel del Conde-Duque, with classical and modern music, zarzuela, dance and film (see Events).
On Saturdays in summer the Madrid Region puts on classical concerts in castles and other monuments in the region (for example, at Manzanares el Real).
The Festival de Otoño (Autumn Festival) begins at the end of September, when the Madrileños are back from their holidays, and enriches the regular cultural programme with concerts (classical, jazz and rock) at various venues, including rock concerts in the bullring at Las Ventas.

Summer and autumn festivals

There are concerts by the town band on summer Sundays in the Templete open-air theatre in the Retiro Park (see Sights from A to Z, Parque del Retiro).

Festival de Flamenco: in the Centro Cultural de la Villa in January.

Flamenco festivals

Flamenco a Corazón Abierto: a flamenco festival throughout the whole of November in the Colegio de Médicos, Calle Santa Isabel 51 (tel. 915385100). Metro: Atocha.

A festival of South American music organised by the Centro Cultural de la Villa (in Plaza Mayor, Las Vistillas, etc.) during the Fiesta de San Isidro in May

Festival de las Américas

Concerts by the band of the Royal Guard: May to June in the Royal Palace (see Sights from A to Z, Palacio Real).

Mozart Festival: in concert halls and theatres in the city (June).

Festival Internacional de Jazz, in the Centro Cultural de la Villa, the Auditorio Nacional and other venues (November).

Jazz festivals

There is a smaller jazz festival in June in the Ateneo (see above).

The Spanish National Ballet has two companies. The Ballet Nacional Español devotes itself to Spanish folk ballets, particularly the flamenco dance, while the Ballet Clásico Nacional offers a classical repertoire and modern choreography. Both companies run an annual season from October to July in the Teatro de la Zarzuela (see above).

Ballet

See Night Life

Music and dance clubs

Information about current programmes can be obtained from the newspapers and the weekly "Guía del Ocio" ("Leisure Guide").

Leisure Guide

See also Events; Theatres; Ticket Offices

Night Life

Madrid's night life knows only one rule: there are no limits to enjoying yourself. And yet the Madrileños enjoy themselves in accordance with certain established rituals. Thus, for example, one should not think of going to a disco before 3 o'clock in the morning. And in some of the "in" hangouts you can be sure that you have come to the right place at the wrong time if you can get in without using your elbows. Beginners should therefore have firmly in their mind the central question: "¿Hay marcha ahora?" ("Where is it at?"). Experienced night-owls will then be glad to show you the way (see Baedeker Special, p. 209). The order in which the following addresses are arranged corresponds roughly to the order in which you are likely to visit the different kinds of night spot in the course of the night.

Daytime

Cafés, tabernas and similar haunts

During the day, in the afternoon, over an aperitif, for a chat with friends over a glass of wine or a drink: a café in Madrid must be prepared for customers at any time of day, for it may be the starting-point or the final stage in a journey through the Madrid night. One condition is essential: the ambience must tempt you to linger. The cafés are usually open from the early afternoon (between 2 and 4 o'clock) to between 1 and 2 in the morning, and on Friday and Saturday to between 3 and 4 (exceptions are noted below). The official closing-time may not always be exactly observed, but if it is there is always the question "¿Y ahora, dónde hay marcha?" ("Where to now?").

There are innumerable cafés, tabernas and bodegas in Madrid to meet the needs of their customers. Here follows a selection of "in" places worth visiting at any time of day or night.

Bruín, Paseo del Pintor Rosales 48. Ice-cream parlour with a terrace.

Café Bailén, Bailén 30. Here you can drink a varied range of coffees, a glass of wine or cocktails prepared according to Caribbean recipes.

Café Belén, Belén 5. A classic café to relax in during the evening or late at night.

Café Comercial, Glorieta de Bilbao 7. A turn-of-the-century classic, with large windows, a well-used interior and a revolving door which has been turning since 1887.

Café Central: see below, *Sitios* with floor shows.

Café Gijón, Paseo de Recoletos 21. open from breakfast time by way of lunch, aperitif time and tapas until after midnight. Another classic old café where friends have met since 1888 to discuss the most progressive ideas in Madrid.

Café Isadora, Divino Pastor 14. Coffees and pacharán (a spirit made from juniper berries) in an ambience that is eternally young.

Café del Real, Plaza Isabel II 2. A classic café immediately behind the Ópera.

Café Espejo: see Restaurants

Nuevo Café Barbieri, Ave María 45. Since it was modern in the 1920s the "new" Barbieri has hardly changed: cast-iron columns, bistro-type tables and a view of the un-Madrid-like Plaza de Lavapiés.

¡A la marcha, Madrileños!

Bajar a Madrid (going into town) is surely stressful enough; but no sooner have millions of Madrileños returned to their suburbs in the evening than they stream back into town – to go to a cinema, for a tapas tour, to spend a long night on the town. Now, in the evening, it can be seen why real Madrileños and Madrileñas are known as *gatos* (cats): city cats with seven night-lives a week. Few other cities have such a full and exhausting night life as Madrid.

Madrid's star began to rise again in the 1980s, when Spain shook off the dead hand of the Franco regime. The 155 m (509 ft) high Torre de Picasso reared up on the Paseo de la Castellana, looking down from a great height on the older skyline round the Plaza de España. Below, in the streets of Madrid, ambassadors like the film-maker Pedro Almodóvar proclaimed to the world the cultural revolt known as the *movida* ("movement") and the reawakened younger generation of Madrileños, with their new heroes, spent their nights in *sitios* ("sites") such as the "Sol" and the "Berlin Cabaret". After forty years of a dictatorship nothing was now forbidden, and the young fiercely defended their right to behave badly. After it had for so long been decreed that olive-stones, used tissues and prawn-shells must be deposited in waste-bins they were now casually dropped in the street. This became a symbol for Madrid's night life. As in Spain's Golden Age, it was an empire on which the sun never set.

"¡A la marcha, Madrileños!" is the chant with which the Madrileños begin their long march through the night, which for many "cats" begins on Thursday and on which sleep is not to be thought of until Monday morning. Real discos do not even open their shutters until three in the morning. Those who want to dance before then can fill in the time in a bar de copas, one of the popular hangouts which cover the transition from evening into night. They can listen to jazz, for example, in the Café Central (Plaza del Ángel 10) or the Populart (Huertas 22), or to flamenco singers in La Soleá (Cava Baja 34) or Casa Patas (Cañizares).

Then, when the discos close in the morning it is time for the "after hours" establishments to open, bridging the period until the next sunset. Each sitio has its own particular time, and new ones are constantly coming into fashion.

Recently air-conditioning has become "in" on hot summer nights. The gente guapa ("beautiful people") now like to sit in ice-cooled sitios with an artificial breeze blowing on their face – though real gatos prefer the airy *terrazas* on the Paseo de la Castellana or the Paseo del Pintor Rosales, or a cool drink at a table outside a bar. Every pavement becomes a sitio – on Plazas Olavide, Santa Ana or Dos de Mayo, in the Huertas or Malasaña quarters, or under the flyover crossing Calle de Segovia, where rock bands play until the first grey light of morning. It is no wonder that the municipal authorities, urged on by irritated householders, have been trying to introduce some kind of closing time and establish "environmentally protected zones". The aim is to control what is now regarded as Madrid's main environmental pollutant: noise, so liberally dispensed by the various music spots and their competing bars and *terrazas*. Under-age youngsters who are not allowed into the bars take over the squares in the Chueca quarter night after night, mixing cola and cheap wine to create an explosive drink and producing headaches for themselves, local people and the authorities concerned with youth welfare. They are the new generation of night-owls in the making, in the continuing battle with the city's silent, sleepless majority.

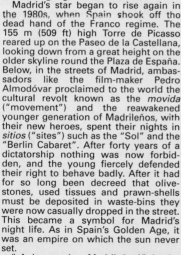

Café del Círculo de Bellas Artes, Alcalá 42. Until 11pm there is an admission charge of 100 ptas. The money is well spent if you want to read in peace or talk with friends in this cultural ambience.

Café del Nuncio, Segovia 9. Coffee in every variation, snacks to satisfy any hunger, well-mixed caipirinhas. From 1.30pm onwards every wish is met in this stylish café with its panelled walls and crystal chandeliers. In summer its terrace in the heart of old Madrid is a delight.

Café Moderno, Plaza de las Comendadoras 1. Cocktails and coffees in the Art Deco interior or on the terrace.

Café de Oriente, Plaza de Oriente 2. Established around the turn of the 19th century with the aim of being *the* café in Madrid. For the odd snack or a coffee on its incomparable terrace, at a corresponding price.

Café Ruiz, Ruiz 11. A classic café in the Malasaña district. For when you feel the need of a coffee, a cocktail or (towards morning) a cup of chocolate, this is a good place to come. You can enjoy your drink either on the terrace or on a red velvet sofa in the interior.

Champañería María Pandora, Plaza de Gabriel Miró 1. If you are on your own you can borrow a book from the library. If you are with friends you can enjoy a glass of wine or cava (a sparkling champagne-style wine).

Los Gabrieles, Echegaray 17. In this taberna with its magnificent décor of azulejos you can meet your friends or watch a flamenco show.

El Gato Persa, Bárbara de Braganza 10. A tearoom with Baroque music, which becomes jazz in the evening. A cosy place to meet a friend amid books.

Horchatería Espronceda, Espronceda 9. Here you can get home-made Italian ice-cream and excellent *horchata* (orgeat) to refresh you on a hot summer day.

Palazzo, Puerta del Sol 8. A classic ice-cream parlour in Madrid's most central square.

Pavilhão Chinês, Lagasca 31. The charm of Lisbon in the centre of Madrid. Every detail is authentically antique.

Salón del Prado, Prado 4. Coffee and cava in an exquisite Parisian ambience, with classical music.

Tetería de la Abuela, Espíritu Santo 18. A tearoom of particular charm.

La Fidula: see under *Sitios* with floor shows

Solesmes, Amnistía 5. Here you can drink your fruit cocktail or cava to soft classical music or Gregorian chant.

Viva Madrid, Manuel Fernández y González 7. Until you have found your way into the crush here between 11pm and 1am you have never really been in Madrid. A café, taberna and *movida* hangout of the early days. On the upper floor, if you can manage to get a table, the atmosphere of old Madrid in a setting of azulejos.

Sitios

There are flamenco shows of very different kinds in very different *sitios*. A *tablao* (flamenco show) usually offers traditional folk dances such as the sevillana, which is often confused with flamenco. In contrast to this fiery dance the establishments known as *peñas* offer what they call the real flamenco, with singing *(cante)* accompanied by a guitar *(toque)*. Many tascas offer now the one, now the other.

Café de Chinitas, Torija 7. A *tablao* with classic shows in the tradition of Málaga. The shows, to the accompaniment of a meal at around 9500 pesetas, change monthly.

Candela, Olmo 2. A bar-taberna in Andalusian style. Some of the great names of *cante* sometimes sing in the *peña* in the basement, but these performances are frequently not open to the public.

Casa Patas, Cañizares 10. Live shows from the lively flamenco scene, changing daily; with dinner.

Corral de la Morería, Morería 17. A *tablao* with flamenco shows.

España Cañí, Plaza del Ángel 14. Taberna with flamenco and flamenco-pop shows. You come here for the atmosphere and the sangría.

Peña Flamenco Chaquetón, Canarias 39. A *peña* in its original form. Only of interest if you want to hear genuine *cante*.

La Soleá, Cava Baja 34. Began as a small *peña,* but is now a large one and has made recordings. Spontaneous flamenco singing in its purest form. No talking allowed during the performance.

Torre Bermejas, Mesonero Romanos 11. Here you can hear the greats of *cante, toque* and *baile* (dancing), and sometimes also traditional folk shows.

Café Central, Plaza del Ángel 10. A bohemian café in the Huertas quarter; jazz bands in the evening. Jazz

Clamores, Alburquerque 14. A classic jazz dive.

El Despertar, Torrecilla del Leal 18. A former grocer's shop in which you can now drink coffees and copas and listen to promising young jazz bands.

Populart, Huertas 22. Atmosphere, sax music, small groups and an ever young audience.

Segundo Jazz, Comandante Zorita 8. One of the few jazz spots in Madrid in which the live performance and not the glass in your hand or the accompaniment by the audience is the main thing.

Café Valvén, Travesía San Mateo 1. A stylish café with cabaret artistes, mimes, salsa parties and rock à la carte. Music and cabaret

Candilejas, Bailén 16. Cabaret, poetry and tarot – accompanied by cocktails and ambience.

Caracol, Bernardino Obregón 18. From flamenco via ethno to salsa. Live, and always in fiesta mood.

Las Noches del Cuplé de Olga Ramos, Palma 51. *Cuplés* (pop songs) and other typical Madrileño types of music. By Olga and her daughter Olga María.

La Redacción, Cervantes 7. A large establishment which has become a springboard for the careers of new *cantautores* (song-writers).

Night Life

★El Sol, Jardines 3. Madrid's best disco, its best place for live rock music, its best *sitio* since the early days of the *movida* and still today.

Classic cafés

La Fidula, Huertas 57. The centrepiece of the establishment is the 200-year-old chocolate machine. Intimate atmosphere, with chocolate from the machine or cocktails to the accompaniment of piano music.

La Flauta Mágica, Alcántara 49. A classic café with its own theatre group, a billiard table and card-playing.

Salón del Prado, Prado 4. Cold dishes, cakes and canapés in a Paris-style café. The tertulias are interrupted only by arias and other classical music.

Late evening to late at night

For quiet hours late at night:

Bécquer, Hermanos Bécquer 10. Creative and classic cocktails in a classic but by no means old-fashioned atmosphere.

El Cock, Reina 16. A quiet place with background music, rather as the Spanish imagine a similar place in Britain. The painter Francis Bacon left his signature on a coaster here.

Cuevas de Sésamo, Príncipe 7. Truman Capote is said to have been a habitué. A *sitio* full of poetry (written on the walls and tables) and curious foreign visitors, who are as keen to drink sangría as to listen to the piano music.

Chicote, Gran Vía 12. Cocktails and tapas of the finest quality.

El Espejo, Paseo de Recoletos 31 (see Restaurants). At night the glass pavilion becomes a stylish Art Nouveau cocktail bar.

El Mundo de Guermantes, San Hermenegildo 22. All the cocktails are named after characters in Proust's "A la Recherche du Temps Perdu".

Bares de copas

After midnight the clubs and *bares de copas* come into their own. For experienced night-owls the night doesn't begin until around 2am.

Barnon, Santa Engracia 17. In the cool draught of the air-conditioning and to mainstream music at disco loudness, the drinks here are whisky and cola or gin and tonic. A few dancers warm up for the discos later.

Café Habana, Infantas 30. Mojitos (first-class Cuban cocktails), habaneras and timba bring the atmosphere of Cuba to Madrid. Many of the customers dance the Cuban samba to perfection.

El Calentito, Jacometrezzo 15. A classic salsa bar.

El Son, Fernando VI 21. Around midnight coffee and rum have their effect; Latin American music from loudspeakers and tapas.

Galileo Galilei, Galileo 100. On two floors in an old cinema. Salsa and ballroom dancing, song-writers and humorists. Live music and bands, always with plenty of ambience.

Honky Tonk, Covarrubias 24. Concerts and fiestas in a former car factory attract mixed and colourful audiences night after night.

Kingston's, Barquillo 29. A *bar de copas* which with its music and its tropical ambience offers an introduction to reggae.

La Nave Va, Trujillos 3. The hull of an old ship, filled night after night, with music of the sixties (blues, jazz or live flamenco on Thursdays). Small and decidedly "in".

No se lo digas a nadie, Ventura de la Vega 7. A designer bar with an unusual name ("Don't tell anyone!"). The pool and billiard tables on the upper floor attract numbers of faithful customers.

*Palacio de Gaviria, Arenal 9. 13 rooms in the elegant ambience of a 19th century mansion, offering a varied range of night life. Tertulias in original Isabelline décor, Argentinian tango, billiards, copas, salsa.

Teatriz, Hermosilla 15. An old theatre magnificently converted by Philipp Starck into a designer night spot, where you can enjoy a copa, a dance on the small dance floor or a snack to satisfy late-night pangs of hunger.

Discos

The number of discos which open when others close is more than can be counted on the fingers of two hands. But because of the fashion-consciousness of Madrileños and Madrileñas and the current practice of the municipal authorities, who are miserly in granting licences but energetic in withdrawing them, they change with considerable frequency. It is advisable, therefore, to consult the weekly "Guía del Ocio" ("Leisure Guide"), available at all news-stands, before setting out.

★Angels of Xenon, Atocha 38. A mammoth disco with go-go girls in cages and celebrated DJs. Lesbians and gays are as much at home here as heteros, who have nothing against the former.

Aqualung, Paseo de la Ermita del Santo 40–48 (Metro: Puerta del Ángel). The clientele a good mix. Refreshing in summer because of the swimming baths.

Archy, Marqués de Riscal 11. A young clientele, who are rediscovering the music of the seventies and eighties.

★Berlin Cabaret, Costanillo de San Pedro 11. A *sitio* which came to the fore in the early days of the *movida*. At the weekend a disco with the inevitable drag queens; during the week a cabaret with a red décor and an appropriately sinful ambience.

Boccaccio, Marqués de la Ensenada 16. One of the classics of the *movida,* forever threatened with closure.

But, Barceló 11. Salsa and merengue, cha-cha-cha and tango.

Café del Mercado, Ronda de Toledo 1. Tropical décor, with groups from the Caribbean playing daily; the dancing is mostly salsa.

Café Valvén: see above, Music and cabaret

Casino Gran Madrid, Carretera de La Coruña, km 28.35. Disco ambience for the not-so-young age groups; night restaurant, gaming.

★Joy Teatro Esclava, Arenal 11. You will get in here around 3am if you are accompanied by Mar Flores, Brad Pitt or the heir to the Spanish throne. If you are not, then correct attire is a precondition of entry, but by itself may not be enough. If the doorkeeper turns you away you need not take it personally. If he lets you in you enter a black disco wonder-world.

KU Madrid, Princesa 1. Unless a fashion show or a publicity show for some product or other takes over the place, the guests most likely to get into this high-class disco are well-dressed people who have just come from a wedding reception. *Pijo,* say the Madrileños: a snob place.

Midday/Midnight, Amaniel 13. A temple of deep and techno music which closes at 6am but reopens at 9 on Sunday mornings and continues until the afternoon.

Pachá, Barceló 11. This disco, dating back to the early days of the *marcha madrileña,* is now the haunt of the rich and beautiful, the *gente guapa*. But it is not *pijo:* the ambience is relaxed. Provided that you are not actually wearing trainers you have a good chance of getting in.

Palace, Plaza de Isabel II. A high-class disco for those who are not quite so young as they were.

Palacio de Gaviria: see above, Cafés and *bares de copas*

★El Sol: see above, Music and cabaret

Terrazas

At temperatures of over 30°C (86°F) in the shade – even in the small hours after midnight – the streets of Madrid fall silent and the action moves to the airy terraces of the cafés and restaurants. The most popular places are on the two wide boulevards, the Paseo de Recoletos and Paseo de la Castellana, with such establishments as the Café El Espejo (see Restaurants), the Café Gijón (see above) and those listed below. Other places to look for a cooling terrace and a refreshing drink are the Paseo del Pintor Rosales, the Plaza de Chueca and the little streets under the Viaducto.

Boulevard, Paseo de la Castellana 37. High prices for a high-class clientele.

Balcón de Rosales, Paseo del Pintor Rosales, corner of Marqués de Urquijo. Its cool situation above the Parque del Oeste makes this rather snob disco, with restaurant and terrace, an inviting place in summer.

Café del Nuncio: see above, Cafés

★Castellana 99, Paseo de la Castellana 99. One of the most "open" *terrazas* on the Paseo de la Castellana, with moderate prices.

Ñ, Paseo de la Castellana 21. Clientele a good mix; reasonably priced drinks.

Homosexual *sitios*

In liberally-minded Madrid the gay scene is not a big issue. Heteros of either sex are neither turned away nor looked at askance in homosexual establishments.

Angels of Xenon: see above, Discos

Café Figueroa, Augusto Figueroa 17. A café of character in which hetero couples feel quite at home.

Club 69, Marqués de Riscal 11, corner of Fortuny. Lesbians, gays and heteros respect each others' preferences in this high-class club and disco.

La Rosa, Tetuán 27. A disco which was originally for women only; but it has now been discovered by gay men, who are still the minority but are happy to dance here.

Café Ruiz: see above, Cafés

Chocolatería San Ginés, Pasadizo de San Ginés 5. Open 7pm to 7am. In the evening respectable ladies and curious tourists meet here; in the morning the clientele consists of workers and night-owls looking for something warm after a long night.

Chocolate con churros/Pastry fritters with hot chocolate

La Fídula: see above, *Sitios*

Nuevo Café Barbieri: see above, Cafés. A stylish setting for an afternoon cup of chocolate.

Parks

Madrid has more than 40 parks, offering visitors rest and relaxation after their sightseeing.

El Retiro (see Sights from A to Z, Parque del Retiro): in the city centre, near the Plaza de Independencia and Atocha Station.

Parque del Oeste (see entry in Sights from A to Z): in western Madrid, near Plaza de la Moncloa, Paseo del Pintor Rosales and the University City (see Sights from A to Z, Ciudad Universitaria).

Jardín de Sabatini: a geometrically laid out park on the north side of the Royal Palace (see Sights from A to Z, Palacio Real), on the site of the former stables.

Casa de Campo (see entry in Sights from A to Z): in the west of the city; Madrid's largest park.

Parque de la Fuente del Berro: in the east of Madrid; laid out in the late 17th century, in the reign of Charles II; area 8 ha (20 acres).

Campo del Moro: the beautifully laid out park of the Royal Palace (see Sights from A to Z, Palacio Real); entrance in Paseo de la Virgen del Puerto. It contains two fine fountains, the Triton Fountain (Tritones) and the Shell Fountain (Las Conchas).

Jardín Botánico (Botanic Gardens): on the Paseo del Prado, near the Retiro Park and the Observatory, with 30,000 species of plants from all over the world (see Sights from A to Z, Jardín Botánico).

Parque de Atenas (area 6 ha (15 acres)): at the foot of the Cuesta de la Vega. It is the counterpart of a park in Athens named after Madrid.

Alameda de Osuna, also known as El Capricho: a former aristocratic estate which is the subject of many stories; 9 km (5½ mi.) from Madrid on the Carretera de la Alameda de Osuna, near Barajas Airport. Particularly attractive features of the park are the little lakes and ponds and the Old People's House.

Parque Enrique Tierno Galván, to the south of Atocha Station, with the Madrid Planetarium (see Museums, Planetario de Madrid).

Parque de la Vaguada y Centro Cívico del Barrio del Pilar: near the

Police

Madrid 2 La Vaguada shopping centre (see Shopping, Souvenirs). Madrid's newest park, it serves the densely populated La Vaguada development. In the park is the new La Vaguada cultural centre (by Javier San José Marqués and Jordi Parcerisas Vázquez, 1982–89).

Parque Juan Carlos II: laid out in the 1990s beside the new Campo de las Naciones exhibition centre (see Trade Fairs) and named after the present king. Twice the size of the Parque del Retiro, with an adjoining golf course.

Police (Policía)

General emergency: tel. 112

Guardía Civil: tel. 062

Municipal Police: tel. 092

Directorate-General of Security
(Dirección General del Area de Seguridad)
Conde-Duque 9; tel. 914100037

National Police: tel. 091

Directorate-General
(Dirección General)
Miguel Ángel 5; tel. 914100037

Post

The Spanish Post Office is responsible for postal services and telegrams but not for the telephone system, which is run by the Telefónica corporation (see Telephone).

Stamps

Stamps *(sellos)* can be bought not only in post offices but also in tobacconists' *(estancos)*, which are identified by a sign showing a stylised yellow tobacco leaf and the letter T and are open until late in the evening.
Foreign mail should be deposited in post-boxes *(buzones;* singular *buzón)* labelled Extranjero, or failing that in a box labelled Provincias. Nowadays, however, most post-boxes are not specially labelled and are used for all mail, whether foreign or local.

Poste restante

All post offices accept poste restante mail *(Lista de Correos)*. When collecting poste restante mail you must produce your passport or other identity document.

Head Post Office

Madrid's Head Post Office in Plaza de la Cibeles is open Mon.–Fri. 9am–midnight.

Telegrams

Telegrams can be handed in at the Head Post Office or tel. 915222000.

Public Holidays (Días feriados)

January 1st	Año Nuevo	New Year's Day
January 6th	Reyes Magos	Epiphany
March 19th	San José	St Joseph's Day
May 1st	Día del Trabajo	Labour Day
May 2nd	Día de la Comunidad de Madrid	Day of Madrid Region
May 15th	San Isidro	Feast day of Madrid's patron saint
June 24th	San Juan	The king's name-day (not every year)
June 29th	San Pedro y San Pablo	SS. Peter and Paul (not every year)
July 25th	Santiago	St James (not every year)
August 15th	Asunción	Assumption
October 12th	Día de la Hispanidad	Commemorating the discovery of America
November 1st	Todos los Santos	All Saints (when November 1st is a Sunday the public holiday is on the 2nd)
November 9th	Almudena	Feast-day of Madrid's patroness
December 6th	Día de la Constitución	Constitution Day (not every year)
December 8th	Inmaculada Concepción	Immaculate Conception
December 25th	Navidad	Christmas Day

Viernes Santo	Good Friday	Movable feasts
Corpus Christi	Corpus Christi	
Jueves Santo	Maundy Thursday (not every year)	

Public Transport (Servicios públicos)

Madrid's underground system, the Metro, is the city's fastest means of transport. There are ten lines, including the orbital line 6, which run from 6.30am to 1.30am on the following day. The rush hours (7–9.30am, 1.30–2.30pm and 7.30–9pm) are best avoided.

Metro

A map of the Metro is given on p. 218.

There is a flat-rate fare of 130 ptas on the Metro. A card with a magnetic strip covering ten journeys costs 900 ptas; it is also valid on the red municipal buses, but not for transfers.

Information: Oficina de Información del Metro; tel. 915225909

Lost property: Metro: Legazpi; tel. 915884346

There are over 150 routes in the municipal bus network (Empresa Municipal de Transportes, EMT), with another 200 routes in the Madrid Region, most of them leaving from the Moncloa Metro station, the Southern Bus Station in Calle Méndez Álvaro and Chamartín Station.

Buses (Autobuses)

The bus fare is 130 ptas. There is also the same ten-journey card costing 900 ptas as on the Metro. Information on bus services: tel. 914019900

EMT runs 20 night bus services (known as *buhos,* "owls"), which all run through the Plaza de la Cibeles. The buses, bearing the letter N, run between midnight and 6am (at midnight, 12.30, 1, 1.30, 2, 3, 4 and 5).

Night buses (autobús nocturno)

Madrid Metro (Underground)

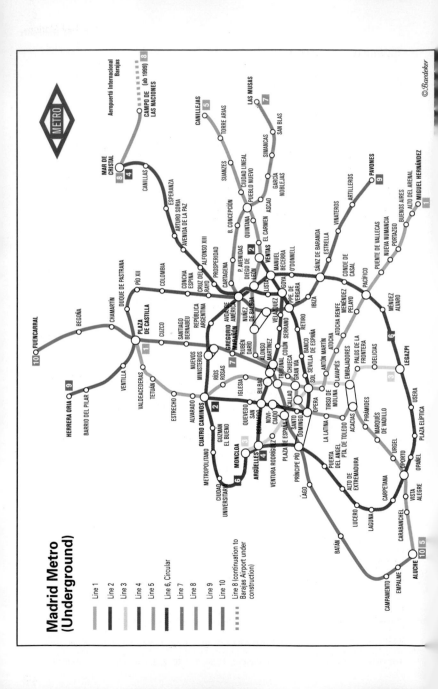

Line 1
Line 2
Line 3
Line 4
Line 5
Line 6, Circular
Line 7
Line 8
Line 9
Line 10
Line 8 (continuation to Barajas Airport under construction)

© Baedeker

Radio and Television

The main radio organisation is Radio Nacional de España (RNE), with five stations broadcasting on FM.
The BBC World Service can be heard until midnight on short wave.

Radio

The state television corporation, Radio Televisión Española, RTVE), has two channels, TVE 1 or La Primera and La 2. The public regional channel, Telemadrid, and three private channels, Antena 3, Telecino and Canal Plus (a pay-TV service which also transmits an interesting uncrypted programme), can also be received on ordinary television sets.

Television

Satellite television is widely available in Spain, but there is little cable television. Satellite television has two digital channels, Canal Satélite Digital and Vía Digital, with sport, film and documentary programmes as well as a wide range of special interest programmes. Most households and hotels can receive on analogue frequencies programmes such as Eurosport, CBN and Euronews.

Satellite, cable and digital television

Rail Stations

The state rail corporation RENFE (Red Nacional de los Ferrocarriles Españoles) has three stations in Madrid, with the same telephone numbers for information and booking. They are linked by Cercanías, the local and suburban railway system, and Chamartín and Príncipe Pío Stations are also linked by Metro line No. 10.

Estación de Chamartín, Calle Augustín de Fozá
This is Madrid's most important station, with lines to northern Spain and France.

Chamartín Station

Estación de Atocha, Glorieta Carlos V
Atocha Station (see entry in Sights from A to Z), or South Station, runs trains to southern Spain and Castilian towns such as Segovia and Toledo. It is also the terminus of the high-speed train AVE to Córdoba and Seville.

Atocha Station

Estación Príncipe Pío or del Norte, Plaza de la Florida
Lines to north-western Spain.

Príncipe Pío Station

Timetable information on trains from any of the stations can be obtained and tickets can be bought by telephoning 913289020. The tickets can either be delivered to your home address or hotel or picked up at the station.
There is also a ticket office at Alcalá 44 (open Mon.–Fri. 9am–1.30pm, 4–7pm, Sat. 9am–1.30pm).

Information

Tickets (billetes) are best bought at least 24 hours before the time of departure in a RENFE office. Although in general it is not obligatory to have a seat reservation ticket (reserva de plaza), it is advisable during the main holiday season and before the major public holidays to buy a reservation ticket along with your travel ticket. After the pre-booking period travel and reservation tickets, if still available, can be bought only at the station half an hour or an hour before departure (with separate ticket windows for different lines).
Tickets bought outside Spain must be validated before setting out on another section of your journey, either in advance at a RENFE office or on the day of travel at the station.

Tickets

Restaurants (Restaurantes)

Lunch is served in Madrid between 1.30 and 2pm, dinner from 9pm onwards. No good restaurant will make exceptions to the rule, though hotel restaurants may sometimes pander to the eating habits of their guests (see Baedeker Special, p. 222). For night-owls there are restaurants which will serve warm dishes late at night. If you are choosing a place for a meal out of the blue there are two useful criteria to apply: a restaurant patronised by many local people is probably a good one, and a look at the menu will help you to decide whether it is in the right price category. We give below a small selection of Madrid restaurants. A reliable restaurant guide for the whole of Spain is the "Gourmettour", published annually, which you can buy in a bookshop.

The following restaurants in our selection are open on Sundays: Asador de Aranda, Casa Mingo, De Funy, La Fonda, El Espejo, La Galette, El Horno de Santa Teresa, José Luis. Hotel restaurants are also open on Sundays.

Restaurants in Madrid (selection)

Gourmet restaurants

Arce, Augusto Figueroa 32; tel. 915225913. Metro: Chueca. Well presented Basque creativity in its purest form, at reasonable prices.

El Amparo, Puigcerdá 8; tel. 914316456. Metro: Serrano. The cuisine of San Sebastián. As is usual in Basque restaurants, you discover each dish afresh – even *rabo de toro* . The "tasting menu" *(menú de degustación)* at around 6000 ptas will give your palate a good general idea of Basque cuisine.

El Bodegón, Pinar 15; tel. 915623137. Metro: Avenida de América. Basque-French cuisine at the highest level in a classic ambience. Here too you can sample the cuisine with a *menú de degustación* (6000 ptas).

El Cenador del Prado, Prado 4; tel. 914291561. Metro: Sevilla and Sol. International cuisine with a Mediterranean stamp in a refreshingly rejuvenated ambience. Unexpectedly reasonable prices.

Club 31, Alcalá 58; tel. 915320511. Metro: Retiro. Classical French cuisine for a select clientele from the world of money and politics.

Goizeko Cabi, Comandante Zorita 37; tel. 915330214. Metro: Nuevos Ministerios. A small restaurant with less inventive cuisine from Bilbao. Luxury for the palate.

Jockey, Amador de los Ríos 6; tel. 913192435. Metro: Colón. In the 1960s this restaurant was the first envoy of French cuisine in Spain, and is now a very formal gourmet restaurant. The biggest and most exclusive but not the best.

★Viridiana, Juan de Mena 14; tel. 915315222. Metro: Retiro. The name is taken from Buñuel's famous film, and the menu has also a touch of surrealism, which is appreciated by the most critical connoisseurs You will need to spend around 10,000 ptas to get an adequate idea of Abraham García's cuisine and bodega.

★Zalacaín, Álvarez de Baena 4; tel. 915611079. Metro: Rubén Darío. The summit of creative Basque cuisine in Madrid. Outstanding meals, for which men are expected to wear a suit; but with menus ranging between 7000 and 9000 ptas you can afford it.

Cabo Mayor, Juan Hurtado de Mendoza II; tel. 913506497. Metro: Cuzco. Noted for the quality of its ingredients, with features of Cantabrian and Navarrese cuisine.

Combarro, Reina Mercedes 12; tel. 915549003. Metro: Alvarado. Solid elegance: the best Galician restaurant in Madrid. Ingredients and prices are much the same as in restaurants of the same type, but here the seafood is guaranteed fresh and is prepared just right.

Las Cuatro Estaciones, General Ibáñez Ibero 5; tel. 915540143. Metro: Guzmán el Bueno. A high-class restaurant whose reasonable prices and casual ambience attract the younger age groups as well as the older. Light international cuisine and a good range of wines.

La Gastroteca de Stéphane y Arturo, Plaza Chueca 8; tel. 915322564. Metro: Chueca. Black magic of creative cuisine, from the shellac dishes to the wall panelling. A bistro which does wonders with Mediterranean raw materials; but it takes some courage to tackle its sea-urchin creations and sorbet of black olives.

★Kikuyu, Bárbara de Braganza 4; tel. 913196611. Metro: Colón. A young team, who go in for minimalism both in the décor and in the cuisine; but it turns out surprisingly well. Up-to-the minute, Mediterranean, light. The ambience is worth a visit in itself. Booking necessary.

El Landó, Plaza de Gabriel Miró 8; tel. 913658253. Metro: La Latina. From the aperitif with pan tumaka and jamón to the milk pudding *(arroz con leche)* as dessert, you are spoiled here with the simplest dishes.

El Mentidero de la Villa, Santo Tomé 6; tel. 913081285. Metro: Colón. The best Basque cuisine: delight for the palate, with small surprises, but full of harmony, as is the ambience. Reasonable prices (lunch menu 2400 ptas).

★El Olivo, General Gallegos 1; tel. 913591535. Metro: Cuzco. As the name indicates, Mediterranean cuisine of the finest quality. If you particularly like any of their olive oils you can buy it in the Oleoteca opposite.

O'Pazo, Reina Mercedes 20; tel. 915549070. Metro: Nuevos Ministerios. The proof that freshly caught fish is delicious even without any nautical trimmings. Elegant and, for a fish restaurant, not cheap.

★Paradís Madrid, Marqués de Cubas 14; tel. 914297303. Metro: Banco de España. Also Paradís Casa de América, Recoletos 2 (Palacio de Linares); tel. 915754540. The only difference in the cuisine of these two branches of the Paradís chain is that in the Casa de América there are sometimes Latin American days. Otherwise both of them offer the finest Catalan cuisine in a cosy avantgarde setting in the Paradís Madrid, in Baroque splendour in the Palacio de Linares or on its pleasant terrace.

★Príncipe de Viana, Manuel de Falla 5; tel. 914571549. Metro: Lima. Superb Basque-Navarrese cuisine, with tried and tested traditional dishes in an elegant setting.

La Trainera, Lagasca 60; tel. 915768035. Metro: Serrano. With his stall in the Mercamadrid market the owner of this Galician restaurant has a direct line to the fish markets of north-western Spain.

Al-Mounia, Recoletos 5; tel. 914350828. Metro: Banco de España. Moroccan cuisine in an authentic setting. Fixed-price menu 5000 ptas.

Eating and Drinking in Madrid

Word of a good restaurant in Madrid gets round as quickly as that of a good film, and as a result almost all restaurants are fully booked at weekends. Even when standing at a tapas bar you may have to use your elbows to convey your tapas or your drink safely from hand to mouth; for Spaniards like going out for a good meal and go out often: so often and so enthusiastically that prices even in top-class restaurants do not get out of hand. It is quite normal, in restaurants such as the Gastroteca de Stéphane y Arturo (Plaza Chueca) or El Amparo (Puigcerdá 8), to get away with a bill of less than 9000 ptas per head without missing out a course or denying yourself a good wine. Spanish cuisine may be not so well thought of as French: the Madrileños do not care.

The astonishing thing about Madrid's culinary culture is that even an average bar-restaurant will offer such a range of fish and seafood that you forget the noise of the traffic outside and could imagine yourself eating in a harbourside restaurant. So many tapas bars offer *percebes* (barnacles), *nécoras* (shrimps) and *gambas* (shrimps) from Huelva fresh from the pot or the plancha that such delicacies seem to be part of the Madrileños' staple diet. But beware: delicacies have their price, as you may discover when you get *la dolorosa* (the bill).

The Madrileños do not of course confine themselves to fish and seafood. The outstanding quality of the ingredients – from the asparagus of Navarre by way of mushrooms from Catalonia and the *carne roja* ("red meat") of Galician cattle to the delicate olive oil of Jaén – is the basis of the delights which Madrid can offer the palate. And to wash the food down there are not only the good red wines of the Ribera del Duero and Rioja and the excellent wines now produced in Valencia and

An everyday sight in Madrid: a cluster of customers outside a bar

Catalonia, as well as the white Albariños, Ribeiros and Ruedas – and also, of course, sherry.

In many countries the introduction of "international cuisine" has liberated the inhabitants from the monotony of their native dishes. Not so in Spain, and certainly not in Madrid. Here as in other European cities you will find a rich spectrum of Asian and Oriental food, pizzas and even sauerkraut; but the variety of regional dishes, in Andalusia or in the rice dishes of Valencia often showing Arab influence, relieves Madrid cuisine of any risk of monotony even without taking account of foreign imports. Moreover Spain has its own gourmet culture. On the one hand there are the creative Basques, represented in Madrid by such top-class restaurants as the Zalacaín (Álvarez de Baena 4) and the

Príncipe de Viana (Manuel de Falla 5), with their light and sophisticated cuisine. The Catalans too make their contribution to the culinary temptations of Madrid. Their cuisine is nearer to that of France: heavier than Basque cuisine, with butter and cream in its refined sauces – although there is also a cult of the lighter olive oil in Catalonia. During the mushroom season the charming Paradís Madrid restaurant (Marqués de Cubas 14) is *the* place to go – rounding off your meal, perhaps, with a boletus ice.

After breakfast, which is usually a fairly Spartan affair, with coffee and toast, a *bollo* (bread roll) or *churros* (fried chou pastry), preferably dipped into thick, hot chocolate, Madrileño stomachs have to wait a long time for lunch, which begins between 1.30 and 3. Consequently by about 11 o'clock the city's cafés and bars are crowded with customers having a second breakfast, and the waiters are kept busy slamming down on the bar counter cups of *café solo, cortado* or *café con leche*. Even those who have had a generous buffet breakfast in their hotel will feel their stomachs beginning to rumble by about 12 o'clock. Fortunately, however, it is now the time for an aperitif, and you can have a *copita de vino* here, a glass of sherry there (ask for a *fino de Jerez)*, or perhaps a *cañita* (small glass) of beer – accompanied, of course, by some small bits and pieces by way of appetisers. These, known in Seville and Bilbao, Valencia and Gijón, and above all in Madrid as *tapas,* are usually provided free along with your drink, with the object of preventing the alcohol from having too devastating effect on an empty stomach. (It is no longer a disgrace in Madrid, however, to have a cola or some other soft drink instead of alcohol). In a bar specifically designated as a tapas bar the tapas are not provided free.

At lunch *(almuerzo* or *comida)* there is much to be said for choosing the three-course fixed-price menu which almost all restaurants offer. It is not only very reasonably priced – ranging from 800 ptas to 7000 (in a top-class restaurant like the Zalacaín), but almost always guarantees variety and quality. After lunch it is still a long time to dinner at about 9.30; but there is a remedy for afternoon pangs of hunger in the form of a *merienda,* an afternoon snack which may be either sweet or savoury. Around 7 o'clock a Madrileño may feel like another cup of chocolate with churros, or in summer a cool and refreshing drink of *horchata* (orgeat), accompanied by something picked up in a *pastelería;* or perhaps he may look into a taberna or bodega where he can have a glass of Rioja or a beer, accompanied by something more substantial in the way of an appetiser – perhaps sherry with spicy table olives or a slice of *chorizo* (paprika sausage)? Punctually at 7 the Venencia (Echegaray 7) opens its old wooden door to meet this need. Not infrequently the 7 o'clock aperitif merges seamlessly into dinner.

There are many reasons for falling into the *tapeo* (tapa sampling) habit. If, for example, you haven't booked a table by Wednesday you won't get one for Friday evening, and certainly not in fashionable restaurants such as the Kikuyu (Bárbara de Braganza 4) or the Viridiana (Juan de Mena 14). But the tapa culture is not merely a expedient for filling in time: it is a whole gastronomic department of its own. There is, on the one hand, the "sitting-down" variant, in which you got to a restaurant, tasca or taberna such as the Casa Ciriaco (Mayor 84) or the Taberna la Salamandra (Alfonso VI 6) and order tapas *para picar* (to nibble), eating a little of many tapas out of the great variety offered. Some establishments specialise in particular delicacies, such as the Pulpería (Pez 18), whose speciality is *pulpo a la gallega* (octopus on paprika potatoes), or the Taberna Bilbao (Costanilla de San Andrés 8), with its *bacalao al pil pil* (salt cod), washed down by first-class wines. But the real tapeo – *lo suyo* – is a tour through a range of different *sitios,* never staying long in any of them but always looking forward to your next port of call, and assuaging your hunger with small bits and pieces so as to leave room for the speciality of the next place on your list.

El Asador de Aranda, Preciados 44; tel. 915472156. Metro: Diego de León. Charcoal-grilled sucking-pig and lamb in fine Castilian style. A good place for children too.

Asador Frontón, Tirso de Molina 7; tel. 913692325. Metro: Tirso de Molina. Basque-style beef from the grill.

La Bola, Bola 5; tel. 915417164. Metro: Santo Domingo. The typical red panelled walls and the attractive ambience combined with the excellence of the cuisine have made this *tasca,* which since 1870 has served one of the best *cocidos madrileños,* popular not only with visitors but with a faithful band of regulars.

Botín, Cuchilleros 17; tel. 912664217. Metro: Sol. According to the "Guinness Book of Records", the oldest restaurant in the world. *Morcilla, chipirones en su tinta* and sucking-pig have been served here since 1725. Its very reasonable fixed-price menu at 4100 ptas attracts large numbers of tourists.

Café de Oriente, Plaza de Oriente 2; tel. 915482010. Metro: Ópera. Independent of the turn-of-the-century café and its terrace, the restaurant offers Basque-Navarrese cuisine, with ingredients fresh from the market, in the ambience of a 17th century convent.

Carmencita, Libertad 16; tel. 915316612. Metro: Chueca. A taberna in which Neruda, Lorca and Benlliure were very much at home. Now more of a bistro serving Basque cuisine; but the exquisite *escabeches* (soused fish) still maintain the old tradition.

Casa de Valencia, Paseo del Pintor Rosales 58; tel. 915441747. Metro: Argüelles. An elegant setting in which to choose from 15 rice dishes, at prices to match. Paella is served with cava or wine.

★Casa Vallejo, San Lorenzo 9; tel. 913086158. Metro: Alonso Martínez. A cosy little bistro with Catalan cuisine. A good place for lunch as well as dinner.

Currito, Casa de Campo, Pabellón de Vizcaya; tel. 914645704. Metro: Lago. Traditional charcoal-grilled dishes such as *carne roja* (red meat) or *besugo* (sea bream). Its terrace is attractive in summer. Prices are on the high side.

★La Dorada, Orense 64; tel. 912702002. Fish dishes in a nautical setting: try their *lubina a la sal.*

El Espejo, Paseo de Recoletos 31; tel. 913082347. Metro: Colón. In addition to its excellent and reasonably priced menu El Espejo offers the attraction of its Art Nouveau interior with a profusion of mirrors. Open on Sunday and in August.

El Estragón, Plaza de la Paja 10; tel. 913658982. Metro: La Latina. A New Age vegetarian restaurant. Tapas bar with meatless *pinchos* (appetisers).

De Funy, Serrano 213; tel. 914576915. Metro: Colombia. Lebanese cuisine in a very attractive setting. Rather out of the way, but it has the advantage of being open on Sunday.

La Fonda, Lagasca 11; tel. 915777924. Metro: Retiro. A very friendly Catalan restaurant in the medium price range. Open on Sunday but closed in August.

La Galette, Conde de Aranda 11; tel. 915760641. Metro: Retiro. Fish and vegetarian dishes in a romantic ambience. Fixed-price lunch menu. Open on Sunday evenings.

Gure-Etxea, Plaza de la Paja 12; tel. 913656149. Traditional Basque cuisine in a classic Basque ambience.

El Horno de Santa Teresa, Santa Teresa 12; tel. 913080102. Metro: Alonso Martínez. Fresh from the market, oven-cooked in traditional Basque style: fish, vegetables and meat *en su punto*. Open on Sunday. Fixed-price menu; reasonable prices.

Julián de Tolosa, Cava Baja 18; tel. 913642057. Metro: La Latina. *Merluza* or *chuletón de buey* as the main dish; nothing else, but of the highest quality. Prices on the high side.

Lerranz, Echegaray 26; tel. 914291206. Metro: Sevilla. Connected with the Cenador del Prado by the back door. Light cuisine; reasonably priced lunch menu.

Lur Maitea, Fernando el Santo 4; tel. 913080350. Metro: Alonso Martínez. The cuisine of Santander; carefully prepared and presented. Two fixed-price dinner menus help to keep costs under control.

Nicolás, Villalar 4; tel. 914317737. Metro: Retiro. Good home cooking, Catalan-style, with the "something" extra which makes a classic Madrid restaurant. The prices entice you to come back.

El Pescador, José Ortega y Gasset 75; tel. 914021290. Metro: Lista. Because Madrid lies so far from the sea, most fish restaurants tend to have this rather overdone quayside décor. The fish and seafood, however, are fresh from the sea. Substantial meals for 6000 ptas.

Redondella, Tortosa 9; tel. 915399410. Metro: Atocha-Renfe. A very normal restaurant with a fixed-price lunch menu near the Centro de Arte Reina Sofía. Office workers and railwaymen on the way to Atocha Station drop in to the tapas bar for a glass of Galician *ribeiro*.

Sal Gorda, Beatriz de Bobadilla 9; tel. 9155395066. Metro: Guzmán el Bueno. Beef, delicate *cerdo ibérico* and vegetables cooked on the *plancha*. A restaurant for every taste; very Mediterranean.

Salvador, Barbieri 12; tel. 915214524. Metro: Chueca. The walls are covered with bullfighting mementoes. The menu at this very typical Madrid tasca includes both *rabo de toro* and *almejas a la marinera*.

Sarrasín, Libertad 8; tel. 915309746. Metro: Chueca. Light Mediterranean cuisine in a light Mediterranean ambience in which gay and heterosexual couples are equally welcome. Reasonably priced lunch and dinner menus.

Bodegas, tabernas and tapa culture

Many Madrid bodegas, tabernas and tascas are so cosy and welcoming that you could stay there until the grey light of morning. Others you make for to drink a glass and then move on. Others again are absolute musts in any real tapa tour in Madrid.

A good route for beginners in the tapa culture would be on the following lines, taking in *sitios* from the listings below: You might begin, for example, in the Taberna de los Cien Vinos (Nuncio 16) with a few *pin-*

Tapa tours

225

chos (perhaps a piece of roast beef or a quiche), move on to Las Austrias (Nuncio 17) for a garlic omelette, look into Almendro 13 (at that address) for a grilled *almendrito* (ham roll), cut yourself a slice of *bacalao* (salt cod) in the Taverna Bilbao (Costanilla de San Andrés 8) and finally establish yourself at a table in La Salamandra (Alfonso VI 6). This will introduce you to Madrid's modern tapa culture and at the same time let you see the quarter round the Plaza de la Paja from its best side.

A classic tour of the Cava Baja area might begin in the Casa Lucio (Cava Baja 35) with a slice of paper-thin *jamón ibérico*. You could follow this up with a beautifully made tomato salad in La Chata (Cava Baja 24), accompanied perhaps by a portion of cheese or rib of lamb. Then on to Díaz y Larrouy (Cava Baja 6) for *pimientos rellenos* (stuffed peppers), and finally to the Posada de la Villa (Cava Baja 9) for a few *croquetas* and tasty *torreznos* (rashers of bacon) to satisfy what remains of your hunger.

Almendro 13, Almendro 13. Metro: La Latina. Finos or a *caña* of beer to wash down freshly grilled morsels on *bocadillos* or *patatas fritas*. A great temple of the new tapa culture of the district.

Las Austrias, Nuncio 17. Metro: La Latina. Seventy wines – only 30 fewer than in its neighbour the Taberna de los Cien Vinos – and *pinchos* with the finest ingredients.

★El Bocaíto, Libertad 6. Metro: Chueca. This classic establishment offers a gastronomic tour of the whole of Spain at its tapa bar.

Casa Alberto, Huertas 18. Metro: Antón Martín. Old Madrilenian from its zinc bar counter to its substantial *albóndigas* (rissoles).

Casa Ciriaco, Mayor 84. Metro: Ópera. The bar at the entrance is always crowded by people drinking *cañas,* waiting for a seat in this old-established tasca where they can get their *picoteo* (a traditional delicacy made from meat and fish).

★Casa Labra, Tetuán 12. Metro: Sol. The Spanish Socialist Party was founded over an aperitif here. If you ever feel hungry between mealtimes, a *pincho bacalao* and a *caña* of beer or a glass of Valdepeñas in the Casa Labra will put you right. You can imagine the state the floor is in; so it is better to look up to the ceiling and study the inscription on it:"*"*The man who drinks properly does the right thing". You can interpret it as you please.

Casa Lucio, Cava Baja 35. Metro: La Latina. Almost a top-class restaurant. Try a slice of paper-thin *jamón ibérico* at its tapa bar.

★Casa Mingo, Paseo de la Florida 2. Metro: Estación del Norte. There has been an abundant flow of cider here daily since 1916. The best accompaniment is a substantial *pollo frito* (fried chicken). In winter you eat and drink inside, but in summer preferably outside.

Cervecería Alemana, Plaza de Santa Ana 6. Metro: Sol. A classic establishment in this lively square. It is particularly proud of its *calamares* and *albóndigas*. Although called German, it has a traditional Madrileño ambience which appealed to Hemingway.

Cervecería Santa Bárbara, Plaza Santa Bárbara 8. Metro: Alonso Martínez. A popular meeting-place before a meal or the cinema for a glass of beer and freshly cooked Huelva prawns. A classic.

La Chata, Cava Baja 24. Metro: La Latina. A classic stop on a tapa tour: tomato salad, cheese, *jamón, cordero asado*.

Cuenllas, Ferraz 5. Metro: Ventura Rodríguez. A designer tapa bar specialising in canapés, delicious morsels on toast.

Díaz y Larrouy, Cava Baja 6. Metro: La Latina. Stuffed peppers and small enchantments with *bacalao*.

La Dolores, Plaza de Jesús 4. Metro: Sevilla. Another canapé specialist, but long before designer tapas were invented. A good place to restore your strength on a tour of the Huertas quarter.

★El Anciano Rey de los Vinos, Bailén 19. Metro: Ópera. Tortilla or canapés to accompany a glass of wine or *torija* (French toast) with a cup of coffee in solid old-world comfort. A good place to have a snack after a visit to the Royal Palace on a Sunday.

★Entrevinos, Ferraz 36. Metro: Ventura Rodríguez. A modern designer taberna. Excellent *embutidos ibéricos (jamón, lomo,* etc.) and fine Crianza and Reserva wines.

La Fuencisla, San Mateo. Metro: Tribunal. One of the best of Madrid's tascas, where you can enjoy its individual style for lunch or dinner.

José Luis, Serrano 89. Metro: Rubén Darío. Also at San Francisco de Sales 14 (Metro: Moncloa) and Rafael Salgado 11 (Metro: Lima). Thirty years ago José Luis brought the Bilbao-style *pincho* to Madrid and was more or less the founder of designer tapa culture here. Open from morning to 1am on the following day.

Posada de la Villa, Cava Baja 9. Metro: La Latina. Whether you sit at a table with friends or stand at the bar, in this old posada the last remains of your hunger will be satisfied with its substantial Castilian dishes in the course of a tapa tour of the Cava Baja.

La Pulpería, Pez 18. Metro: Noviciado. Octopus on paprika potatoes, with a glass of beer or fine white Ribeiro wine from Galicia. Crammed full every evening with hungry young people.

Taberna del Alabardero, Felipe V 6. Metro: Ópera. A respectable old taberna in turn-of-the-century style, the haunt of well-to-do bohemians. You can eat your tapas and drink a full-bodied Crianza wine either at a table on the terrace or in the dining room. Particularly good on *rabo de toro* and *merluza*.

★La Taberna de Antonio Sánchez, Mesón de Paredes 13. Metro: Tirso de Molina. You can't find *ola gitana* or *rabo de toro* better done than in this most Madrilenian of Madrid's tabernas. Spitting on the floor has been prohibited since 1830, when *torrijas* cost 15 centimos.

Taberna Bilbao, Costanilla de San Andrés 8. Metro: La Latina. A pleasant place to look in at; a representative of the new tapa culture.

La Taberna de los Cien Vinos, Nuncio 16. Metro: La Latina. Every *pincho* is a delight. Try one or more of its hundred wines.

Taberna La Salamandra, Alfonso VI 6. Metro: La Latina. A new *sitio*, painted bright yellow, in one of the recently renovated streets behind the Plaza de la Paja. An important staging-post on a tapa tour of La Latina.

La Venencia, Echegaray 7. Metro: Sol. Open 1.30–3.30pm and from 7.30 to after midnight. The very essence of Jerez de la Frontera. The best of finos from wooden casks, with spicy table olives.

Late-night dining	Boñar, Cruz Verde 16; tel. 915310039. Metro: San Bernardo. Substantial León-style cuisine until 3am. Seating for over 250.
	Champañería Gala, Moratín 22; tel. 914292562. Metro: Antón Martín. Paella and cava on a fixed-price menu until 2am.
	Capirén, Plaza de la Marina Española 4; tel. 915411177. Metro: Ópera. A smart bistro, open daily 9pm–3am.
	La Carreta, Barbieri 10; tel. 915327042. Metro: Chueca. Tango and steaks from the grill until 5am.
	L'Obrador, Segovia 17; tel. 913664834. Metro: La Latina. Italo-French cuisine until 3am.
See also	Food and Drink; Night Life; Business Hours, VIPS

Security

In Madrid, as in all big cities, there is always some risk of theft or robbery. It is wise, therefore, to take sensible precautions.

You should never leave anything of value in a car, particularly one with a foreign registration number, parked in the street or in an off-street parking garage. When leaving the car you should remove the car radio and leave the glove-box and boot cover open, so that the car is seen to be empty.

Watch out if you have a puncture. Thieves sometimes contrive to puncture the tyre and then offer to help in changing the wheel. You should politely refuse any such offer of help and make sure that no one can get at the luggage when you are removing it from the boot to the interior of the car to take out the spare wheel.

Valuables (passport, money, etc.) should be carried on your person. You should carry only a small quantity of cash; larger sums, as well as cheques, should be deposited in the hotel safe. If you want to draw money from an automatic telling machine choose one which is within the bank building rather than outside and bolt the door from inside. If possible, have someone with you when you leave the bank.

If you are physically attacked it is better to offer no resistance.

Thefts and break-ins to a car should be reported at once to the police: this is necessary to support a claim to your insurers. If you lose your passport you should apply to your embassy or consulate for a replacement document. Bag snatching is common in Madrid.

Loss of Eurocheques	See Currency
Emergencies	See entry

Shopping

Shopping quarters	See Baedeker Special, p. 231

Shopping centres and arcades

Department stores	All branches of the department store chain El Corte Inglés (including Preciados 3, La Vaguada) offer an overwhelming range of goods. For books, newspapers, periodicals and computer software: FNAC (Preciados 28; Metro Callao)

Madrid 2, La Vaguada, is the city's largest shopping centre (architect César Manriques), with an area of 220,000 sq. m (241,000 sq. yds). Situated in the northern district of El Pilar (Metro Barrio del Pilar), it has more than 250 shops (open Mon.–Sat. 9.30am–10pm).

Madrid 2, La Vaguada

Until 1982 the Mercado Puerta de Toledo (Ronda de Toledo 1) still sold fish. After extensive renovation (architects Martín Domínguez, Jesús Peñalba and Ricardo Aroca) its area of 2.5 ha (6 acres) is now occupied by highly exclusive shops, including designer boutiques and antique shops, as well as galleries which run exhibitions, conferences and other cultural events (open Tue.–Sat. 11.30am–9pm, Sun. 11.30am–3pm).

Mercado Puerta de Toledo

The Galería del Prado (Plaza de las Cortes 7) has an area of 4350 sq. m (46,825 sq. ft), with 38 exclusive shops.

Galería del Prado

The Jumbo 24 shopping centre at Avenida Pío XII 2 in northern Madrid (near Chamartín Station) is open 24 hours a day. From foodstuffs to DIY, nearly everything you want is to be found here.

Jumbo 24

Moda Shopping, on Avenida del General Perón, is a modern shopping centre with 78 shops, cultural institutions and banks.

Moda Shopping

This shopping arcade, with many high-class shops and a popular bar and restaurant on the roof, has two entrances, one at Paseo de la Castellana 34, the other at Calle Serrano 61 (Metro Núñoz do Balboa).

ABC Serrano

Specialist stores

In recent years young Spanish couturiers have begun to make a name for themselves. A number of avantgarde fashion houses have opened in the Chueca quarter to the north of the Gran Vía, for example in Calles Almirante, Conde de Xiquena, Argensola, Santa Teresa and Justiniano. You need to keep your eyes open to find them, since the shops have only small windows and the entrances are sometimes hidden. The following is a selection of addresses:
Adolfo Domínguez, Serrano 18 (for men and women; much sought-after avantgarde creations by Spain's star designer from Galicia)
Agatha Ruiz de la Pada, Marqués de Riscal 8 (for men and women; one of the most established women designers)
Ararat, Almirante 10/11 (for women; unusual and extravagant fashion, often by young designers)
El Caracol Cuadrado, Justiniano 8 (collection of creations by leading fashion designers)
Dafnis, Paseo de la Habana 174 (exclusive women's fashion)
Ekseption, Velázquez 28 (progressive fashion and party wear)
Elena Benarroch, Zurbarán 16 and Ortega y Gasset 10 (exclusive and progressive fashion for women)
Gallery, Piamonte 18 (avantgarde fashion for men)
Jesús del Pozo, Almirante 9 (ready-to-wear and bride's wear)
Kenzo, Ortega y Gasset 15 (avantgarde fashion for men and women)
Loewe, Serrano 26 (for women), Serrano 34 (for men) (classic and luxury outfitters, leather goods, accessories)
Massimo Dutti, Princesa 79, Goya 73, etc. (reasonably priced classic fashion for men and women)
Pedro Mirago, Almirante 20 (avantgarde fashion for men and women)
Roberto Verino, Claudio Coello 27 (Galician star designer for men and women)
Supreme, Hermosilla 102 (party wear)
Sybilla, Collejón de Jorge Juan 12 (one of Spain's star women designers; unusual, colourful and yet simple creations for women)

Fashion

Shopping

Vacas Flacas, Claudio Coello 24 (unusual fashion in Arte Povera style – using remnants and unusual materials)
Zara, Princesa 45/63, Gran Vía 32, Velázquez 49 (classic and casual fashion for women at reasonable prices)

Shoes

Gaitán, Jorge Juan 13 (bespoke and hand-made shoes)
Caligae, Calle Augusto Figueroa 27
Ezrupulus Net, Calle Almirante 7 (unusual shoes)
Camper, Calle Ayala 13 (fashion shoes)
Alpargatería Antigua Casa Crespo, Divino Pastor 29 (alpargatas and other esparto wickerwork)

Sweets

For unusual sweets:
Casa Mira, Carrera de San Jerónimo 30
La Pajarita, Villanueva 4
Caramelos Paco, Toledo 55
Pastelería Mallorca, Serrano 6, Bravo Murillo and Velázquez 59
Pastelería Niza, Argensola 24

Wine

Bodega de los Reyes, Reyes 6 (attractive and well-stocked wine store near Plaza de España)
Mariano Aguado, Echegaray 19 (good, well-stocked wine store near Plaza de Santa Ana)
Santa Cecilia, Blasco de Garay 72 (supermarket for wines and spirits)
El Rincón del Cava, María de Guzmán 43 (specialises in Catalan sparkling wines)
Mariano Madrueño, Postigo de San Martín 3 (wines and spirits)

Honey

El Colmenero, General Álvarez de Castro 9 (wide range of flower honeys)
La Moderna Apicultura, Rodríguez San Pedro 37

Ham

Museo del Jamón, Paseo del Prado 44, Carrera de San Jerónimo 6, Gran Vía 70, etc.
Mercado de la Paz, Ayal 28 (e.g. Stall 63, La Boulette, delicious jamón ibérico de Bellota from different parts of Spain)

Olive oil

La Oleoteca, Juan Ramón Jiménez 37 (belongs to the owner of the El Olivo restaurants – see Restaurants – where you can sample the different kinds of olives)

Cheese

La Dehesa, Argensola 21 (in addition to its excellent cheeses and the right wines to go with them, also sells olive oil and other delicacies)
El Palacio de los Quesos, Mayor 53 (unbeatable range of cheeses)

Antiques (antigüedades)

Madrid is one of the centres of the European antiques trade. Its range extends from the El Rastro flea market to the leading auction houses, from pictures by way of jewellery and everyday objects to books and period furniture. The following is a selection of shops in the area round the Cortes and round the Plaza de Santa Ana:
Deogracias, Carrera de San Jerónimo 34
Abelardo Linares, Plaza de las Cortes 11
Antonio Serraon, Plaza de Santa Ana 10
Arte de Reloxes, Plaza de Santa Ana 10
Suarte, Calle del Prado 8
Brunswick, Calle del Prado 12
Martín Franco, Calle del Prado 10
Salafranca, Plaza de las Cortes 7
Sotheby's Calle del Prado 18
Patrick Moore, Calle del Prado 23

In the El Rastro flea market, round Plaza de Cascorro, on Plaza

Shopper's Paradise

Madrid has the undeserved reputation of being an expensive place. This reputation goes back to the period in the early eighties when the peseta was much over-valued, but is not borne out by the exchange rate at which the euro is being introduced into Spain. It is true that in high-class fashion houses like Loewe, an old-established brand name recently rejuvenated, or Dafnis you can spend a fortune – as Madrileñas and Madrileños in the right social circles like to do. It is true also that less well-off citizens also love luxury. But when you can get a pair of high fashion lady's shoes for around £50 luxury is evidently a relative term.

If you want to buy a first-class Rioja wine, air-dried Iberian ham, the best La Mancha cheese or olive oil for the most refined palate, you will be surprised to find how the price compares with what you would pay at home. Moreover the people of Madrid, particularly the women, are inveterate bargain-hunters. For them the end-of-summer sales begin in July – before the real summer season. And at such establishments as Zara (Princesa 45/63, Gran Vía 32 and Massimo Dutti (Princesa 79, Goya 73, etc.) – in the fashionable Calle Princesa as well as the select Salamanca quarter – you can buy reasonably priced fashion articles next door to some of the great names of fashion.

For the window-shopper and the impulse buyer Madrid offers an overwhelming variety of temptations. If you don't know what you want or where to get it you will either be totally lost or you will end up in one of the many branches of the Corte Inglés department store chain. But if you are interested in fashion you should not miss the chance of an expedition round some of the Spanish houses, which since the boom years of the 1980s have come out of the shadow of their great European counterparts and gained an international reputation.

The heart of Spanish avantgarde fashion is to be found in Calles Almirante and Piamonte in the Chueca quarter. Here you will find Jesús del Pozo's workshop and shop (Almirante 9), Excrupulus Net (Almirante 7), with the hippiest shoes, and the very latest from Toni Miró at Gallery (Piamonte 18).

The large international couturiers and Spanish fashion leaders such as Adolfo Domínguez (Serrano 18), Loewe (Serrano 26 and 34), Dafnis (Paseo de la Habana 174) and Elena Benarroch (Zurbarán 16 and Ortega y Gasset 10) are to be found in the Salamanca quarter, between Calles Serrano and Príncipe de Vergara, rubbing shoulders with antique and furniture shops. In Calle Claudio Coello are Madrid's elite art galleries. Off Claudio Coello opens Callejón de Jorge Juan, the finest 150 metres of shopping street in the city, with the incomparable women's fashion of Sybilla (No. 12).

More conventional shopping areas are the Gran Vía and the district round Calle Preciados, extending down to the Puerta del Sol. Here, round the Corte Inglés department store, specialist shops selling everything from toys to workaday fashion. Another similar shopping area is along Calle Princesa in the Argüelles district. A more traditional shopping quarter is on the Puerta del Sol and Plaza de Pontejos and in the Calles Mayor and Arenal. Here you will find, alongside video shops and burger bars, specialist shops selling lace and fabrics, fans and mantones (shawls), flamenco gear, confectionery, militaria, stamps and music.

The Rastro quarter round the Ribera de los Curtidores is famous for its flea market, but it also has specialist shops selling second-hand photographic equipment, excellent antique shops in the Galería Piquer (Ribera de los Curtidores 12), basketwork, wrought-iron articles and much more besides.

Round the Plaza Mayor the shops are still rather as they were in the seventies: hats and underwear for Him, bras for Her, domestic requirements and bed-linen. But here too there are excellent shops selling Spanish craft products (El Arco de los Cuchilleros, Plaza Mayor 9; El Caballo Cojo, Calle Segovia 7).

General de Rey and on the Ribera de los Curtidores are other antique shops:
Antigüedades Asia, Calle del Carnero 4
Antigüedades Arienza, Calle del Carnero 17
Antigüedades del Siglo 20
Galerías Piquer, Ribera de los Curtidores 29 (Art Nouveau), in a shopping arcade with several antique shops
Alonso Ojeda, Ribera de los Curtidores 12, in a shopping arcade with several antique shops
L. Carabe Palacios, Ribera de los Curtidores 12
Crimea, Ribera de los Curtidores 12
J. Miranda, Ribera de los Curtidores 13
P. Mateos García, Plaza General Vara de Rey 10
Nuevas Galerías, Ribera de los Curtidores 12
Ortiz Hurtado, Ribera de los Curtidores 29
Ruiz Santiago, Ribera de los Curtidores 29
J.C. Ruiz Perria, Plaza General Vara de Rey 10

In the Salamanca district and round the Paseo de la Castellana there are also shops selling antiques, objets d'art and period furniture:
María Gracia Cavestany, Jorge Juan 14
López de Aragón, Jorge Juan 9 (specialises in old azulejos)
Luis Carabe, Lagasca 36
Fernando Durán, Serrano 8 (a famous auction house)
Espinosa, Núñez de Balboa 42
Gambara, Ortega y Gasset 33
Serrano Cinco, Centro de Arte y Antigüedades, Serrano 5
Rica Basagoiti, Padilla 30
Berkowitch, Velázquez 4
Rey Fernández Latorre, Claudio Coello 35
J. Serrano Pombo, Claudio Coello 43
Stop, Núñez de Balboa 32

Toys	Sánchez Ruiz, Gran Vía 47 Lola Berlin, Corredera Alta 32 Imaginarium, Núñez de Balboa 52 Pérez Vallejo, Gran Vía 11 (bookshop with paper houses and cut-out paper figures)
Postcards and posters	Postcards, posters, old prints and town plans: Librería Jiménez, Mayor 66, and Imagenes, Huertas 47 (see below, Bookshops) Casa Postal, Libertad 37 (postcards and old prints) Sótanos, Gran Vía 55 (contemporary town views)
Guitars and fiddles	José Ramírez, Concepción Jerónima 5 (open 9.30am–8pm, Sat. 9.30am–1.30pm; Jul. 1st–Sep. 30th, 9.30am–4pm) Paulino Bernabé, Cuchilleros 8 Manuel González Contreras, Mayor 80 Guitarras, Mayor 66 Evilio Domínguez Hernández, Virgen de Lluch 88 Fernando Solar, Divino Pastor 24 (fiddle-maker)

Bookshops (librerías)

Madrid has an overwhelming abundance of bookshops. Once concentrated round the Puerta del Sol and in the Gran Vía, they are now to be found all over the city.
La Casa del Libro, Gran Vía 29 (on six floors, the largest stock of books in Madrid)
Crisol, Juan Bravo 38
La Tarántula, Sagasta 28
Fuenteteja, San Bernardo 48 (one of Madrid's oldest bookshops).

Librería Rafael Alberti, Tutor 57

Librería de la Escalinata, Escalinata 7 (specialises in 16th–18th century books)

Second-hand books

El Renacimiento, Huertas 49 (also prints of all periods and countries)
Librería Viuda de Rodríguez, San Bernardo 27 (specialises in bullfighting, art and hunting literature and books on Madrid)
Librería de San Ginés, Pasadizo de San Ginés 2 (both old and new books)
Librería de Bibliófilos Españoles, Plaza San Martín 3
There are several bookshops, new and second-hand, in Calle Libreros.
Librería Jiménez, Mayor 66 (old prints)
On Cuesta de Claudio Moyano (see Sights from A to Z, Jardín Botánico) there are numbers of stalls selling both new and second-hand books.

Librería Gaudí, Argensola 13

Architecture, art, film and theatre

Xarait, San Francisco de Sales 32
Naos, Quintana 12
Antonio Machado, Fernando VI 17
Alphaville, Martín de los Heros 14 (books, periodicals, postcards and posters on films)
Cuéllar, Benito Gutiérrez 17 (many foreign books)
La Avispa, San Mateo 30 (theatre, dance and film)
El Corral de Almagro, Almagro 13
León Sánchez Cuesta, Serrano 29
Patrimonio Nacional, Felipe 5/Plaza de Oriente (books on buildings and art objects under the protection of the National Monuments Board)

Camelot, Gaztambide 20 (Spanish and foreign comics, science fiction)

Comics

Madrid Comic, Gran Vía 55 (many foreign comics)

Librería de Mujeres, San Cristóbal 17

Women's bookshop

Marcial Pons, Plaza Conde del Valle de Suchil 8 (Spanish and foreign books and periodicals)

History

León Sánchez Cuesta, Serrano 29

Taléntun, Núñez de Balboa 53 (children's books for all ages)

Children's books

Phoebe, Fernández de los Ríos 95 (publication and sale of maps; large stock of guidebooks)

Maps and travel literature

Tierra de Fuego, Duque de Liria 4
La Tienda Verde, Maudes 38
Años Luz Libros, Francisco de Ricci 8

La Librería, Señores de Luzón 8 (books and posters on Madrid)

Madrid

Librería Jiménez, Mayor 66 (old prints and town plans)
Sótanos, Gran Vía 55 (contemporary posters)

Librería Náutica Robinson, Fernando el Católico 63

Nautical

Blanco Montejo, Lope de Rueda 27 (British Admiralty charts; charts from all over the world)

Kier, Velarde 1

Esoterica, the occult

Librería San Pablo, Plaza Jacinto Benavente 2 (also records, videos, maps)

Religion

Librería Deportiva Esteban, San Martínez Paz 4

Sport

Mundi-Prensa Libros, Castelló 37

Economics

Librería Agrícola, Fernando VI 2 (specialises in agriculture)

León Sánchez Cuesta, Serrano 29 (also history, art and literature)

Other specialist shops	Casa Diego, Puerta del Sol 12 (typical Spanish fans, screens and sticks) Casa Jiménez, Preciados 42 (shawls, scarves and kerchiefs) Justo Algaba, La Paz 4 (bullfighters' costumes) Palacios y Museos, Goya 48 (reproductions and copies of museum objects) Seseña, Santa Cruz 23 (capas – typical Spanish cloaks – for men and women) Maty, Maestro Victoria 2 (sevillanas costumes for children and adults)
Arts and crafts	Almost all types of Spanish arts and crafts are represented in Madrid. Craft workshops are found mainly in the old town, shops in the Malasaña quarter (see Sights from A to Z, Plaza del Dos de Mayo), round Calles Almirante and Huertas, in La Vaguada shopping centre (see above, Shopping centres) and on the Puerta de Toledo. A representative range of craft products can be seen in the Fundación de Gremios, Avenida del Cardenal Herrera Oria 278. A selection of shops selling selected work by various craftsmen: El Arco de los Cuchilleros, Plaza Mayor 9 (new Spanish craft products in a wide range of materials) Centro Cultural Islámico, Salvador de Madariaga 4 (craft products from the Islamic world in Madrid's mosque) Sala Adamá, Avenida Felipe II 24 (work by potters from all over Spain)
Wax and candles	Cerería Ortega, Toledo 43
Pottery and ceramics	El Caballo Cojo, Segovia 7 Ars 31, Divino Pastor 16 (mainly South American crafts)
Basketwork	El Pozo, Almirante 30 (work also carried out to order)
See also	Markets; Business Hours

Sightseeing Tours

Madrid Visión	Information about organisers of city sightseeing tours can be obtained from travel agencies, hotels and tourist offices. The official city tour, Madrid Visión (tel. 917671743 and 913020368) at present costs 1700 ptas; day ticket with unlimited changes 2200 ptas; reduction of 40% for children between 4 and 14. The first bus of the day leaves Calle San Bernardo 19 at 9.45. You can join the bus at any Madrid Visión stop (e.g. in Plaza de España).
Guided tours	There are guided tours of the historic districts of Madrid (in English) on Saturday mornings, starting at 10am from the municipal tourist information office in the Plaza Mayor (see Information). The cost is at present 500 ptas. Information can also be obtained from municipal information offices (see Information).
See also	Excursions

Sport

Parks and sports centres	Madrid's parks and sports centres offer ample facilities for keeping fit in whatever way you prefer. There are plenty of opportunities for jogging. There is boating on the lakes in the Retiro Park and the Casa de Campo.

There are numerous basketball and football pitches (mostly tarmac). Roller-skating and roller-blading are widely popular. There is a mountain bike track in the Casa de Campo. A public sports centre in which tennis and squash courts can be hired and which has a swimming pool and facilities for a variety of other sports is the Polideportivo de Aluche, Avenida del General Fanjul; tel. 917061781; Metro: Aluche.

There are facilities for swimming in a number of reservoirs round Madrid (see below, Water sports), in rock pools on the Manzanares in its source area at La Pedriza, a nature park near Manzanares el Real, in pools on the Río Eresma between Valsaín and the Venta del Diabolo, under the north side of the Sierra de Guadarrama (along N 601), and in the Las Presillas reservoir on the Arroyo de Santa Ana, in the valley of the Río Lozoya, which can be reached from El Paular, near Rascafría, by way of the Puente del Perdón.
Bathing

Bowling Chamartín, Estación de Chamartín; tel. 913157119.
AMF Bowling Center, in the Centro Comercial La Vaguada; tel. 917301811. Metro: Barrio del Pilar.
Bowling

See Sights from A to Z, Las Ventas, and Baedeker Special, p. 164
Bullfighting

There are regular motorcycle races, including world championship events, as well as car races on the Circuito de Jarama (25 km (15 mi.) north of Madrid on the Burgos road: see Sights from A to Z, Sierra de Guadarrama).
Car and motorcycle racing

To fish in reservoirs or mountain streams you must have a *licencia fluvial*. For information on how to obtain a licence and how to get in touch with an angling club, ask the Federación Española de Pesca, Calle Navas de Tolosa 2; tel. 915328353.
Fishing

Information: Federación Madrileña de Deportes Aéreos, Calle Ferraz 13; tel. 915475922.
Information on hang-gliding: Escuela de Ala Delta Hombres Pájaro, Calle Pez 27; tel. 915328250.
Flying

See Sights from A to Z, Estadio Santiago Bernabéu and Estadio Vicente Calderón
Football stadiums

The only public golf course in the Madrid area is the Campo de Golf Alivar de la Inojosa, near the Parque Ferial; tel. 917211889.
Golf

See Sights from A to Z, Hipódromo de la Zarzuela (at present closed)
Horse racing

See entry
Swimming pools

Cotos, little place in the Sierra de Guadarrama (see entry in Sights from A to Z), 7 km (4 mi.) from Nava Cerrada, is a good base from which to climb to the Laguna de Peñalara, below the peak of that name. The climb is possible even in summer, with a chair-lift to help you on your way.
A popular climbing area in the Sierra de Gredos is the Macizo de Gredos, a huge granite massif, with Mt Almanzor as its highest peak, which forms a barrier between the plateaux of Old and New Castile. Another good climbing area in the Sierra de Guadarrama is the massive bulk of La Pedriza. Information: Federación Madrileña de Montañismo, Calle Apodaca 16; tel. 914480724 and 915938074. Hill walks and climbs, winter sports trips and mountain bike excursions are organised by Deporte y Montaña de la Comunidad de Madrid, Calle Sagasta 13; tel. 915943034, and Sportnatura Aire Libre, Avenida Donostiarra 4; tel.
Walking and climbing

Estadio Vicente Calderón, home ground of Atlético Madrid

914036161. A wide range of walking and climbing guides can be found in Madrid's bookshops (see Shopping, Souvenirs).

Water sports

Most of the reservoirs round Madrid either supply the city with drinking water or are nature reserves, and access is not permitted for other purposes. There are, however, three – San Juan, El Atazar and El Vellón – which offer facilities for a variety of water sports.

Winter sports

The mountain regions of central Spain offer excellent conditions for winter sports, but the ski resorts in this region, particularly in the Sierra de Guadarrama, within 50 km (30 mi.) of the capital, are hopelessly over-crowded at weekends. The main skiing areas in the Sierra de Guadarrama are the Puerto de Navacerrada 1860 m (6103 ft): see Sights from A to Z, Sierra de Guadarrama), with 12 cableways and lifts, and the nearby resorts of Cotos and Valdesquí on the pass road to Rascafría. The pistes begin at altitudes of up to 2200 m (7200 ft). These resorts are best reached on the mountain railway from Cercedilla, which itself is reached on the Cercanías line from Madrid.

The Sierra de Gredos to the west of Madrid, whose highest peak is Almanzor (1592 m (5223ft)), is mainly for experienced skiers, and is well provided with mountain huts.

Other sports facilities

There are municipal sports centres in all Madrid districts, with facilities for a wide variety of sports. Information from the Instituto Municipal de Deporte; tel. 914635498.

Swimming Pools

Most of Madrid's baths and swimming pools belong to housing estates and clubs and are not open to the wider public.

There is a public swimming pool of Olympic standard in the Polideportivo del Canal de Isabel II, run by the Comunidad de Madrid, at Avenida de Filipinas 54; tel. 915339642 (open June to August).

In Plaza de la Cebada is a municipal bath, La Latina (tel. 913658031).

At Villanueva de la Cañada, to the west of Madrid, is Aquopolis, a pool with artificial waves and giant chutes and flumes. It can be reached by bus (No. 626) from Las Rozas/Majadahonda.

Taxis

Madrid's taxis are white, with a diagonal red stripe on the front doors, the city's heraldic bear on the rear doors and the letters SP *(Servicio público)* on the front and rear bumpers. When a taxi is free there is a green light on the roof and the sign "Libre" behind the windscreen.

Taxis can be picked up at a taxi rank, hailed in the street or summoned by telephone. The numbers to call are:
914475080 (Radio-Taxi),
915478200 (Radio-Teléfono Taxi),
914459008 (Tele Taxi) and
914051213 (Radio Taxi Independiente).

The basic fare is 175 ptas, plus 85 ptas por kilometre. There are supplements of 150 ptas on Sundays and public holidays, at night and for journeys to or from rail and bus stations, 350 ptas for journeys to or from the airport and 50 ptas for each item of luggage. Waiting time is charged at the rate of 1650 ptas per hour, which is also the basic charge for longer trips outside Madrid.

Fares

Telephone (Teléfono)

The national telephone company, Telefónica, has recently been privatised, and is now liable to competition from other private companies.

Another recent change is that all telephone numbers must include the local dialling code, even for calls within the same area. All Madrid numbers, therefore, now begin with 91, and there are nine figures in all numbers. Numbers beginning with 900 are toll-free.

There are public payphones all over the city, most of then in open cabins. They are operated by 25 or 100 peseta coins or by a telephone card *(tarjeta)*, which can be bought in tobacconists' shops and newsstands. At Gran Vía 30 and Paseo de Recoletos 41 are telephone offices open 24 hours a day, with numerous telephones. Telephone calls from hotels are charged at considerably higher rates.

Directory enquiries (within Spain): 1003
Directory enquiries (international): 025
Time: 093
Wake-up call: 096
Telegrams: 91522000

Useful telephone numbers

Calls from the United Kingdom to Spain: dial 0034, followed by the 9-figure number
Calls from the United States or Canada to Spain: dial 01134, followed by the 9-figure number

International dialling codes

Calls from Spain to the United Kingdom: dial 00, wait for a loud continuous tone and then dial 44, followed by the area dialling code without its initial zero

Calls from Spain to the United States or Canada: dial 00, wait for a loud continuous tone and then dial 1, followed by the area dialling code.

Theatres (Teatros)

In the Teatro de la Zarzuela around 1900

Madrid's theatres show both an attachment to tradition and a readiness to accept new forms. Their range extends from the performances of the classical repertoire in the National Theatre by way of the zarzuela (the traditionally Spanish form of operetta) to modern productions and puppet shows in the Teatro Pradillo. There are performances both in the city's theatres, more than 30 in number, and in various cultural centres. The following is merely a brief selection of Madrid's most important theatres.

Teatro Nacional María Guerrero (home of the Centro Dramático Nacional), Tamayo y Baus 4; tel. 913194769 (Metro: Banco de España or Colón). See Sights from A to Z, Teatro Nacional María Guerrero.

Teatro Real (Theatre Royal), or Teatro de la Ópera, Plaza de Oriente; tel. 915160660 (information), 915160606 (tickets) (Metro: Ópera). See Sights from A to Z, Teatro Real; Music.

Teatro de la Comedia (home of the Compañía Nacional de Teatro Clásico), Calle del Príncipe 14; tel. 915214931 (Metro: Sevilla).

Sala Olimpia (Centro Nacional de Nuevas Tendencias Escénicas), Plaza de Lavapiés; tel. 914677662 (Metro: Lavapiés). An international Festival of Puppet Theatre is held here in spring in certain years.

Teatro Pradillo, Pradillo 12; tel. 914169011 (Metro: Concha Espina; buses 16, 52). Modern productions, choreographies, programme for children, puppet plays.

Teatro de la Zarzuela (Teatro Lírico Nacional), Jovellanos 4; tel. 915245400 (Metro: Sevilla). See Baedeker Special, p. 133.

Teatro Español (home of the Compañía de Teatro Municipal), Plaza de Santa Ana; tel. 914296297 (Metro: Sevilla). See Sights from A to Z, Teatro Español

Teatro Calderón, Atocha 18; tel. 913691434 (Metro: Tirso de Molina).

Leisure Guide

For information about the programmes of the various theatres, see the newspapers or the weekly "Guía del Ocio" ("Leisure Guide").

See also

Cultural Centres; Events; Music; Ticket Offices

Ticket Offices

Concert and theatre tickets can be ordered by telephone from the Caja de Madrid (tel. 902488488) or the Caja de Catalunya (Teleentradas; tel. 915383333). Tickets for football matches, cinemas and bullfights can be obtained from Localidades Galicia at Plaza del Carmen 1; but it is better to go direct to the box-offices *(taquillas)* of the football stadiums and bullrings.

Time

From October to March mainland Spain is on Central European Time (an hour ahead of Greenwich Mean Time). From March to October it is on Central European Summer Time (2 hours ahead of GMT). The exact dates of the change-over are announced in the media.

Tipping (Propina)

Although a service charge *(servicio)* is included in hotel and restaurant bills, hotel staff and waiters, as well as taxi-drivers and the attendants who show you to your seat in a theatre, cinema or bullring, expect a tip *(propina)* of the order of 5–10 per cent of the bill. In bars and restaurants, a tip should be left on the bar counter or the table.

Trade Fairs (Ferias)

With numerous congresses, over 50 trade fairs and both national and international exhibitions every year, Madrid has since the 1980s become a major centre for events of this kind. Many of them, such as FITUR, the world's second largest trade fair of the tourism industry (held in January/February), or ARCO, the International Contemporary Art Fair (February), are held annually; others, like the fashion show Pasarela de Cibeles, twice yearly.

The Parque Ferial de Madrid, also known as the Campo de las Naciones, is Madrid's new exhibition centre of the 1990s (architects Jerónimo Junquera, Estanislao Pérez Pita, Mark Fenwick, Liliana Obal and Francisco Javier Sáenz de Oíza). It lies to the north-east of the city, 3 km (2miles) from Barajas Airport, in the Olivar de la Hinojosa area (Hortaleza district). It can be reached on the M 40 motorway or on Metro line 8, extended to Barajas Airport in 1999. It has 10 ha (25 acres) of indoor exhibition space, plus another 3 ha (7 acres) in the grounds.

Parque Ferial de Madrid

Within the Campo de las Naciones site, in addition to the exhibition pavilions, are the Parque Juan Carlos I, a park twice the size of the Retiro, a Palace of Congresses (architect Ricardo Bofill), the Teatro de la Vaguada, a luxury hotel complex, a shopping centre, an artificial lake, a golf course and other sports facilities.

Smaller events continue to be held in the old exhibition grounds in the Casa de Campo (see entry in Sights from A to Z), which has 4 ha (10 acres) of exhibition space.

Madrid's central trade fair and exhibition organisation is IFEMA (see below).

Info/IFEMA
Parque Ferial Juan Carlos I, E-28042 Madrid
Tel. 917225180

Information

Patronato de la Feria del Campo (Ayuntamiento de Madrid)
Avenida de Portugal, Casa de Campo, E-28013 Madrid
Tel. 815889393

Cámara de Comercio e Industria de Madrid
Huertas 13, E-28012 Madrid
Tel. 914293193

Congresses

Most congress organisers, including almost all the 85 hotels which have congress and seminar facilities, belong to the Madrid Convention Bureau:

Madrid Convention Bureau
Señores de Luzón 10, E-28013 Madrid
Tel. 915383500

The Palacio de Congresos in the Paseo de la Castellana, with a façade designed by Juan Miró (1980), could originally accommodate congresses of 3000 people without using its main exhibition hall (2000 sq. m (21,529 sq. ft)), but since a fire in 1995 only part of the building can at present be used.

Palacio de Congresos de Madrid
Paseo de la Castellana 99, E-28046 Madrid
Tel. 913378100

A selection of events

January: Intergift – Salón Internacional del Regalo (gifts); Fitur (Tourism Fair)
February: Pasarela de Cibeles (International Fashion Show; held also in September); ARCO International Contemporary Art Show); Exponautica (Boat Show)
March: Expo Ocio (Leisure Fair); Ofitec (office equipment; until May); Retromóvil (veteran and vintage cars; date varies)
April: Expofranquicia (Franchising Fair; sometimes in May); Feria Internacional del Mueble (furniture); Expomúsica (musical instruments)
May: Semana de la Alimentación (food and wine; biiennal); Almodeda (auction houses and galleries)
June: Salón del Vehículo de Ocasión (second-hand cars)
September: Pasarela de Cibeles (see under February)
October: Liber (International Book Fair)
November: Feriarte (art and antiques)

Travel Documents

Personal papers

For entry to Spain British, US and Canadian visitors need only a valid passport; no passport is required for a stay of up to 3 months.

British visitors, like other European Union citizens, do not require a visa for a stay of more than 3 months, but must obtain a residence permit *(tarjeta de residencia),* valid for up to 5 years. For this purpose they must produce evidence that they have sufficient resources to maintain themselves, in the form either of a job contract or an account with a Spanish bank, or a certificate of marriage to a Spanish citizen. They should apply to the following agencies:

Ministry of the Interior: for information tel. 900150000
Policía Nacional
Pasaje Maestros Ladrilleros, Plaza de la Remonta (Metro: Tetuán)

Car papers

Most national driving licences and car registration documents are accepted in Spain, though it is sometimes an advantage to have an international driving licence. EU citizens staying in Spain for more than 3 months must have their national driving licence registered in Spain. If the licence is not the new standard EU type there is a charge of 2500 ptas.

Jefatura Provincial de Tráfico
Calle Arturo Soría 14
Tel. 900123505

Transport
Directorate

Car insurance

Foreign drivers should get a "green card" from their insurers, together with a bail bond as a precaution in case of an accident, which might otherwise lead to the car being impounded.

All visitors should ensure that they have adequate insurance cover. On health insurance, see Medical Aid.

Personal
insurance

It is advisable before leaving home to make photocopies of your travel documents and to keep them separate from the documents themselves. If your documents are lost or stolen this will make it easier to get replacements.

Viewpoints

The Montaña del Príncipe Pío (see entry in Sights from A to Z), rising above the Manzanares, is the highest point in south-western Madrid. From here there are fine views of the Royal Palace, the Casa de Campo, the church of San Francisco el Grande and, farther away to the north, the hills of the Sierra de Guadarrama.

Montaña del
Príncipe Pío

From the cafeteria (at present closed) on the 18th floor of the Edificio España, in the Plaza de España, there are superb views of the Royal Palace, the old town, the Gran Vía, the Templo de Debod (see Montaña del Príncipe Pío) and the Casa de Campo.

Edificio de España

From the gardens of Las Vistillas (above Calle Segovia at the corner of Calle Bailén; Metro: Ópera) there are views of the Manzanares, the Almudena Cathedral and, away to the north, the Sierra de Guadarrama.

Las Vistillas

From the Casa de Campo there are views of south-western Madrid. The finest views of the Royal Palace, the Almudena Cathedral and the skyline of the Plaza de España are to be had from the cableway over the park (Teleférico; station in Paseo del Pintor Rosales; Metro: Argüelles).

Casa de Campo

The only building open to the public offering a view over the whole of western Madrid is the Faro de Moncloa (see Sights from A to Z, Ciudad Universitaria). It is open Tue.–Sun. 11am–1.45pm, 5.30–8pm.

Faro de Moncloa

When to Go

Madrid is attractive at any time of year. February and October usually have settled, sunny weather. In spring and autumn temperatures in the city are at their most agreeable, though in some years there are persistent showers of rain. May, June and September are the months for enjoying your meal or your drink on café terraces and other open-air establishments. In July and August temperatures not infrequently rise

to 40°C (104°F) in the shade. In August many restaurants and shops are closed.

In winter temperatures in Madrid may well fall below freezing point; but lasting frost is likely only near the mountains.

See Facts and Figures, Climate

Climate

Youth Hostels

Visitors who are members of youth-hostel associations affiliated to the International Youth Hostel Federation can find accommodation at reasonable prices in Spain's youth hostels *(albergues juveniles)*, which are usually open from July to September. The maximum stay in any one hostel is three days. During the main holiday season it is advisable to book in advance. For information contact:

International Youth Hostel Federation
Fountain House, Parkway, Hertfordshire AL8 6JH
Tel. (01707) 324170

Instituto de la Juventud España/Red Española de Albergues Juveniles
Calle José Ortega y Gasset, E-28006 Madrid
Tel. 913477700, fax 914018160

◀ *From the cableway in the Casa de Campo there are good views of the Manzanares (here canalised), the Royal Palace and the Almudena Cathedral*

Glossary

Ajimez: a double-arched window.

Alcázar: a Moorish fortress, frequently taken over and extended by Christian rulers.

Almohads: members of a puritanical Muslim sect, originally Berbers, who ruled Spain from the mid 12th to the early 13th century.

Almoravids: a fanatical people of Berber origin who extended their rule over much of Spain in the 11th century.

Arabesques: a type of curvilinear decoration, with intertwining leaf, flower and geometric designs; often in the form of a frieze.

Artesonado: a coffered wooden ceiling, probably of Almohad origin, which was popular in Christian Spain until the 15th and 16th centuries.

Ayuntamiento: Town Hall.

Azulejos: glazed tiles, originally blue *(azul)*.

Capilla Mayor: chancel of a church, containing the high altar.

Catalan Gothic: a form of Late Gothic which flourished in Sicily, under Spanish influence, in the 15th and 16th centuries.

Catalan Gothic Churrigueresque: an elaborately decorative form of Baroque, with a riot of fanciful ornament.

Ermita: hermitage; chapel.

Herreran style: a Spanish Renaissance style, post-Plateresque and pre-Baroque, named after Juan de Herrera (1530–97), architect of the Escorial.

Isabelline Gothic: an ornamental form of Late Gothic developed in the reign of Isabella the Catholic.

Isabelline period: the Romantic period in Spain, in the reign of Isabella II (1833–68).

Morisco: a compulsorily converted Muslim in medieval Christian Spain.

Mozarab: a Christian under Muslim rule in Spain. The Mozarabs developed a characteristic architectural style influenced by Arab models, with such features as the horseshoe arch.

Mudéjar: a Muslim in Christian Spain. The Mudéjar style in architecture is seen in buildings built by Moorish craftsmen for Christian rulers and in later buildings under Moorish influence. Characteristic features are the horseshoe arch and the artesonado ceiling.

Paseo: promenade.

Peña: a type of flamenco show.

Plateresque: a highly charged decorative style developed in the late 15th and the 16th centuries, with a combination of Late Gothic and Mudéjar influences.

Reja: an iron screen or grille.

Retable: reredos, altarpiece.

Sillería: choir stalls.

Tablao: a flamenco show.

Tertulia: a meeting of friends for conversation; a discussion group.

Index

Index

Imprint

112 illustrations
11 maps and plans, 1 large plan of Madrid

Original German text: Dr Karl W. Biehusen, Genoveva Dietrich, Thomas Hirsch, Friedrich Huber, Frank Lang, Anja Schliebitz, Reinhard Strüber

Editorial work: Baedeker-Redaktion (Anja Schliebitz)

Cartography: Franz Huber, Munich; Mairs Geographischer Verlag, Ostfildern (city plan)

General direction: Rainer Eisenschmid, Baedeker Ostfildern

Source of illustrations: AKG-Berlin (6); Baedeker-Archiv (12); Dietrich (1); Eisenschmid (1); Hirsch (1); Lade (2); Laif (1); Mauritius (4); Schapowalow (2); Schleicher (77); Schuster (3); ZEFA (1)

Front cover: Images Colour Library. Back cover: AA Photo Library (R. Strange)

English translation: James Hogarth

3rd English edition 1999

© Baedeker Stuttgart
Original German edition 1998

© 1999 The Automobile Association
English language edition worldwide

Published by AA Publishing (a trading name of Automobile Association Developments Limited, whose registered office is Norfolk House, Priestley Road, Basingstoke, Hampshire RG24 9NY. Registered number 1878835).

Distributed in the United States and Canada by:
Fodor's Travel Publications, Inc.
201 East 50th Street
New York, NY 10022

Licensed user:
Mairs Geographischer Verlag GmbH & Co.,
Ostfildern-Kemnat bei Stuttgart

Printed in Italy by G. Canale & C. S.p.A., Turin

ISBN 0 7495 2184 8

Principal Sights of Tourist Interest

Notes

Notes

Notes